Domestic Disturbances

Domestic Disturbances

Re-Imagining Narratives of Gender, Labor, and Immigration

BY IRENE MATA

University of Texas Press, Austin

First edition, 2014
First paperback edition, 2015

Requests for permission to reproduce material from this work should be sent to:
    Permissions
    University of Texas Press
    P.O. Box 7819
    Austin, TX 78713-7819
    http://utpress.utexas.edu/index.php/rp-form

♾ The paper used in this book meets the minimum requirements of ANSI/NISO Z39.48-1992 (R1997) (Permanence of Paper).

Library of Congress Cataloging-in-Publication Data

Mata, Irene, 1972–
    Domestic disturbances : re-imagining narratives of gender, labor, and immigration / by Irene Mata.
        pages cm
    Includes bibliographical references and index.
    ISBN 978-0-292-77131-4 (cl. : alk. paper)
    1. Hispanic American women—Social conditions.   2. Women immigrants—United States—Social conditions.   3. Women household employees—United States—Social conditions.   4. Women foreign workers—United States—Social conditions.   5. Hispanic American women in literature.   6. Hispanic American women in mass media.   7. United States—Emigration and immigration—Social aspects. I. Title.
    E184.S75M388   2014
    305.48'868073—dc23

                                                                                        2014016665

    ISBN 978-1-4773-0984-1 (paperback)
    doi:10.7560/771314

*For my mother and all of the immigrant women who raise
their children in cultures not their own*

Contents

Acknowledgments

As with most academic projects, this book is the result of the encouragement and support of many individuals. I would like to begin by offering my sincerest appreciation for the work of the cultural producers who have made this project possible. Thank you to the incredible artists who granted me permission to use their work: Laura Alvarez, Adela Arellano, and Debora Kuetzpal Vasquez. Quiero expresar mis más sinceras gracias y profundo agradecimiento a Elvia Claudio por compartir su historia de lucha, perseverancia, y esperanza, y por permitirme a compartir sus experiencias con el resto de la comunidad.

This book was made possible by the financial assistance of various sources. When I was a graduate student, my research was partially funded by a University of California, San Diego Center for the Study of Race and Ethnicity Dissertation Research Fellowship and a UCSD Literature Department Year Long Dissertation Fellowship. In its later stages, this project was supported by a Susan and Donald Newhouse Center for the Humanities Fellowship and by multiple Wellesley College Faculty Research Grants. The Newhouse Center, under the direction of Carol Dougherty and the coordination of Jane Jackson, provided me with a place to think and write, and fostered a space for collaboration and conversation that was truly stimulating.

There are many individuals whose help has been instrumental in my journey through multiple academic institutions. At New Mexico State University, I was incredibly lucky to work with amazing mentors like Catrióna Rueda Esquibel (who first introduced me to Chican@ literature), Alison Giffen and Diane Price Herndl (who trained me to be a feminist educator), and Diane Bass, Maria Guerra, and Jan Farmer (three amazing women who became my family in Las Cruces). At the University of California, San Diego, I had the opportunity to work with individuals who challenged me to think of literature beyond the written words on a page. I am thankful for the unwavering support of Rosaura Sánchez and the members of my dissertation committee: Lisa Lowe, Shelley Streeby, Michael Davidson, and Jorge Huerta. I am indebted to my colleagues in the Women's and Gender Studies Department, who have created a home for me at Wellesley College. Thank you to Sealing Cheng, Elena Creef, Rosanna Hertz, Charlene Galarneau, Nancy Marshall, Susan Reverby, and Sima Shakhsari for their mentoring, their support, and their willingness to always listen. A special thank you to Betty Tiro and Marisa Shariatdoust for their constant assistance in the daily navigating of the institution and their steadfast friendship.

Thank you to my amazing research assistants, Silvia Galis-Menendez and Lourdes Mendoza, for all of their help in preparing this manuscript for publication. I am incredibly grateful to all of my students (too numerous to list), who consistently push me to be a better teacher, mentor, and scholar. From my first day in the classroom, they have inspired me and sustained my spirit.

I am thankful for the friendships that have shaped my life and my work. Thank you to my writing group, Charlene Galarneau and Tanya McNeill, for keeping me on track and generously offering suggestions. I am indebted to Linda Heidenreich and Elena Creef for their invaluable feedback on previous versions of this manuscript. Thank you to Rusty Barceló and Mari Castañeda for their guidance and wise *consejos*. I am grateful for the mentoring, love, and support offered so unselfishly by Chris Guzaitis, Linda Heidenreich, and Rita Urquijo-Ruiz. Thank you to Aisha M. Beliso–De Jesús, my newfound sister in the cold Northeast, and her family for helping me create *familia from scratch*.

My trajectory as a scholar began at home, in a small house filled with the sounds of English and Spanish, the sights of syncretic images, and the smells of Mexican food. Since I was raised in an immigrant household in the El Paso–Juárez border area, the straddling of cultures has always been a way of life for me. I am forever grateful to my family for teaching me the value of tradition while at the same time teaching me the importance of challenging traditions that cause harm. Thank you to my father, Guadalupe Ernesto Mata, for instilling in me a love of the written word and to my mother, Irene Martinez de Mata, who taught me that knowledge isn't always found in a book. I am indebted to my sisters/best friends, Ernestina Mata Hernandez and Marisela Mata, whose unwavering support helped sustain me through the difficult student years and who have kept me grounded when I needed it most.

I am indebted to various individuals who helped me raise a family while pursuing my education and writing this book. Thank you to Ryan Van Wyhe for years of unwavering support and for being an amazing co-parent. I am grateful to my extended family, including Nancy and Terry Markus, Josie and Matthew Horton, and Chris Guzaitis (my village).

Mil gracias to Genevieve Rodriguez, who, like a good community organizer, challenges me to constantly question what I think I know. From her I have learned the importance of finding love in every act of resistance and the value of individual actions of opposition. She reminds me every day that writing about activism and change isn't enough—we must live it. I am indebted to her for introducing me to Elvia Claudio and the amazing community organizers in San Antonio. Most importantly, I thank her, *mi corazón*, for bringing love, laughter, and oh so much color into my life.

And finally, the most heartfelt thank you to my beautiful and brilliant children, Alyssa Marie Flores and James Matthew Flores, for their years of patience and support and for teaching me the meaning of unconditional love. They have had to endure countless birthday parties attended by graduate students instead of other children, dinner conversations where ideology and representation are staples, and numerous debates around what shows we watch on television. I am indebted to Alyssa and James for their willingness to move across the country, leaving behind friends and family and the warmth of the desert sun. They have blossomed in this untraditional childhood and inspire me daily to try and make the world around us a better place for them.

Domestic Disturbances

Introduction

In Lin-Manuel Miranda's 2008 Tony Award–winning musical *In the Heights*, the character Abuela Claudia asks the question, "What do you do when your dreams come true?" as she reveals to the audience that she has won the lottery. While the dream of winning the lottery is one shared by many, Abuela Claudia's song "Paciencia y Fe" is not a simple expression of celebration. Instead, Miranda uses the song to give us Abuela Claudia's story of immigration and labor. We learn that she and her mother left the warmth and familiarity of La Vibora in Havana, Cuba, many years before for a cold and dreary life in the United States, a decision based on economic necessity. In her emotional musical narrative, Abuela Claudia recalls the difficulties of living in New York City, including finding housing, searching for work, and learning to speak English. Abuela Claudia's moving song becomes her immigrant narrative, explaining to the audience the reason for migration and the struggles she and her mother encountered in their transition.

While the phrase "paciencia y fe" (patience and faith) is repeated throughout the composition, the song is very much about the frustration of having one's dreams deferred. Abuela Claudia's family's life was one of work and hardship, and the only inheritance left behind for her was the combination of her memories and her mother's dreams. The song ends with mention of a decision the audience doesn't learn about until Abuela Claudia's duet with Usnavi, the protagonist of the play and the young man she helped raise as her own grandchild. In the song "Hundreds of Stories," she makes plans with Usnavi to divide the winnings in three in order to share with Usnavi and his cousin Sonny. She wants to return to the Caribbean and enthusiastically sings of the "seaside air" and of opening with Usnavi a beachside bar, a place where they will make new memories.[1] Even though they are at least a generation apart and Usnavi's family is from the Dominican Republic, not Cuba, they share a lifetime of work and the memories and dreams of parents long gone. At the center of these is the notion of "home," and it is this notion that lies at the heart of their own dreams of creating new stories in a place far removed from their difficult life in Washington Heights. For Abuela Claudia, home continues to exist in a place where "the sea meets the sky," an island where she and Usnavi will create their own stories of home.

Abuela Claudia's story in Miranda's production gives us a glimpse into the complicated narrative of immigration shared by many. While her story includes the hardships faced by those who immigrate to the United States, her chronicle is important because of what is conspicuously absent from her narrative: an impetus for immigration based on the "American Dream." Instead of seeing a representation of the decision to leave Cuba as a quest for success in the "land of opportunity," the audience gets a clear understanding of the need for economic survival that forced Abuela Claudia and her mother to leave their home. Of even more significance is the fact that Abuela Claudia's dream is to return to a "home" that lies outside of the space she has inhabited for the majority of her life. Even though Washington Heights has been the location in which she resides, it and the United States are not the spaces she considers home. The dream of winning the lottery holds for her the promise of creating her own stories in a place she sees herself as truly belonging.

Abuela Claudia's immigrant narrative does not fit comfortably into the rhetoric of assimilation and upward mobility at the center of the ideology of achieving the American Dream. Instead, her story offers an audience a version of immigration and notions of home that complicate the conventions of a popular genre and raise questions about the complexity of immigration narratives in our current historical moment. The type of immigrant narrative that has enjoyed favor for more than a century has traditionally been one that promotes an image of the United States as a nation of immigrants, where hard work and perseverance will translate to individual success. At the heart of this literary tradition is the desire to be embraced by one's adopted country and an emphasis on creating a better home for oneself within the borders of the "land of opportunity." Unfortunately, such an idealized narrative has been out of the realm of reality for multiple immigrant groups, whose "difference"—be it racial, religious, cultural, or class based—cannot be easily subsumed under the rhetoric of "American." Through a representation of alienation and class struggle, Miranda's character Abuela Claudia illustrates the limitations of the traditional immigrant narrative and offers an alternative version, one rooted in hardship and disappointment. The aspiration in her narrative is not for the achievement of the American Dream, but for the creation of a space where she will finally feel at home, a space that does not exist within the constructed—physical or ideological—boundaries of the nation.

A Contentious Topic

The issue of immigration is one of the most visible and contentious topics of debate in the national arena, with everyone from right-wing pundits like Sarah Palin to alternative rockers like Zack de la Rocha offering their opinions. While immigration reform took a backseat during President George W. Bush's terms because of the events of September 11, 2001, and the subsequent war, the debate around immigration once again entered the national spotlight after he left office. With the country in a recession, it comes as no surprise that the practice of scapegoating immigrant workers is once again popular. What is new is the extent to which misinformation and opinion are being disseminated through multiple electronic venues such as internet blogs and social-networking sites. Along with more traditional forms of media, new media platforms have invited their audiences to participate in the debate. The ease with which it is now possible to share news stories, blogs, and articles has allowed for a broad circulation of views on immigration reform. Similar to the use of vitriolic rhetoric against Mexicans/Mexican Americans (both citizens and noncitizens) during the Great Depression, we are witnessing a resurgence in anti-immigrant sentiment and policies on a much wider scale.

The clash of pro- and anti-immigrant groups over Arizona's 2010 Support Our Law Enforcement and Safe Neighborhoods Act (SB 1070) is illustrative of the larger debate around immigration, labor, and citizenship.[2] The law makes "the failure to carry immigration documents a crime and give(s) the police broad power to detain anyone suspected of being in the country illegally" (Archibold). Opponents of the law consider it a legalized form of racial profiling and worry about the effect of such a discriminatory piece of legislation on the Latin@ community. While the legislation is currently being challenged on multiple grounds by the Justice Department and by coalitions like the one formed between the Mexican American Legal Defense and Education Fund, the American Civil Liberties Union, and the National Immigration Law Center, the anti-immigrant sentiments of the law have moved beyond the boundaries of Arizona. The multimedia political news source *Politico* analyzed the 2010 gubernatorial races and found that "of the 37 gubernatorial races this year, candidates in more than 20 states have endorsed adopting a strict Arizona-style immigration law or passing legislation that makes it harder for illegal immigrants to live, work and access basic public benefits in their state," and states like Georgia have passed laws based on SB 1070 (Budoff Brown). The emergence of such draconian policies is disturbing, but, as evidenced by a history of exclusionary immigration policies, not new.

Even before the passage of SB 1070, the state of Arizona had found itself in the middle of the immigration discussion when the decision was made to construct a nearly 2,000-mile-long wall between the United States and Mexico to stop the influx of undocumented immigrants into the country. One month before the passage of the Secure

Fence Act, signed into law by President Bush in October 2006, the *Arizona Daily Star* in Tucson sent an investigative team along the nearly 2,000-mile U.S.–Mexico border in an attempt to provide its readers with an understanding of the issues surrounding the immigration debate. The *Star*'s four-part series, entitled "Sealing Our Border: Why It Won't Work," follows a group of journalists in their journey from San Diego to the Gulf of Mexico in a report that looks at the economic, cultural, and physical geography of the border.

One of the most intriguing parts of the series, "The Legacy of Gatekeeper and Hold the Line," investigates the role that the construction of physical barriers has played in keeping out undocumented immigrants. Through various interviews, the report represents diverse views regarding the militarization of the border and provides a comprehensive look at the conflicting sides of the debate. Of particular interest is an interview with Border Patrol Agent Christopher Bauder, who is identified as having patrolled the San Diego Sector for over nine years. Bauder believes that Operation Gatekeeper has been unsuccessful and that closing off the border will ultimately fail because the real issue in the immigration debate is employment, not border security. Based on his observations, Bauder claims that "ninety-five percent of the people that cross the border are coming to find work." Bauder's statement emphasizes the economic relationship that exists between immigration and labor. For Bauder, the resolution to the immigration problem lies in going after businesses that hire undocumented workers. Even though Bauder and those like him who argue for a crackdown on employers understand the relationship that exists between labor and immigration, the discourse he utilizes is contained within a rhetoric of immigration that emphasizes its effects on the nation and the importance of maintaining nation-state boundaries.[3]

While there are multiple positions on the immigration debate, one thing that most vocal proponents and opponents of immigration have in common is the emphasis they place on the domestic consequences of the growing number of immigrants. Scholars like Vernon Briggs and conservative political right-leaning groups like Numbers USA and the Center for Immigration Studies claim that undocumented immigration adversely impacts the United States because immigrants take away jobs from "real Americans" and place undue strain on government resources. Briggs contends, in particular, that undocumented workers hurt the African American working class by competing for its jobs and, in the process, suppressing wages. Some opponents of immigration rely on the racist rhetoric that situates immigrants as too different (read "inferior") from white Americans and see the growing number of immigrants as a threat to the culture of the nation—a culture they see as based on the mythology of a homogeneous white citizenry. On the other hand, pro-immigrant organizations like the Cato Institute and the Pew Research Center's Hispanic Trends Project maintain that immigrant workers are a necessary part of the national economy and contribute to the well-being of the nation through their labor and the taxes they pay. These organizations tend to see immigrants as adding to the cultural diversity of the country, a diversity based on liberal ideas of multiculturalism (which run the danger of glossing over important differences). Both sides of the argument concentrate their debates on the effects that immigrants have on the country, but they situate immigration within the boundaries of labor and the nation, in isolation from the geopolitical realities that influence immigration patterns. In explaining why people "choose" to immigrate to the United States, many employ the rhetoric of the United States as the land of opportunity, a place where dreams can come true. This rhetoric, however, makes the assumption that the American Dream is a possibility for all and obscures the changes that have occurred under a new global regime of interconnected economic and political networks.

My interest in the current immigration debate lies in understanding how cultural productions engage in the discussion of immigration and participate in the circulation of ideologies regarding immigration and labor—specifically through their depiction of immigrant women workers. One of the most effective ways of reading these representations is through a study that deconstructs the conventional immigrant story, an anachronistic narrative that continues to be perpetuated both in cultural productions and in the general debate about immigration.[4] The traditional immigrant narrative, a genre in American literature that became popular during the late nineteenth and early twentieth centuries, continues to be used today in describing the process of the "Americanization" of immigrants.[5] The tale is ultimately a narrative of progress, acting as an ideological tool that attempts to contain the experience of immigrants within a story line that promotes the idea of achieving success, i.e., the American Dream, through hard work and perseverance. Often left out of such a conventional narrative are stories of structural racism, sexism, and classism, obstacles that many immigrants find insurmountable, regardless of how hard they work. As a tool of analysis, the traditional narrative of immigration is no longer a useful framework for tracing the ventures of modern immigrants, nor for determining the differences that exist among immigrant populations. Instead, the schema becomes useful in a project of deconstruction and creation of alternative narratives. In fact, new narratives are challenging these "success stories" and act as a stepping-stone to new schemas of narration that more accurately engage the realities of contemporary immigrant experiences. The purpose of my project is twofold: to read the conventional immigrant narrative as a type of ideological system of containment whose organizing logic can be challenged and ultimately dismantled; and to identify the creation of a Latina genealogy of immigrant literatures that provides oppositional narratives that offer decentralized accounts of power and exploitation.

A Literary Tradition

The majority of scholarship on the immigrant-narrative genre has tended to look at canonical texts like those of Mary Antin, William Carlos Williams, and Anzia Yezierska and has been limited to written works. While the analysis of these texts has been instrumental in understanding the immigration histories of some European immigrants and in identifying the conventions of the genre, it has tended to overlook the differences between a European immigration experience and those of non-European immigrants. For example, literary critic William Q. Boelhower, in his essay "The Immigrant Novel as Genre," identifies the macroproposition of the immigrant novel thus: "An immigrant protagonist(s), representing an ethnic world view, comes to America with great expectations, and through a series of trials, is led to reconsider them in terms of his final status" (5). In her/his journey toward achieving the "final status," the protagonist must reconcile the tension between the old world and the new. That reconciliation can take the shape of various outcomes, ranging in degree from attempting to hold onto old-world culture in the new world, to completely assimilating into the new world, leaving the old world behind.[6] Boelhower also identifies the schema of the narrative in the protagonist's quest for reconciliation. The narrative, written in the traditional linear structure, follows the protagonist through three stages, or phases: expectations, contact, and resolution. The immigrant's story usually begins in the phase of expectations, which can occur in the old world or the new world and is the moment of the immigrant's dream, the moment of imagining the possible new world. It is in this stage that the immigrant protagonist is often the most invested in the ideology of the United States as "America," the land of endless opportunity. Following the stage of expectations is that of contact, where the protagonist faces various experiences and trials in the new world. These trials often take the form of economic struggle, hard labor, and discrimination based on being a new arrival. The challenges survived during the contact phase ultimately lead to the final phase, resolution, where the protagonist either achieves assimilation or becomes alienated, and, according to Boelhower, it is this alienation that "leads the protagonist to idealize the old world—either through an attempt to preserve his old world culture, even though he may be assimilated into the new world, or through a stiff criticism of an alienating set of experiences in America" (5).

To understand the organizational logic behind the structure, we must begin with an understanding of the historically popular immigrant story. Getting to the heart of this literary tradition allows those invested in challenging cultural systems of power the opportunity to contest the logic through a project of deconstruction. The conventional structure of the immigrant narrative functions as an ideological tool that masks struggle and oppression to keep intact the myth of the nation as the "city on a hill." The schema identified by Boelhower functions as a form of "systematizing thought," to use Michel Foucault's terminology, and as such can be analyzed and dismantled. When we insert subjugated histories and contest the structure of the schema of this master narrative, the fissures in the conventional narrative widen into much larger ruptures that cannot be easily subsumed under the narrative's organizing logic. Through these cracks come forth narratives of immigration that question our assumptions about the processes of diasporic movement and our national construction of citizenship and belonging. The centering of these often-marginalized stories allows cultural producers to create oppositional narratives that challenge the ideological containment of the traditional schema.

So what is at stake in analyzing the conventional immigrant narrative? Even though Boelhower identifies the organizing structure of the dominant immigrant narrative, he leaves unsaid a discussion of the ideological work the schema is performing. If we look at the narrative structure of the traditional immigrant story as simply a literary convention, we run the risk of overlooking the power the narrative has had in creating and perpetuating commonly held assumptions about immigration and how the traditional narrative has been employed to render invisible those stories that do not conform.[7] It is no coincidence that the rhetoric of the American Dream remains so entrenched when discussing the question of immigration. While identifying the schema is a useful undertaking, we must push the deconstruction project further to truly understand the intervention that new immigration narratives are making and the disruption they pose to the national rhetoric of meritocracy. The first step in dismantling the ideologies of the immigrant narrative lies in recognizing the system on which it is created—the foundation on which the ideology is built. The most important element of the traditional immigrant narrative is its reliance on a steadfast belief in the possibility of achieving the American Dream—a dream of attaining economic success while enjoying the freedoms and privileges of living in a democratic and egalitarian society, in a nation that promises "liberty and justice for all."

The notion that if one just works hard enough, one will be successful is a powerful aspect of the dream. Inherent in this ideology is the idea of meritocracy, the belief that what one gets out of the system is relational to what one puts into it. A person is successful based on individual merit, "generally viewed as a combination of factors including innate abilities, working hard, having the right attitude, and having high moral character and integrity" (McNamee and Miller). Under a system of meritocracy, a nation's resources are allocated and distributed based on the merit of individuals. If a person is unable to achieve economic success, it is seen as a failure of the individual, a lack either of drive or of ability or a deficiency of character. Absent from this construction are forces that impede one from succeeding based on individual merit. The simplistic structure of meritocracy does not account for important "social gravity" factors—including inheritance, access to education, and discrimination—that keep an individual within a specific class location regardless of merit.[8]

Another significant aspect of the American Dream ideology lies in the notion of choice and the belief that if people choose to work hard, they can be successful. However, the success or failure of the individual's accomplishments in this scenario is connected to the concept that the nation-state creates relatively equal opportunities for all its citizens. The American Dream ideology is dependent on the imagining of the nation as egalitarian, a space where all dreams are achievable for everyone. The success stories paraded to keep us invested in this ideology are also the stories used to differentiate the United States from the rest of the world. After all, isn't this dream the reason that immigrants choose America? While the rhetoric of the United States as the land of opportunity remains ever present, the reality of the widening gap between the rich and the poor, the increase in poverty, the continual problem of unemployment, and the rise of hate groups tells a different story. If this dream is achieved by so few, why does it continue to enjoy such popularity? Why does the idea of the American Dream continue to permeate so many aspects of our culture?

To understand the function of the American Dream ideology as part of a larger construction of the nation, we need to identify it for what it is: a myth. While the word "myth" is used to describe everything from creation stories to religion, I want to employ a definition of it based on Roland Barthes' understanding of it as a system of communication, a "form" (*Mythologies* 109). For Barthes, myth is a message, an ideology, and as such, can be read and deconstructed. Barthes points out that the power of myth lies in its ability to naturalize, to "transform history into nature" (*Mythologies* 129). If we employ Barthes' practice of reading myth as a system of meaning, we can begin to read the American Dream as a powerful ideological tool that lies at the center of the traditional immigrant narrative. We can recognize how this idea of success obfuscates the role played by structures of power in creating opportunity and privilege. By looking at the American Dream as a constructed ideology, a myth, we can begin to deconstruct the traditional immigrant narrative and investigate how the narrative itself is a myth, a set of ideologies about the nation and belonging.

Deconstruction of the myth of the American Dream is dependent on inserting invisible histories and uncovering marginalized narratives. In his discussion of genealogy, the local, and the return of knowledge, Michel Foucault outlines his notion of "subjugated knowledges." For Foucault, it is the emergence of subjugated knowledges, the "historical contents that have been buried or masked in functional coherences or formal systematizations," along with "a whole set of knowledges that have been disqualified as inadequate to their task or insufficiently elaborated: naive knowledges, located low down on the hierarchy, beneath the required level of cognition or scientificity," that can lead to a discursive critique of organized systems of power (7). The combination of alternative scholarly knowledge (which has been omitted from traditional histories) and marginalized local knowledge (which has been disqualified and dismissed as inferior) disrupts the systemic ordering and separation of knowledge and knowledge production. The conventional immigrant narrative operates based on a dependence on an ideologically constructed history—a history that privileges a specific construction of the nation as a democratic and meritocratic state. Left out of this official history are the stories of struggle and oppression of those groups that remain in the periphery. In employing both of these types of subjugated knowledges to critique official discourses, the possibility of disrupting structures of power becomes a new reality.

The importance of deconstructing the traditional immigrant narrative and incorporating subjugated knowledges to create a new narrative lies in the oppositional possibilities that the practice entails. In *Methodology of the Oppressed*, Chela Sandoval argues,

> To shift from the condition of legitimized citizen and faithful consumer of ideology
> to another location . . . means that one must learn to take in, decipher, and decon-

struct ideology using a formal mode of analysis. One willingly perceives the image, but then, removing oneself from its system of life, its composition is revealed as a structured appropriation of previous meanings and forms: the life of dominant ideology is thus undone. (103)

If we analyze the conventional immigrant narrative from a position in the margins, from a position that questions the myth of upward mobility and assimilation, the power of the narrative is undermined.

Once we read the traditional immigrant story as a myth, we can begin to recognize the possibilities of using the narrative to undermine conventional ideologies. In her discussion of the "methodology of the oppressed," Sandoval maps out the five strategies that have aided the survival of marginalized groups under various systems of oppression: "the technologies of semiotics, deconstruction, meta-ideologizing, democratics and differential movement" (146). Using the technology of semiotics, or the reading of signs, to deconstruct signs is a two-pronged strategy of resistance. Meta-ideologizing challenges dominant cultural forms through the appropriation of existing ideologies, or what Sandoval terms the "*ideologization of ideology itself*" (108). The technology of democratics brings together existing techniques for the purpose of egalitarian social change. The fifth technology, differential movement, allows for the operation, maneuvering, and progression of the other four technologies that make up the methodology of the oppressed. These techniques, or "oppositional technologies of power," allow for a decentering of power that makes possible the movement toward recognizing the oppositional possibilities that exist in alternative narratives of immigration. By reading new narratives as examples of a "methodology of the oppressed," we read in them alternative histories and narratives of immigration that challenge the ideological enclosure of the traditional immigrant schema.

On Acculturation and Assimilation

The persistent inflow of Hispanic immigrants threatens to divide the United States into two peoples, two cultures, and two languages. Unlike past immigrant groups, Mexicans and other Latinos have not assimilated into mainstream U.S. culture, forming instead their own political and linguistic enclaves—from Los Angeles to Miami—and rejecting the Anglo-Protestant values that built the American dream. The United States ignores this challenge at its peril.

» Samuel P. Huntington, "The Hispanic Challenge"

Integral to a discussion of the immigrant narrative is the emphasis it places on assimilation. In the traditional narrative, the goal of assimilating into the dominant American society is an important marker of success and, as evidenced by Samuel Huntington's sentiments above, proof of national belonging. While an assimilationist narrative provides an uncomplicated ending that gestures toward a happily-ever-after conclusion, theories of assimilation and acculturation are anything but simple. Herbert J. Gans' distinction between the two terms, one he argues was part of the conventional usage in the 1940s at the University of Chicago, is "based on the difference between culture and society and, accordingly, acculturation refers mainly to the new-comers' adoption of the culture . . . of the host society . . . assimilation . . . refers to the newcomers' move out of formal and informal ethnic associations . . . into the nonethnic equivalents accessible to them in that same host society" (877). In other words, "acculturation" means adopting certain aspects of the host country's culture that the immigrant views as favorable or useful while retaining the immigrant's connection to his or her own culture. "Assimilation," however, implies a rejection of one's culture to be absorbed into the larger, hegemonic mainstream. While assimilation has enjoyed certain moments of popularity, many now view it as a negative process and prefer a more acculturationist model. In their defense of assimilation theory, Richard Alba and Victor Nee provide a review of canonical accounts of assimilation and trace the popular theories surrounding the subject. From discussion of earlier conceptions of assimilation, like Milton Gordon's "structural" assimilation and W. Lloyd Warner and Leo Srole's "straight-line" assimilation, to more recent conceptions, like socioeconomic assimilation and residential/spatial assimilation, Alba and Nee's essay highlights the complexity of the construction and the changes that the field of study has undergone.

For Gans, the polarization between acculturation and assimilation is unnecessary since he believes that the labels have been misleading and that "so-called assimilationists have actually been emphasizing acculturation (becoming American culturally but not necessarily socially)" (876). He introduces the term "ethnic retentionists" to refer to individuals "who avoid acculturation and instead retain their ethnic ties" (876). Gans, however, also rejects positioning acculturation and ethnic retention as necessarily polar and instead argues for a reconciliation of the two positions based on his argument that "even when second and third generation ethnics may have become almost entirely acculturated, they still retain a significant number of ethnic ties . . . and cannot be said to have assimilated . . . This is not at odds with ethnic retention theory, which mainly argues that ethnic social ties are being retained, but which pays less attention to ethnic cultural retention. Thus, the two positions differ less in empirical reality than in debate" (876). Gans' distinction is important as it points to the gap that can exist between empirical research on a subject and the discussion that takes place around it. In this project, I rely on the more traditional conception of assimilation because of the popularity it continues to enjoy in our national discourse on immigration. The acceptance of Huntington's thesis on the inability or unwillingness of Mexican immigrants to assimilate illustrates the continued dependence on a simplistic assimilation/non-assimilation binary. For the most part, cultural producers are not interested in the complexities of assimilation/acculturation, but instead continue to flatten the topic to provide simple and easily consumed plotlines.

Just as the dominant rhetoric of the immigration debate fails to fully encompass the complexities of the current immigration and labor situations, the traditional immigrant narrative is unsuccessful in representing the changing immigration experience. The schema that Boelhower identifies is based on an ethnic model of difference that functions well in analyzing the more traditional white immigrant stories, but doesn't meet the needs of immigrant stories of people of color who cannot simply assimilate because of the issue of race or who do not see assimilation as something to be desired.[9] The traditional schema's inability to easily translate to narratives of people of color also illustrates the limitations of the conventional immigrant paradigm in describing more recent immigration patterns and experiences.[10] Despite the real differences in immigration patterns and experiences, popular cultural productions continue to use the dominant immigrant narrative as a basis for the representation of the immigration of people of color; revisions of this narrative, on the other hand, are being undertaken by authors who are challenging its story line. As Lisa Lowe has argued, "Cultural productions emerging out of the contradictions of immigrant marginality . . . intervene in the narrative of national development that would illegitimately locate the 'immigrant' before history or exempt the 'immigrant' from history" (*Immigrant Acts* 9). Cultural productions about marginalized immigrant communities whose immigrant experiences are not necessarily stories of progress serve to disarticulate the dominant immigrant narrative and ensure the visibility of different immigrant patterns that have influenced the formation of the United States as a heterogeneous nation.

A Global Framework

The conventional paradigm of the immigrant story is based on a clear geographical and ideological distinction between the old world and the new world, a differentiation that positions the United States as the preferred location. The new world is supposed to represent modernity, while the old world stands for antiquated ideas that must be rejected in order for the immigrant subject to transition into a subject of modernity.[11] In revising the dominant narrative of immigration to include the different realities of immigrants of color, a new immigrant story should not only challenge the conception that one must reject the old world in favor of life in the new world, but ultimately reject the constructed distinction between the old world and the new world. The emphasis on creating new immigrant stories that more closely illustrate the lasting relationship that exists, not between old world and new world, but between countries of origin and host countries, and between new and earlier immigrants, allows the narratives to go beyond being just individual stories.[12] The story of Abuela Claudia is just one of many immigrant narratives that portray the connection that remains between immigrants' adopted country and the home they have left behind. These new narratives become cultural productions that demand a new way of representing immigration, a representation that rejects the old/new world binary in favor of a model that reframes the experience in terms of immigration relationships that exist within a connected global network. In such a representation, the links that exist between the country of origin and the host country become more clearly evident and immigration is seen as a condition that is not necessarily precipitated by the desire to achieve the American Dream, or one that ends with arrival in the United States. Abuela Claudia's story and her dream of returning to the Caribbean, the place she still considers home, make a strong argument for a more complex narrative structure and displace the United States as the preferred site in which to create one's home.

The relationship between the country of origin and the host country can be much more easily understood if conceptualized as fitting into what scholars such as Immanuel Wallerstein refer to as a world-system. Within a world-systems analysis, the theory of modernization—one that is predicated on the constructed spatial/temporal differences between nation-states—is rejected in favor of studying countries within an interconnected global system.[13] The world-systems analysis rejects the binary between modern and premodern/less modern and the hierarchy that such a binary makes implicit. Instead, Wallerstein argues for an understanding of the current capitalist global system as being predicated on the extensive division of labor that occurs between what he refers to as the core states and the peripheral areas. The core states exploit the peripheral areas through a range of methods, including the exporting of peripheral areas' natural resources and raw materials and the importing of manufacturing industries to employ cheap labor.[14] By referring to economically dominant countries as the "core," Wallerstein is underscoring the imbalance of power that exists between the core and the periphery, while emphasizing the interconnectedness of the two areas. When the new immigrant narrative is situated as occurring under a world-system, the movement of people across constructed national boundaries is no longer described as occurring between spatially and temporally differentiated areas, but instead as taking place within a global system that is based on various economic and political relationships.

The acknowledgment of the relationship between the immigrant and the two countries s/he inhabits becomes an important tool in understanding the changes that have taken place in the immigration patterns of the United States. In her work on immigration and globalization, Saskia Sassen stresses the importance of understanding immigration beyond domestic policies and the internal effects of the movements of diasporic peoples. Sassen argues that while conditions of poverty, unemployment, and overpopulation do play a role in migration, they alone do not promote the large-scale emigration we are currently seeing, and it is important to understand the processes that transform these conditions into a "migration inducing situation" (*Mobility* 6). A focus on the more commonly acknowledged conditions of migration ignores the internationalization of production and migration in favor of an analysis that focuses on the domestic—making immigration a domestic problem for the host (receiving) country and isolating the process from the more global relationship between the sending and receiving countries, or the periphery and the core. In her analysis of the Dominican Republic, Haiti, and Mexico, Sassen argues that these countries "accentuate, first, the fact that U.S. business, military, or diplomatic activities were a strong presence in countries that have significant migration to the U.S." and that "secondly, it is important to emphasize that the combination of poverty, unemployment, or underemployment with the emergence of objective and ideological linkages probably operates as a migration inducing factor" (*Mobility* 9). The increase in migration to the United States can only be accurately studied if the connections—be they military, economic, or ideological—between sending countries and U.S. foreign policy are fully understood.

While the traditional schema of narration may be useful in analyzing immigrant narratives that take place during the early part of the twentieth century, the composition of immigrants to the United States has changed drastically to include many non-Western populations.[15] The Immigration Act of 1965 led to an increase in migration from non-European countries, an unforeseen result of the policy's empha-sis on family-reunification immigration. Sassen maintains that the 1965 act "should be seen in combination with military and economic policies facilitating a wide range of U.S. activities abroad" (*Mobility* 6). The increase in economic intervention and military campaigns in Latin America during the second half of the twentieth century created what is now referred to as "new enclosures." The term "enclosure" refers to the movement that began in the fifteenth century in which English peasants were forced off common land and into wage labor.[16] "New enclosures" is now used to describe the ways in which disadvan-taged populations have been separated from various means of pro-duction, like their land, and forced to migrate to cities or immigrate to countries dependent on cheap labor, like the United States.[17] Sassen connects the process of separating the worker from the land and the creation of a migrating class of labor:

> Capitalism transforms land into a commodity. Because land was the basis for pre-capitalist modes of subsistence, its transformation into a commodity created a mass of landless peasants with little alternative to becoming part of the rural or urban labor reserve . . . labor reserves willing to be mobilized into the labor market. (Mobility 33)

Along with economic restructuring, U.S. military intervention in Lat-in America and the Caribbean has also created a mass displacement of people that has affected immigration.[18] The creation of "new en-closures" in the current world-system serves to further illustrate the correlation that exists between the core and the periphery.

The ideological containment performed by the conventional immi-grant paradigm and the national debate on immigration functions to downplay or erase the initial reason for immigration and disregards the connection between the core and the periphery. Both the debate and the conventions of the genre place an emphasis on the economic opportunities (i.e., the American Dream) and the democratic, meri-tocratic system the United States offers immigrants (i.e., the "city on a hill"), but they ignore the reality of the role that U.S. foreign policy, alone and in conjunction with the International Monetary Fund and the World Bank, has played in restructuring countries of origin. Ul-timately, the United States itself should be held accountable for the migration into the country.

The resolution at the end of the traditional immigrant narrative and the national debate on immigration both assume that a level of assimilation is the ultimate goal that is eventually to be achieved. Proponents and opponents of immigration both take for granted that an immigrant's life will automatically be more successful in the United States. Again, the reality of immigrants of color, both documented and undocumented, resists such an easy resolution. Boelhower's narrative schema is insufficient in describing the experience of immigration under our present world-system. It is a very general schema that does not consider the very complicated relationships the immigrant subject must navigate before, during, and after emigration. Within such a schema, important issues that make up the current immigrant experience—such as an immigrant's un/documented status, or a sending community's dependence on remittances (money sent home by workers who have emigrated), or the militarization of constructed national boundaries—are completely absent. Even though some contemporary critics have attempted to insert narratives of immigration by people of color into the U.S. literary canon, they do not directly challenge many of the assumptions present in the traditional immigrant narrative schema.[19]

In contemporary cultural productions, new oppositional narratives are central in understanding and capturing the experience of immigrant workers. Instead of providing a linear narrative of progression of immigration, I argue that certain contemporary immigrant narratives of people of color provide us with a representation of immigration as a set of continuous conditions that do not end or begin with the physical arrival of the immigrant into the new country. Like theories of modernization, the older schema of narration is based on a continuum of progress and temporal movement. A country is said to go from premodern to modern, just as the protagonist of the traditional narrative goes from the phase of expectations to a final resolution, or from being a subject of the periphery to the possibility of becoming a citizen of the core. The linear movement in the story is easily mapped out through the narrative. Unlike the line of progression in these narratives of progress, oppositional narratives resist being diagrammed on a steady upward slant, but instead call for an illustration of the various conditions that immigrant subjects encounter. There is no simple beginning or ending. Instead, these stories represent the negotiating of relationships and experiences, including the impetus for emigration, the journey and crossing of the border, and the relationship of the immigrant subject to family, community, and labor. These continuous relations can exist simultaneously and are not necessarily experienced chronologically or in different spaces; in other words, they take place in the core and in the periphery. There is no unequivocal temporal or ideological separation between the host country and the country of origin. By insisting on an understanding of the movement of peoples across constructed boundaries, as occurring under a world-system of connections, the revised narratives challenge the ideological closure of the narrative of progress and immigration being redeployed by popular representations of immigration and the current debate on immigration reform.

I want to further emphasize the role that work and the struggle for survival play in becoming an immigrant subject by reading the alternative narratives through the lens of labor. In paying specific attention to gender, through an analysis of texts dealing explicitly with female immigrant protagonists and characters, I also want to place new immigrant narratives within the changing gender composition of emigration under globalization. By employing a reading of texts through a contemporary immigrant narrative of labor, while also using, to borrow Henry Louis Gates Jr.'s term, a "culture-specific methodology" that places at its center race, gender, and class, I find that a much more historically situated analysis of immigration and labor becomes possible.

Oppositional Narratives of Immigration and Labor

Genealogy is, then, a sort of attempt to desubjugate historical knowledges, to set them free, or in other words to enable them to oppose and struggle against the coercion of a unitary, formal, and scientific theoretical discourse . . . the project of these disorderly and tattered genealogies is to reactivate local knowledges . . . against the scientific hierarchicalization of knowledge and its intrinsic power effects.

» Michel Foucault, "7 January 1976" (10)

In his discussion of subjugated knowledges, Foucault argues that genealogy plays a pivotal role in the excavation of buried histories and obscured local knowledges. For Foucault, the role of the genealogist is not to ignore historical sequences or to reject knowledge, or to replace this organizing system with our own, but instead to recognize the "tyranny of overall discourses" (8). Genealogies are about "insurrection of knowledges . . . against the centralizing power-effects that are bound up with the institutionalization and workings of any scientific discourse organized in a society such as ours" (9). In this project, I position Latina cultural producers as an example of genealogists who incorporate marginalized histories to challenge the construction of the nation as an egalitarian meritocracy that offers all immigrants the opportunity to achieve the American Dream. Through their centering of histories of oppression and injustice, Latina genealogists provide new narratives of immigration that put forth decentralized accounts of power and exploitation. The accounts incorporate local and marginalized knowledges for critical inquiry and encourage audiences to question assumptions about labor, migration, and gender. By approaching texts offered by producers of nontraditional cultural productions, we can uncover the oppositional possibilities their narratives present. While expanding the parameters of the genre, the alternative texts challenge problematic and potentially dangerous representations of immigrant bodies and complicate the simplistic rhetoric that surrounds our current immigration debate. The work of such writers and artists humanizes individuals who are often rendered just numbers by popular media, pundits, and politicians. These narratives, I argue, now constitute a Latina genealogy of immigrant literature and provide a powerful body of counternarratives that confront the ideological project of the conventional immigrant narrative, while inserting into the nation's awareness immigrant bodies most often rendered invisible and undesirable.

One of the first critical representations of the physical crossing of the U.S.–Mexico border is found in Gregory Nava's 1980 film *El Norte*. In the critically acclaimed film, Nava provides a horrific visual representation of economic and military enclosures that prompt the migration of brother and sister Enrique and Rosa Xuncax from Guatemala. The Guatemalan army, to protect the interests of coffee growers, terrorizes any worker who attempts to organize or to resist extreme labor exploitation, and the Xuncax siblings must flee their home country to avoid being executed.[20] While not all contemporary immigrant stories so clearly illustrate the reasons for emigration, an important aspect of oppositional narratives is their representation of the conditions under globalization that act as the impetus for emigration. Many of the narratives mention the inability to earn a living in the country of origin, due to the lack of work or the substandard wages that make survival virtually impossible. Some place emphasis on emigration taking place to avoid violence, while others represent the reasons for it as various displacements. The conditions behind the diasporic movement of the immigrant protagonists is not always made apparent, yet these new stories of immigration and labor reject conscription into the older conventional narrative that usually situates the decision to immigrate within the ideology of progress that envisions the United States as the land of opportunity. Oppositional narratives show that the motives behind the decision to immigrate are economic and political factors that exist within the present phase of late capitalism. In the process, they make visible the connection between the United States and an immigrant's country of origin, which is absent in the conventional narrative.

The phase of expectations no longer exists in its previous form; instead, the impetus for immigration becomes a quest for survival and not the pursuit of an ideological "promised land." Now people emigrate because they have no choice—they are pushed out. Many have been the victims of new enclosures created by the global restructuring of resources and industries. Some leave their homes as a result of natural disasters, while others are forced to flee the violence of wars and armed conflicts. The United States' reliance on cheap labor provides immigrants with the possibilities of work and economic survival. However, while many hope for better lives here, there is no longer a universal expectation of immigrating and achieving the American Dream. Within the new global network of immigration, the immigrant subject is much more aware of the economic realities of living in the United States and is no longer naïve like Enrique and Rosa Xuncax of *El Norte*, who believed that American streets are paved with gold. Immigrants have emigrated and returned, corresponded with those left behind, and exported cultural productions, actions that have altered the ways in which the immigrant subject sees the United States. Because of the mass movement of people and the immense sharing of information, today's immigrants enter the country with a more realistic understanding of the challenges they will face as workers in this country.

Another characteristic of oppositional immigrant narratives that illustrates the changing composition of immigration in the contemporary moment is the emphasis on what I refer to as the navigation of spatial liminality during the movement from citizen of one nation to immigrant in another. As border crossers, to use Gloria Anzaldúa's concept, immigrants must constantly make their way through a space that exists in the margins, belonging neither here nor there.[21] Their arrival in the United States does not presuppose an instant incorporation into the nation, so immigrants must learn to traverse the margins to which working-class immigrants of color are most often banished. In a world where immigration laws no longer effectively function to keep out diasporic peoples, the journey to the host country and the crossing of the constructed borders of the nation become an important aspect of the immigrant paradigm. No longer is it assumed that the immigrant is entering the United States through official channels, or through the previous ports of entrance, like Ellis Island. Now immigrants are entering through official and unofficial channels, facing a new set of challenges and perils. Some texts choose to emphasize the journey that undocumented immigrants are confronted with as they make their way to the border of the United States. Traversing the terrain that lies between the site of departure and the border, the immigrant subject must negotiate the liminal space that denies her an official status and defines her as an object that must be apprehended or kept out. Other texts choose to focus on the difficulties experienced by the immigrant at the point of crossing the border. As a site of state oppression and violence, the border gets represented in Latina narratives as one more aspect of the immigrant experience with which immigrants must contend.[22] In such cultural productions, the centering of undocumented individuals' stories works to incorporate into the genre of the immigrant narrative individuals who are relegated to the margin. Instead of reducing immigrants to the image of "criminals," the stories of these individuals humanize them. The alternative stories offer oppositional narratives that challenge the invisibility of diasporic people.

In the current age of immigration, the undocumented status of immigrants cannot be reconciled under the old narrative of immigration. Instead, the new immigrant paradigm proposed by a Latina literary genealogy pays close attention to the undocumented worker's constant state of living in the precarious position of being "unofficial." Living in fear of detection is an aspect of the immigrant experience that does not exist within the old paradigm's phase of contact and is an important marker of the changes that have occurred in the process of immigration to the United States. Several texts represent the inhumanity of classifying human beings as "undocumented" and forcing them to exist in a marginal space of constant hiding. Others represent the intensification of exploitation that takes place when a domestic worker is undocumented. While cultural producers sometimes do not clearly identify their immigrant protagonists as documented or undocumented, under the present movement of people across national boundaries, official documentation can no longer be assumed.

The conditions of immigration for many people of color do not end at the point of arrival in the United States, but continue to influence the life of the new immigrant subject, an aspect of the experience to which Latina writers pay close attention. In the older model of immigration, the protagonist is often represented arriving in a new world, most often surrounded by a different culture and language. The sense of alienation encountered by the immigrant functions to cement the distinction between old and new world, and plays an important role in helping to linearly develop the narrative of the immigrant as a story of progression. In our current state of globalization and transnational movement of peoples, it is unlikely that an immigrant will be unable to find a community of fellow immigrants. Cities like El Paso, Los Angeles, New York, and Chicago provide immigrants with enclaves where they can make connections and find help in negotiating their way through the U.S. economic and political system.[23] Within the older model of narration, the contact phase often positions the immigrant as the "other," a process that occurs as soon as the immigrant arrives in the country. In the immigrant communities that now make up a vital part of urban spaces, the new immigrant is no longer the "other" but is instead just "one more." It is only when the immigrant subject leaves the community of immigrants that she is confronted with being the "other," but as soon as she returns to her immigrant community, she again belongs.[24] The oppositional narratives represent a fluidity in the position of the immigrant subject that is absent in the former narratives' conception of the contact phase. Many immigrants are also comfortable in urban spaces, dispelling the myth of the periphery as existing outside the core in a premodern state. The heavy industrialization of Latin America and the Caribbean has facilitated the movement of individuals from rural areas to cities in countries of origin, and from those home cities to cities in host countries like the United States. Alternative immigrant narratives more effectively encompass these changes and represent the conditions of immigrant communities existing in the margins of cities. They are uncovering the creation of community, not for the sake of creating separatist spaces, but in an effort to combat the prejudice and discrimination often faced in the world outside of the immigrant community.

Current immigrant stories by Latina cultural producers also illustrate the changes in familial relations that make up the immigrant experience. Women—who are a growing part of the transnational immigrant community—often leave behind children in the care of their home communities. Unlike men, who frequently migrate and leave children behind with mothers, these immigrant women must depend on extended families and community members to help raise their children, further reinforcing the link between host and country of origin. As a result of the mass migration of women, the practice of immigrating for work and sending money home has become a major source of income for countries in the periphery. Barbara Ehrenreich and Arlie Russell Hochschild point out that "the governments of some sending countries actively encourage women to migrate in search of domestic jobs, reasoning that migrant women are more likely than their male counterparts to send their hard-earned wages to their families rather than spending the money on themselves" (7). Not only do these remittances help support the families left behind, but they aid in the overall economy of the home country.[25] While some women return to their countries of origin and others eventually send for their families, many are forced to raise their children from afar.[26] The phase of contact in the traditional narrative cannot adequately encompass the relationships that exist between a female immigrant protagonist and her family under the current conditions of globalization. While nation-states might try to ignore/erase the role that women immigrants now play in national economies, oppositional narratives are centering the contributions these women make to the global economy and positioning their laboring bodies as integral to the functioning of multiple national governments.

In the older immigrant story, labor often plays an important role in helping the immigrant protagonist achieve success through hard work and in the process perpetuates the myth of an American meritocracy. Contemporary narratives of labor and immigration instead represent labor and the protagonist's position as a worker in direct relation to the immigrant condition. The space of labor is now positioned as a microcosm for the exploitation of the worker under a capitalistic system that takes advantage of the undocumented immigrant's liminal position in the United States. Latina narratives focus attention on how the intersection of the protagonist's being a woman, a person of color, and an immigrant (often undocumented) influences her experience in the workplace. The conditions of labor represented emphasize the racism and exploitation faced by the immigrant protagonist, and while popular texts attempt to reconcile the abuses of the laborer under the ideology of assimilation and success, most of the oppositional narratives do not offer a clear resolution to the difficulties experienced by workers in the space of labor. Instead of situating labor as a stepping-stone to economic success and as a way of achieving the American Dream, the contemporary narrative represents the laboring space as the place where ideologies of race, class, and gender get played out. In the case of domestic work, the insular walls of the home as laboring space help to contain not only the exploitation of the worker but also the physical and emotional violence to which many domestic laborers are subjected.

Even though many of the contemporary narratives being discussed in the subsequent chapters follow a linear structure in narrating the story of the immigrant worker that culminates in the resolving of various conflicts at the end of the text, they do not always offer a simple resolution. Some of the texts attempt to provide a happy ending by portraying a certain level of assimilation or, more accurately, acculturation; others challenge the audience at the closing of the narrative by instead gesturing toward the protagonist's continual negotiation of the immigrant condition. Instead of the easy solutions advanced by the conventional narrative of immigration and assimilation, oppositional immigrant narratives point to a continual experience of immigration under a structure of late capitalism that often begins anew with the constant movement of the individual. The new immigrant subject does not always come to the United States with the idea of settling down forever, and some choose to return home after the conditions of the original immigration change or after earning enough money to return. Some return home disillusioned by their inability to negotiate a racist system based on exploitation. Others, however, are forcibly ejected from the nation through the process of deportation. At the point of deportation, the movement of the individual might be southward, but there is always the possibility of a new journey to the north, gesturing to the continuous cycle of immigration.

In what follows, I contend that texts by certain Latina cultural producers are providing a specifically Latina genealogy of new immigrant narratives that more closely engage the conditions of immigration occurring in late capitalism. I position these texts as challenges to stereotypical representations of immigrant workers promoted by popular cultural productions, like Hollywood-produced films. I argue that major Hollywood film producers redeploy the discourse of the old narrative of immigration in an attempt to advance the ideology of the nation as the land of opportunity. In these popular cultural productions, it is imperative that the challenges faced by the immigrant be simply resolved. The realities of exploitative labor cannot so easily be subsumed into the narrative, so those difficulties must be dealt with in a way that makes them simple and unproblematic. By providing the protagonists of the films with problems and conflicts they can fix, the cultural productions can justify happy endings for audiences. In giving audiences the requisite happily-ever-after conclusion, current Hollywood films perpetuate the dominant immigrant narrative and head off any discomfort that audiences might feel about immigrant workers, effectively acting as an ideological form of containment to ensure that the myth of the "city on a hill" remains intact. Each of the cultural productions that I situate as counternarrative to conventional Hollywood movies emphasizes different aspects of the new immigrant narrative being proposed. By mapping out how each cultural production situates the immigrant experience, we can examine how Latina cultural producers are representing the local, marginalized narrative of those who remain relegated to the periphery. The oppositional possibilities of the texts become evident. The work of these cultural producers builds on the project of theorizing the border undertaken by Anzaldúa in the 1980s. The understanding of the border as constructed, as "una herida abierta" (an open wound), and the acknowledgment of the processes of immigration as complex and continuous, expands the project of theorizing the border beyond the physical demarcation between nations (Anzaldúa 25). The specific crafting of narratives around the lives of women draws our attention to the marginalized stories of female immigrants and the particular role gender plays in the movement of individuals across national boundaries. The narratives of opposition included in my analysis incorporate the stories of women, labor, and movement that social scientists have been studying for some time now.[27]

To understand the legacy of the traditional immigrant narrative and uncover the ideological work being performed by the schema, I start in chapter 1 by comparing three very different texts that provide conventional stories of immigration. I begin with an analysis of a canonical Chicano text, José Antonio Villarreal's *Pocho*, positioning it as an example of the traditional immigrant narrative and reading it alongside the 2004 Hollywood-produced film *Spanglish*, directed by James L. Brooks. By analyzing the texts together, I look at how the conventional immigrant narrative has been employed by earlier texts and how later films continue the tradition of casting the immigrant story as a narrative of progress and upward mobility. This chapter also illustrates the role that gender plays in constructing immigrant bodies in representation.

In my second chapter, I examine representations of immigrant workers in the space of the home. I argue that the representations of these workers in texts by Latina writers reject the message of success present in the Hollywood films. The texts analyzed in the first chapter perpetuate the ideology of the immigrant narrative as a narrative of progress, while texts by Latina writers challenge stereotypes about domestic workers through an inclusion of stories told from the perspective of marginalized voices and promote a new literary genealogy. The film *Spanglish* stands in stark contrast to the representations of domestic labor and gendered immigrant bodies advanced by Lucha Corpi's novel *Cactus Blood*, Anayansi Prado's documentary film *Maid in America*, and the plays *Latina*, by Milcha Sánchez-Scott, and *Living Out*, by Lisa Loomer.

Chapter 3 shifts the discussion of immigrant domestic labor to the public space of the hospitality industry. I juxtapose three Hollywood movies—Wayne Wang's *Maid in Manhattan*, Wes Anderson's *Bottle Rocket*, and Ken Loach's *Bread and Roses*—with Esmeralda Santiago's novel *América's Dream* and Marisela Norte's spoken-word piece "Act of the Faithless" to analyze the various representations of domestic labor that take place in the transnational space of global cities. In this chapter, I expand the conversation on domestic labor to include janitorial work and housekeeping in the sphere of the hotel industry and office buildings. Loach's film provides an opportunity to discuss the multiple forms of resistance taking place through the unionization of immigrant workers in the public realm of domestic labor.

The final chapter analyzes the strategic move of positioning immigrant workers as superheroes and the role that new technology plays in creating new Latina narratives of immigration. By looking at the *Superheroes* photo series by Dulce Pinzón alongside Laura Alvarez' multimedia series *Double Agent Sirvienta* and Anayansi Prado's *Maid in America*, we can investigate the role that resistance to invisibility plays in several examples of visual culture. The move to position workers often marginalized and made invisible by their labor and immigration status as heroic and bigger than life rejects the common rhetoric that represents laboring immigrant bodies as a waste or a drain on our national resources. These cultural producers offer new and exciting representations of immigrant narratives that expand the parameters of the genre.

While I have organized my chapters according to the different conditions I have identified in my argument, I have done so for the sake of creating a sense of coherence. I do not mean to imply that the current conditions of immigration occur in a linear/temporal fashion or to re-create a linear schema of narration. Trying to identify one unified organizing schema would re-create the disciplining of knowledge that the project of genealogy is trying to challenge. I also am not arguing that the literature, film, and other media that I analyze in this book exist completely outside of dominant ideologies, but the texts do provide more complex representations of contemporary immigration and labor. Instead of claiming that the counternarratives that I discuss are somehow more "authentic" or "real," I want to read these works as offering a different perspective or representation of what has become a popular literary convention. I hope that by reading literature by writers of color through the lens of a new immigrant paradigm, I can contribute to a growing dialogue on what it means for individuals to live under the current global conditions of immigration and the role that cultural productions play in challenging or perpetuating anachronistic models of movement through national boundaries. As a whole, the texts offer a Latina canon of oppositional narratives that challenge the ideological construction of the nation while expanding the theorization of the border. Through their insertion of narratives of oppression, injustice, and hardship—subjugated knowledges—Latina artists/authors are creating a powerful cultural legacy of resistance.

CHAPTER ONE

Dream a Little American Dream
A Traditional Story-Book Romance

> My mom has the mentality that many undocumented individuals have, and that is they love this country as much as they love their own. They love America because of the opportunity their children could have . . . Education and opportunity is the reason we cross the border. Give me a chance, America, to show that you have raised me right, that even if I was not born from your womb, I was still raised by you. I have learned how to be an American, but mostly I have learned to love this country as mine.
>
> » Carla, quoted in *Undocumented Students* (7)

On May 19, 2007, the UCLA Center for Labor Research and Education held a conference to inform students and community members about the California and federal Development, Relief, and Education for Alien Minors (DREAM) Acts.[1] The conference included the testimony of twelve undocumented high school and college students—testimonies the organizers hoped would put a human face on the issue. The quote that opens this chapter is an excerpt from the testimony of Carla, one of the students. Carla's plea for acceptance and recognition as "American" is a heart-wrenching illustration of the complicated construction of citizenship and national belonging. Her narrative indicates that "education and opportunity" are the reasons that individuals like her mother chose to immigrate to the United States. With both of the legislative acts' focus on education, it is no surprise that rhetoric about the United States as the land of opportunity is strongly present in the testimonies of the young people. Carla's words, however, also point to the contradictory position in which she finds herself. Even though she has excelled in school and has been a "good" resident of California, her undocumented status denies her the opportunity to be a true American. While she might see herself as American, the legal system, which defines the criteria for citizenship, rejects her claim.

Because both DREAM Acts focus on the education of immigrants, we can read the testimonies of these young people as existing within a larger discourse of immigration and national belonging. The emphasis on education and hard work in the testimonies is an important strategic move that positions these young people as worthy of being embraced by the nation and counters the mainstream conception of "undocumented immigrant" as synonymous with "dangerous criminal." Carla's testimony relies upon implicit, shared understandings about how immigrant narratives should work—she is on the path to success and wants the chance to achieve the dream so many others have enjoyed. While Carla's narrative of immigration is not fiction, her story and those of her fellow presenters are informed by fictive narratives and include some of the same elements that have made the genre of American immigrant literature so popular. The ideology of the United States as the "land of opportunity" and the "promised land," important aspects of older immigrant narratives, continues to exist. The discourse of upward mobility through hard work and perseverance, a longtime staple of immigrant narratives, remains a pervasive part of our national ideologies. To understand how this traditional narrative of immigration continues to influence our current cultural imagination, we must first recognize the basic structure of the narrative and the ways in which it has evolved.

I read José Antonio Villarreal's *Pocho* (1959) as an example of a classic Chicano text that closely follows the organizational logic of the traditional, canonical narrative of immigration, a narrative that was cinematically represented and reproduced almost fifty years later by James L. Brooks' *Spanglish* (2004). Although the novel closely follows the more masculinist structure of the bildungsroman while the film deploys a woman as its protagonist, there are some very basic similarities between the two cultural productions, including a strong emphasis on the United States as the ideological "promised land" and on the role of education in assimilating immigrants. Analyzing these two cultural productions as examples of the traditional immigrant narrative allows for an uncovering of the enduring aspects of the narrative while identifying the changes and adaptations it has undergone that allow it to remain so relevant today. Together, the texts also offer a point of comparison for the new immigrant narratives that will be discussed in subsequent chapters.

A Traditional Narrative

"Traditions" which appear or claim to be old are often quite recent in origin and sometimes invented.

» Eric Hobsbawm, *The Invention of Tradition* (1)

The image of the United States as a nation of immigrants is an enduring one that permeates multiple aspects of our national imaginary. A key element of this image is the construction of the nation as a traditionally welcoming place for the world's less fortunate, but worthy, people. An important ideological tool in this construction has been an immigrant narrative that seeks to explain a diverse immigration history while glossing over ruptures that challenge the notion of the United States as an egalitarian nation of immigrants. While this immigrant narrative is often associated with literary tradition, the parameters of the narrative are not contained within the confines of the written page. The popularity the narrative continues to enjoy illustrates the longevity of this rhetorical tradition, and its multiple manifestations in cultural productions provide for an opportunity to deconstruct the story's organizing logic while also identifying fissures in the structure. By positioning the immigrant narrative as part of the longer story of constructing the nation, its ideological power becomes visible.

In his introduction to *The Invention of Tradition*, historian Eric Hobsbawm takes on the challenge of reframing the ways in which certain European traditions commonly believed to be ancient and enduring are actually much more modern productions. These traditions include some that are older and formally instituted as well as emerging traditions that have enjoyed a quick adoption. For Hobsbawm, the term "invented traditions" is "a set of practices, normally governed by overtly or tacitly accepted rules and of a ritual or symbolic nature, which seek to inculcate certain values and norms of behaviour by repetition, which automatically implies continuity with the past" (1). Hobsbawm's introduction invites us to think critically of how the notion of "tradition" becomes synonymous with "ever-present" and "enduring." He argues for an understanding of "tradition" as a process of invention through repetition and reference to the past.[2] The concept of "invented traditions" lays down a theoretical map for an investigation of rituals and practices that participate in the creation of a national imaginary.

The importance of Hobsbawm's notion of "invented traditions" to this project rests on the potential of deconstructing the concept of "tradition" in the production of cultural texts. By positioning the traditional immigrant narrative within a theoretical framework that challenges the notion of "traditional" from the outset, the ideological project of the genre becomes more easily discernible and therefore de-familiarized. Repetition of narrative tropes is identified and disrupted. In his discussion of the importance of studying the invention of traditions, Hobsbawm argues that the "history which became part of the fund of knowledge or the ideology of nation, state or movement is not what has actually been preserved in popular memory, but what has been selected, written, pictured, popularized and institutionalized by those whose function it is to do so" (13). Viewing a paradigmatic immigrant experience through a theoretical lens that questions its historical veracity allows for a framing of the immigrant narrative as part of a larger, institutional process of socialization and not just as a simple story of individual success. It further provides the opportunity to delve beneath the institutionalized story of immigration to uncover marginalized stories that have been preserved and circulated in alternative communities.

The idea of the United States as a "city upon a hill" has been a prevailing ideological tool in perpetuating the notion that this country is a place of enlightenment, a model of morality and democracy for all others to follow. The phrase in reference to this country was first uttered in a sermon by Puritan immigrant John Winthrop aboard the ship bringing him to the shores of what would become America. It is often this Puritan image that gets universalized as the immigrant experience that helped make the United States a "nation of immigrants." Politicians, in proclaiming the moral superiority of the United States, have relied heavily on Winthrop's rhetorical construction of America. What is important to acknowledge is that under such a construction, the nation is very specifically imagined as a community created by a white migration from Europe, a migration being led by men who sought to break the chains of tyranny. To create a more egalitarian space, these founding immigrants relied on an intellectual history of Western ideas of enlightenment that evolved into a myth of Anglo-Saxon superiority. Historian Reginald Horsman argues that the "Englishmen who settled in America at the beginning of the seventeenth century brought as part of their historical and religious heritage a clearly delineated religious myth of a pure English Anglo-Saxon church . . . They shared with their fellow Englishmen an elaborately developed secular myth of the free nature of Anglo-Saxon political institutions" (1). The reliance on this myth of religious and governing superiority helped create the image of Americans as "favored by Providence" to spread their message of civilization (Horsman 83).

Today, the United States continues to be constructed as a place of opportunity for economic success and a home for democratic ideals and personal freedoms. The ideological power of Winthrop's construction of the future United States as the "city upon a hill" has not waned since he first uttered these words in 1630. In fact, in attempting to glorify American exceptionalism, President Ronald Reagan, ironically a strong anti-immigration proponent, often invoked Winthrop's phrase in his own political discourse.[3] In his 1975 radio address "Images," Reagan claimed that "you don't have to travel too far in the world to realize that we stand as a beacon, that America is today what it was two centuries ago, a place that dreamers dream of, that it is what Winthrop said standing on the deck of the tiny Arabella . . . 'We shall be as a shining city for all the world upon the hill'" (quoted in Hanska 160-161). His statement might seem contradictory with his anti-immigration policies, but it closely follows the tradition of casting the United States as a nation of immigrants. More than just perpetuating the erasure of peoples of color, Reagan's words invoke a history of immigration that has been constructed as white and Western European. The tradition of American immigration remains rooted in a longer historical project of racial formations that continues to ignore narratives that digress from the Anglo-Saxon paradigm. Under the invented logic of the nation as the "city upon a hill," any realities that do not conform to this image remain marginalized, lying outside of the narrative's parameters. The discomfort created by narratives of disruption, which include accounts of unpleasant realities of hardship and injustice, preclude their inclusion within traditional representations of immigration.

A Narrative Tradition

[By using] earlier texts as benchmarks, we will increasingly be able to note not only the ruptures in the discourse but also the links and differences between what was produced in the late nineteenth century and what has been produced in the twentieth century.

» Rosaura Sánchez, "Ideological Discourses in Arturo Islas's *The Rain God*" (114)[4]

The practice of situating narratives of immigration within the discourse of the United States as the "promised land" is prevalent in a larger literary tradition that creates and promotes chronicles perpetuating this ideology. To destabilize the notion of "tradition" within the genre, the identification of narrative repetition becomes necessary. In his work on immigrant narratives, literary critic William Boelhower identifies the schema of narration most often followed in traditionally structured stories. The story's linear breakdown into the temporal phases of expectations, contact, and resolution illustrates the constructed aspect of works in the genre and the powerful ideology of the United States as the "promised land" that persists in this narrative form. The phase of expectations is an important one in the traditional immigrant account because it sets up the initial reason for movement in the story, that is, for the protagonist's leaving her/his home country for the new world. In the conventional immigrant narrative, economic struggle tends to be a popular reason for immigration, with the myth of the American Dream, financial success, as a powerful beacon luring those less fortunate to the nation's shores.

The traditional narrative concentrates a majority of its plot development on describing the immigrant's experiences in the phase of contact. This phase includes the new immigrant's encounters with individuals and the social and governmental structures of the new nation. These are typically challenges faced by the immigrant that function as a form of initiation into the new-world culture. Included in this phase are depictions of labor, descriptions of language acquisition, and accounts of racism and prejudice faced by the protagonist. While the trials and tribulations encountered are often daunting in the hegemonic narrative, the protagonist must overcome them in order to make the complete transition from the old world into the new. The contact phase facilitates conflict, where the dreamy expectations meet unexpected difficulties and the road to success suddenly looks much harder. This is the temporal stage under which immigrants prove themselves worthy of becoming citizens of the new nation. The convention of the contact phase works well ideologically with the American Dream idea of success through hard work, no matter how great the obstacle. Under such a model, the immigrant's ability to overcome obstacles ensures eventual victory.

In the dominant immigrant paradigm, the phases of expectation and contact advance the story line to a culmination in the last phase, resolution. It is in this final stage that the conflicts and challenges faced by the immigrant are resolved in a way that makes possible several endings. The immigrant can fully assimilate into the larger mainstream, having severed all ties with the old world and embraced the modernity of the new world. The immigrant can also assimilate into the new-world culture but at the same time keep certain cultural practices of the old world, cultural practices that can be easily incorporated into the greater new-world culture.[5] In some stories, however, the protagonist does not assimilate but chooses to live on the margins, in an ethnic enclave where s/he can attempt to live based on the old-world culture. In this last scenario, the immigrant chooses not to give up old-world ideals, and in her/his isolation from the new world lies the lack of resolution of the narrative. The question of assimilation as a possibility, or in some cases impossibility, is never addressed. Under such a model of immigration, the narrative ensures a conclusion to the immigrant story that is commensurate with the protagonist's successful or unsuccessful assimilation, as if it were an individual choice. What follows is a reading of two texts that share a narrative structure that comfortably follows the organizing logic of the traditional immigrant story. While the productions focus on protagonists of color, their duplication of the immigrant paradigm perpetuates the myth of white American exceptionalism ushered in by Winthrop's words almost four centuries ago.

A Literary Precursor

America is God's Crucible, the great Melting-Pot where all races of Europe are melting and re-forming! Here you stand, good folk, think I, when I see them at Ellis Island, here you stand in your fifty groups, with your fifty languages and histories, and your fifty blood hatred and rivalries. But you won't be long like that, brothers, for these are the fires of God you've come to . . . Germans and Frenchmen, Irishmen and Englishmen, Jews and Russians—into the Crucible with you all! God is making the American.

» Israel Zangwill, *The Melting Pot* (1908; quoted in Nahshon 288)[6]

One of the most well-known Chican@ texts in U.S. literature is José Antonio Villarreal's *Pocho*. Published in 1959, the novel has been hailed as the "'beginning' of the Chicano novel" by Ramón Saldívar (*Chicano Narrative* 60). There is no doubt that *Pocho* holds an important position in the Chican@ literary canon. The time of its publication is significant as it comes at the tail end of an important historical shift for the Mexican American community.[7] Before the civil rights activism of the 1960s came a decade of a growing Mexican American middle class and a shift from Mexicanism to Americanism (Garcia 310–314).[8] As Richard A. Garcia points out in his study of the Mexican American middle class in San Antonio, the shift in ideology occurred during McCarthyism, when being critical of the nation was constructed as disloyal and potentially communist (310). In her essay on ideological discourses and literature, Rosaura Sánchez argues that "a study of both earlier and recent narratives will allow us to track down evolving ideological discourses and cultural practices" (115).[9] If we historically situate the novel, it becomes possible to read *Pocho* as a product of its time, a text that reflects the importance of conformity.[10] As such, the novel provides us with the opportunity to analyze the deployment of the immigrant narrative in Mexican American literature during a time when assimilation was a popular ideology within the community. At the same time, examining *Pocho* helps us see the ways in which its narrative schema continues to function in much later texts.

Villarreal's *Pocho* employs the traditional structure of the immigrant-story genre, following the lives of both the first- and second-generation members of an immigrant Mexican family and culminating in the formulaic resolution. Even though the text's protagonists are men of color, the organizing logic of the story follows the paradigmatic model and replicates ideologies of American exceptionalism. While *Pocho* was published over forty years after the Mexican Revolution (1910–1917), the text places the immigration of the family in the early part of the twentieth century, during the revolution's tumultuous years.[11] *Pocho* tells the tale of Juan Rubio and his family, who leave Mexico and eventually settle in the agricultural fields of Santa Clara, California. The narrative follows the coming-of-age story of Richard Rubio, the only son of the family, from his birth in Brawley, California, to his enlistment in the U.S. Navy. The story begins with Juan Rubio's account of fighting in the revolution and his immigration to Texas and eventual settlement in California. Juan's narrative provides the reader with the family's history and the circumstances around Richard's birth. The narrative begins by telling the stories of the protagonist's family, but ultimately shifts to document a young boy's quest to become an assimilated citizen of the nation.

The phase of expectations is an important one in the organizing structure of the traditional story of immigration, and it plays a significant role in *Pocho*. Juan and later his wife, Consuelo, leave Mexico to escape the violence of the revolution and to search for the better economic opportunities the United States represents. For the phase of expectations to function, the host country must offer the immigrant an opportunity to accomplish something s/he is unable to achieve at home, and the impetus for immigration must be connected to the immigrant's expectations. In *Pocho*, the Mexican Revolution offers a strong impetus for migration that can easily be subsumed under the ideology of immigrating for a better life. Richard's family ends up in the United States in search of the type of life they can no longer hope for in Mexico. The most effective way of ensuring that the United States is situated as the land of opportunity, where the family can hope to achieve the American Dream, is to construct a binary distinction between the old world and the new world. The novel represents Mexico as the old world, the country of origin as existing in differing spatial and temporal phases.

In *Pocho*, we get a representation of Mexico not only as a backward country, but as a violent space filled with death and corruption. The first part of the novel is told through the perspective of Juan, who describes his home country as being in the midst of chaos. The dream of the revolution has died, and all of the democratic ideals and hopes for a new nation that Juan had fought to gain have been destroyed with the death of the Mexican Revolution's hero, Pancho Villa.[12] The ideas Juan has held about democracy, however, are represented as extreme. He recalls,

> We took the Chinese and the Spaniards and killed them in bunches, and everyone said we were massacring chinitos and gachupines simply because of their nationality, and the truth was that we did it because we could not trust them. They would have inherited the city we liberated, and someday we would have to return and fight for it again. That is the only way to save México. (27)

For Juan and his compatriots, Mexico belongs to "Mexicans," and anyone who doesn't fit into this rigidly constructed notion of citizenship is suspect. The biologically deterministic definition of a "real" Mexican excludes "chinitos" and "gachupines," populations whose immigrant ancestry would be visible through racial markers.[13] His image of a new Mexican democracy as being based on the annihilation of anyone considered untrustworthy—or more importantly, foreign—stands in sharp opposition to the liberal notions of democracy and nationality represented by the ideology of the United States as the "city upon a hill," the beacon of hope and equality for all people of the world.[14] In contrast to the myth of American exceptionalism, Mexico's racial formations signify an adherence to undemocratic principles of inequality. Villarreal's representation would have his reader believe that, unlike immigrants to the United States, who are imagined as being welcomed into the nation's fold, foreigners in Mexico cannot function as part of the new nation envisioned by revolutionaries like Juan Rubio. Juan's lack of remorse for the bloodshed and his attempts to rationalize it as a necessity for the success of the revolution help to further represent Mexico as a country full of brutal individuals who cannot grasp the true meaning of democracy. Unlike the American Revolution and its heroes, who are cast as noble, insightful men who sought to unshackle the nation from the grips of tyranny, the Mexican Revolution and its actors are represented as being cruel, brutal, and totalitarian. Ultimately, by reproducing mythologies of American exceptionalism, the text reduces Mexico's revolution to a failed experiment.

The myth that positions the United States as the providential nation, the land where true democracy was birthed, is part of a larger ideology of American exceptionalism that proved foundational to the imperialist practices begun under the doctrine of Manifest Destiny, practices based on a construction of a racial system that privileged whiteness. The construction was specifically grounded on the creation of an imagined community rooted in an Anglo-Saxon heritage.[15] To justify the multiple expansionist projects taken on during the nineteenth century, politicians and intellectuals undertook the challenge of creating a racial order that positioned white Americans as superior and responsible for spreading the American ideals of democracy. In the case of the racial construction of Mexicans, the justification of the annexation of Texas and the Mexican-American War demanded a formulation of this population as inferior to white Americans. The description of Mexicans by American politicians as "semi-barbarous hordes" and as "imbecile and indolent" helped make the case for these two actions.[16] The ideological construction of Mexicans as racially inferior also positioned the Mexican government as unstable and ineffective because of the "inadequacies of an inferior population" (Horsman 220).[17] It was this subordinate position of Mexicans—as lower on a racial hierarchy and incapable of ruling themselves—that helped justify the Mexican-American War to an American population.[18]

In *Pocho*, the representation of a failed Mexican revolution perpetuates the much older narrative of Mexican inferiority. It is this chaotic and dysfunctional space of violence that Juan Rubio is forced to flee to avoid being captured by corrupt government officials. While he loves the idea of the Mexico for which he had been fighting, Juan must join the mass of immigrants escaping the violence of the revolution. Their entrance into the new nation, however, is not one of welcome.

The image of the Statue of Liberty, with her torch acting as a beacon, is a powerful visual in the construction of the United States as the "promised land." The "Mother of Exiles," as she is named in Emma Lazarus' poem, has become the physical embodiment of the ideology of the United States as a welcoming nation for the "huddled masses yearning to breathe free." She is the visual manifestation of the concept that the United States is a "nation of immigrants." However, her position on the East Coast, on Ellis Island, very specifically welcomes a certain immigrant—one arriving from Europe. Her message of welcome is geographically and metaphorically absent for those immigrants who enter the nation from the south.[19] These immigrants are constructed as racially and culturally different and are not included within the discourse of the "huddled masses" embraced by the Statue of Liberty. Based on this historical construction of Mexicans, it is easy to see how more modern constructions of immigrants from our southern neighbor continue to be formulated as undesirable. What gets created is a binary between "good" immigrant (white) and "bad" immigrant (not white)—a model to which our current immigration debate closely adheres.[20]

While *Pocho*, as a whole, follows the narrative of the individual assimilation of the traditional immigrant, a narrative disruption occurs that illustrates the complicated position of immigrants from the south. Villarreal pays close attention to the difference between the expectations of immigrants and what they actually encounter:

> *Thus Juan Rubio became a part of the great exodus that came of the Mexican Revolution . . . They came first to Juárez, where the price of the three-minute tram ride would take them into El Paso del Norte—or a short walk through the open door would deposit them in Utopia. The ever-increasing army of people swarmed across while the border remained open, fleeing from squalor and oppression . . . The bewildered people came on—insensitive to the fact that even though they were not stopped, they were not really wanted. (15–16)*

Villarreal represents these emigrants as leaving Mexico to escape the poverty and violence of a nation in chaos. They view the United States as their "Utopia," and the border remains fluid enough to allow their entrance into the new nation. Their expectations are consistent with the expectations phase as the first phase in the conventional narrative of immigration.

Within the framework of the more paradigmatic immigrant story, the expectations of the immigrant subject are not necessarily rooted in fact, but are based on the ideological construction of the United States as the utopian "land of opportunity."[21] These "bewildered people" are represented as being unaware of the difficulties they will encounter once they enter the host country.[22] The disruption in the narrative occurs in Villarreal's representation of these immigrants as undesired, as "not really unwanted." This ideological crack in the narrative is, however, overlooked and subsumed under the more imposing structure of the immigrant paradigm. In fact, these individuals become the foil that positions Juan Rubio and his family as an exception to this mass of "bewildered" and "insensitive" immigrants.[23] While the Rubio family will face similar difficulties, their actions in the face of these challenges will function to illustrate the exceptional character of the Rubio men. Their struggles are important in the schema of narration because they separate the expectations phase from the contact phase and provide the narrative with a linear structure of development that follows the protagonist on the path to becoming a subject of the new nation.

On First Contact—Proving One's Worth

The Americans were once scattered all over Europe; here they are incorporated into one of the finest systems of population which has ever appeared . . . The American ought therefore to love this country much better than that wherein either he or his forefathers were born. Here the rewards of his industry follow with equal steps the progress of his labour; his labour is founded on the basis of nature, self-interest . . . From involuntary idleness, servile dependence, penury, and useless labour, he has passed to toils of a very different nature, rewarded by ample subsistence. This is America.

» J. Hector St. John de Crèvecoeur, *Letters from an American Farmer*[24]

The second phase in the traditional narrative schema provides accounts of challenges faced in order to illustrate the worthiness of the immigrant subject. Through hard work and perseverance, the immigrant earns a place in the new nation, with labor playing a vital role in the quest for upward mobility.[25] In *Pocho*, Juan Rubio becomes part of the immigrant workforce that helps build the country's infrastructure. After leaving the El Paso area, Juan finds his way to Los Angeles, where "he helped build the tall buildings, and was one day buried in a sand slide, but he survived" (28). Like that of the immigrant characters in di Donato's *Christ in Concrete*, Juan's labor in the construction of Los Angeles helps to historically situate the work of immigrants in the construction of the United States' urban spaces. Once the family is reunited in California, the Rubios become part of the migrant labor force that works the fruit and vegetable fields to survive. Richard's story enters the narrative and he recounts a youth filled with poor people coming and going, but also with the family's involvement in movements of resistance, including the unionization of farm workers. While the attempts to organize the various agricultural labor groups do not fully succeed, the text's focus on what the organizers were trying to accomplish illustrates the exploitation to which workers were subjected.[26]

Even though the Rubio family is forced to work hard to ensure their economic survival, they are rewarded for their hard labor. The idea of success through hard work—a success demarcated by an upward mobility defined by consumption of goods—is an integral part of the ideology of the American Dream, and this ideology gets perpetuated in *Pocho*. In fact, the Rubios achieve an important milestone in realizing that dream: they become homeowners.[27] For the Rubios, purchasing a house means more than just buying into the American Dream. Their purchase conforms to the connection popularly constructed between citizenship and consumption. Through their purchase, the Rubios are buying a piece of the nation and setting down roots—claiming a space of their own. The Rubios' homeownership further functions to sever the family's connection to Mexico and ends Juan's dream of returning to his country of origin, although Juan "was unaware that he was fashioning the last link of events that would bind him to America and the American way of life" (129). While Juan had constantly spoken of returning home, by becoming a homeowner he provides his son, Richard, with a tangible piece of inheritance that is supposed to make Richard's life more successful. The ideology behind homeownership further perpetuates the idea of the "American way of life" as predicated on a process of consumption. In purchasing a home, the family can be seen as becoming part of "America," but ironically, becoming homeowners does not protect them from their tenuous position as immigrants.[28]

Educating the New Citizen

> The training of future citizens is the first duty of the public schools . . . Schools are the focal points of civilization.

> » *New York Times*, 1906 (quoted in Fischer et al. 7)

Part of the function of the traditional immigrant narrative is to neutralize any tensions that exist between old- and new-world ideas and beliefs. The most effective way of ensuring the transition from dated old-world ideas to the enlightenment of new-world thought is through the education of the immigrant subject. In their introduction to *Identity, Community, and Pluralism in American Life*, Fischer et al. underscore the role that education played in negotiating questions of diversity and difference in the face of growing immigration from southern and eastern Europe: "Policymakers and educators placed a good deal of emphasis on assimilating the foreigners into their homogeneous vision of American society, especially through a system of public education in which common American values and expectations could be imposed" (xii). These "foreigners" were, for the most part, immigrants whose ethnic difference was constructed as surmountable through a "proper" education. They could be assimilated into the image of a "common America" because their European origins elevated them in a racial hierarchy that privileged whiteness. Nonwhite immigrants faced a harder time inserting themselves into this racialized structure.

As an exemplar of the traditional immigrant narrative, *Pocho* places a strong emphasis on the role that education plays in Richard's quest to become a productive member of the nation. Richard's relationship to education illustrates the tension between the "civilizing" mandate of the school system and immigrants of color, but in the novel, schooling still functions as a way of initiating him into the new world. Although his family works the agricultural fields around Santa Clara, unlike the children of other migrant workers Richard is able to attend school on a regular basis.[29] Like many immigrant children, Richard is often teased for being different. He is picked on for the contents of his lunch, called "Frijoley bomber" and "Tortilla stranger" (47). Instead of withdrawing, Richard recalls that "for almost a year, he had purposely eaten where he could easily be observed, refusing to be driven into hiding because they laughed about the food he ate" (47). School is not represented as an embracing space of learning, but Richard refuses to allow those around him to deter him from getting an education. While Richard has a deep respect for knowledge, he thinks very little of those who are supposed to be teaching him that knowledge: "Sometimes I read things in books that show me teachers are wrong sometimes. I guess they think we're too dumb to know about two sides to a story" (71). Richard is represented as a strong and intelligent young boy who is smarter than even his own teachers. While Richard has the advantage of being born in the United States, his citizenship does not guarantee him the education he needs to be successful. It becomes the task of the individual boy to educate himself, even if that means rejecting the authority of those around him.

Richard's initial experiences with education are positive because the teachers are able to recognize his intelligence. At school, what he refers to as "old-country manners" make him a favorite among his teachers. He is "also a good student, and [stands] near the top of his class without seemingly trying" (103). As Richard grows older, he becomes disenchanted with his teachers, who do not understand how to guide such a smart boy, and with the school system, but not with education itself.

In the same way in which labor becomes a way of physically proving that one is worthy of being a national subject, education becomes a means of verifying one's acceptance of new-world ideas. When Richard enters high school, he no longer has teachers to mentor him and must rely on his own sense of importance to fight an unfair tracking system:

> And the adviser in the high school, who had insisted he take automechanics or welding or some shop course, so that he could have a trade and be in a position to be a good citizen, because he was Mexican, and when he insisted on preparing himself for college, she had smiled knowingly and said he could try those courses for a week or so, and she would make an exception and let him change his program to what she knew was better for him. She'd been eating crow ever since. (108)

Richard and the adviser have differing ideas of what type of education he should be pursuing, but it is important to notice the ways in which the adviser positions knowledge of a trade as an integral part of being a good citizen. Her racism, however, reduces Richard to just another Mexican whose possibilities for life extend only to blue-collar labor and limits her ability to see the potential in him.[30] With no real support, Richard must take the initiative to create his own opportunities through continuing his education. In effect, *Pocho* upholds the notion of a race-blind immigrant narrative in which the individual (if good/strong/determined enough) can overcome structural inequalities.

Individuality and Pulling Oneself Up by the Bootstraps

> The bootstrap is a simple invention: a strap, sewn to industrious footwear to help pull them on. Often underappreciated, it is a vital attachment to rubbery galoshes and cumbersome riding boots. But colloquially the strap has even greater significance. To "pull oneself up by the bootstraps" is to better oneself by one's own unaided efforts . . . In America, the strap signifies a national vision: in this land of opportunity, the rugged, self-reliant individual must lift himself out of poverty to attain the once unattainable. American mythology fits all its greats with bootstraps.

> » Alexander Ewing, "On Bootstraps"[31]

In addition to education, Richard's incorporation into the nation is heavily predicated on masculinity and the notion of individuality. Following the tradition of young boys discovering their place in the world through the bildungsroman, Richard turns to books to learn to mold himself into the model of acceptable American masculinity.[32] In an important narrative development, Richard is given Horatio Alger's books to help guide his education.[33] In *Pocho*, the project of learning how to be a productive citizen of the nation is one that relies heavily on the messages garnered from books. Alger's popular stories of poor young men who are capable of overcoming their economic disadvantages through strong moral character and hard work provide Richard inspiration while simultaneously situating his story within a longer history of individual struggle and success—a masculinist tradition. *Pocho* closely abides by Alger's lessons of creating one's own success based on notions of hard work, education, and individuality. Alger's texts emphasize the "pulling oneself up by the bootstraps" mentality that focuses very much on the idea of the self-reliant individual.[34]

The message of upward social mobility through hard work is an integral part of the nation's myth of the American Dream. For the young Richard, success and the achievement of the American Dream come with the rejection of the old-world values that are retained by his family. To embrace the ideas and beliefs of the new world, Richard must ultimately give up his connection to the immigrant family and become an individual.[35] He comes to see his family as a burden that keeps him from fully living up to his potential. His parents are represented as good but uneducated immigrants whose thoughts and ideas are still entrenched in an old-world mentality. Richard's mother, Consuelo, especially, is portrayed as simple and naïve. The young immigrant boy's family and upbringing becomes another obstacle that must be overcome on his immigrant journey. While his father often vocalizes old-world ideas, it is Richard's mother who gets portrayed as the very personification of ignorance.

The portrayal of Consuelo clearly illustrates the well-defined masculinist framework at play in the novel's development of its male protagonist. During a conversation with Consuelo, Richard condescendingly refers to her reasoning as "silly" and realizes that his mother thinks less about everything than he does: "it occurred to him that his mother always followed rules and never asked the why of them" (62). In contrast to Richard, whose superior intellect and individuality allow him to think for himself, Consuelo can only do what she is told. Several times the novel describes arguments Richard has with his mother because of her inability to understand what he has learned.[36] She confesses to him, "I have told you I understand very little. I know only that you are blasphemous and you want to learn more in order to be more blasphemous still—if that is possible" (64).[37] Villarreal chooses to have the character of the mother emphasize her own ignorance, and juxtaposes this with Richard's embrace of new-world learning.

The novel reduces Consuelo to the stereotype of the ignorant woman who cannot possibly function without the guidance and support of a man. Even when Consuelo attempts to embrace new ideas that are seen as a rejection of an old-world thought—e.g., when she tries to assert her rights as a woman and not just a wife—Richard dismisses her efforts. For Richard, his mother lacks the intelligence necessary to fully understand how the United States functions. After all, she is just a woman.

Although he loves his mother, Richard believes that a family cannot survive when the woman desires to command, and he sees his mother as like a starving child who has become gluttonous when confronted with food. She has lived so long with the tradition of her country that she cannot help herself now, and she abuses the privilege of equality afforded the women of her new country (134). Richard views Consuelo as incapable of leading the family because of her ignorance, and this is because of his own patriarchal ideas about the family structure: that only a man can successfully "command" a family. For Richard, his mother is too much a product of the old country, and hence is not worthy of the true equality offered by the new country.

The fact that Richard dismisses his mother's attempt to become a more assertive woman as misguided illustrates an important contradiction in the text. Richard wants to be a modern citizen of the new

41

nation, but his position as male in the household is better served if his mother continues to exist in the role of the self-sacrificing mother/wife of the country of origin. It is fine for other women— non-immigrant women—to assert their claims to equality, but having his mother stand up to his father threatens Richard's conception of the superiority of men in their family. As long as the message of gender equality remains outside the structure of his family, Richard can accept it. However, when such a message permeates his immigrant home and creates fissures within the established structure of his family, Richard must find ways to reject it. Villarreal employs the binary between old/new world to ease the tensions the emerging ideology of gender equality creates in the narrative, a strategy that comes at the expense of his female characters.[38] As an educated man, Richard reverses the positions of his adult mother and himself and situates himself as superior to her based not only on their levels of education but also on a gender hierarchy that benefits him.

From the very beginning, Richard's body is constructed as hypermasculine, and it is this masculinity that provides him with the license to infantilize his mother. In an effort to illustrate his exceptionalism as being based not only on his intellect but also on his constructed gender, the text places a huge emphasis on Richard's male body. When he is born, Juan Rubio is overwhelmed by the birth of his "manchild," his only son, the one whose "genitalia seemed enormous in proportion to the little body" (31). Juan is so proud of his ability to have fathered a visibly endowed son that he is reduced to tears. The text dismisses the importance of Juan's previously born children—all girls—and reduces masculinity to the presence of a penis that ultimately secures Richard's position in the family hierarchy. The male child's penis becomes a larger metaphor for the power that the phallus will grant Richard—a power Juan sees as his own masculine bequest to his male progeny. While Mexican culture is represented as more patriarchal than the United States', Richard's male privilege is, in fact, guaranteed in both cultures and his misogyny goes unchallenged. The novel would have its reader believe that Consuelo is incapable of fully understanding the transitions she must undergo to become a "real" American because she lacks a penis.

Eventually, Richard's development into a "real" American man must come through a separation from his family members, who are reduced to representing the "less-enlightened" country of origin. The emphasis on the individual illustrates the gendered aspect of the narrative since individuality, in the traditional immigrant narrative, is marked as "masculine." The text divorces the protagonist from the "feminine" influence in his life to facilitate his transformation into a national subject. The women in Richard's family are seen as unfit candidates for absorption into the nation who must therefore be rejected. Their femininity and inability to leave the home confines them within a gender construction that reduces them to dependents. When Juan abandons the family, Richard replaces his father as head of the household and the women of the family become reliant on Richard for their financial protection.[39] The novel represents Richard's new status as the patriarch as a necessary development in his journey to become a "real man," which in this case means providing for the women in his family—women incapable of caring for themselves. While a burden, Richard's position is also one of power that further elevates him in the familial hierarchy and portrays his masculinity as more evolved than Juan's. Unlike his father, Richard does not shun the financial responsibility of providing for the family. Instead, he rejects what his mother and sisters represent. Villarreal's emphasis on Richard's struggle to be an individual ultimately positions him against his family's notion of community, one seen as archaic and residual. In the narrative, individuality and masculinity play important roles in the protagonists' becoming members of the nation.

Culmination of Hard Work

While *Pocho* offers moments of contradiction and ambiguity in its protagonist's quest to assimilate, the novel advances an ending that comfortably fits within the model of the canonical schema of narration. In the traditional immigrant narrative, the phase of contact is followed by the phase of resolution, where the immigrant subject achieves a level of assimilation or acculturation, or completely rejects the new world and lives in self-imposed isolation. This last stage in the narrative attempts to solve any conflicts or contradictions introduced during the contact stage. Usually it means overcoming hardships and prejudices in order to transition from immigrant subject to a subject of the nation. In this case, the novel culminates with the protagonist making decisions that will ultimately affect the rest of his life.

In *Pocho*, we don't have an optimistic ending to the protagonist's story, but are instead left with Richard's continual quest to define his place in the nation. Ironically, in his pursuit to separate himself from his family, he ends up enlisting in the U.S. military: he joins an organization that demands complete adherence to rules and regulations and the absorption of the individual into the unit. Unlike the family he leaves behind, this community is one of men, based on a strict policing of gender and masculinity that will help Richard develop into a "real" American. Because the United States is participating in World War II, enlisting in the military becomes an option for Mexican Americans like Richard.[40] The military provides Richard with the opportunity to sever the connections with his family—and the femininity and weakness they represent—at last.[41] He realizes that enlisting is wrong, "all very wrong that he should use the war, a thing he could not believe in, to serve his personal problem," but enlisting offers Richard the chance to fulfill his financial duties as the patriarch of the family while physically separating himself from it (186).

The decision to enlist not only breaks Richard's connection to the family and the old world, but also makes him an active member of the new world through his military service for the nation.[42] While he might not be invested in the war, by joining the U.S. Navy he asserts his position as a male citizen of the nation and fights for the country in the same manner that his father once fought for the Mexican Revolution. He continues the masculinist legacy of his father, but this time in service of a nation represented as worthy of protection. Richard demonstrates his loyalty to the nation through his military service and the possible sacrifice of his life—the highest calling to masculine men. By enlisting, Richard becomes a true son of America, protecting the country just as he takes care of the family—providing for both his physical home and his homeland.

The traditional narrative structure and organizational logic that *Pocho* follows continue to be used today to describe the stories of new immigrants. The linear progression of the text, the various experiences in the phase of contact, and the resolution it offers are all aspects that we can see in contemporary immigrant narratives that continue to employ the ideologies of the American Dream. By reading the film *Spanglish* through the same lens of the paradigmatic immigrant narrative, we can see how this more recent cultural production perpetuates an older narrative of immigration and assimilation, and we can also see the ways in which gender functions even more explicitly within the masculinist conventions of the immigrant story portrayed in mid-twentieth-century American fiction.

Same Old Story—On the Silver Screen

Released forty-five years after *Pocho*'s publication, James L. Brooks' film *Spanglish* offers its own version of the paradigmatic immigrant tale, illustrating the flexibility and longevity of the narrative form and its ability to incorporate ever-more-modern ideologies of race, gender, and immigration. Audiences today are much more likely to be familiar with the film, which was intended for a mainstream release, than with Villarreal's novel. *Spanglish* was critically acclaimed, heavily promoted—it had an estimated production cost of $80 million—and featured an all-star cast that included Adam Sandler, Téa Leoni, Paz Vega, and Cloris Leachman.[43] The narrative of the film follows Flor Moreno and her daughter, Cristina, as they emigrate from Mexico to the United States in an effort to create better lives for themselves. In her attempt to provide for and protect Cristina, Flor ends up becoming a domestic worker for the Claskys, a privileged but dysfunctional family made up of John and Deborah Clasky, their children, Bernice and Georgie, and Deborah's mother, Evelyn. The story is told from Cristina's perspective, as she discusses how important her mother's influence has been in creating her sense of identity in an admission essay for Princeton University. The title is a reference to the ways in which the film attempts to fuse the two different families, with their diverse languages and cultures, bringing them together to create a new, multicultural way of interacting and understanding each other that transcends cultural barriers.

From the outset, the film visually positions Flor and her daughter as "good" immigrants: pretty, polite, and most importantly, harmless. They are not part of the dangerous mob of brown bodies invading the United States from the south—an invasion that pundits and politicians warn is currently taking place. In fact, the first time we see Flor and a young Cristina is in a scene that offers the audience a quaint picture of their Mexican home and a glimpse of the strong relationship between the mother and daughter. Flor has decided to finally emigrate after having been abandoned by Cristina's father. For her, the United States provides an "opportunity for change" from the lives they are currently living. The scene takes place in their Mexican home, which is a brightly colored and beautifully decorated abode. There is no sense of poverty or economic difficulty present. The scene presented to the audience is quite different from the original scene in the screenplay of the film. In the script, included in the film's DVD version, Cristina and her mother must leave Mexico to escape the poverty and desperation Flor's criminal husband left them in when he was incarcerated. The filmed version, however, rewrites the script to provide the audience with a much more palatable version of immigration, one that positions Flor as a "good" domestic. Both versions represent Mexican men as deviant, as either criminal or irresponsible, and as bad fathers/husbands.[44] In the film, it is easy for the viewer to assume that Flor decides to relocate to the United States simply because it offers better opportunities; the film erases the reality of poverty and desolation that forces countless immigrants to leave

Mexico every day. Instead, the film perpetuates the expectation of the American Dream as the motivation for immigration while providing the audience with a protagonist beautiful enough to distract from the stereotypically ugly concept of immigration.

Crossing the Border

> Give me your tired, your poor,
> Your huddled masses yearning to breathe free,
> The wretched refuse of your teeming shore.
> Send these, the homeless, tempest-tost to me,
> I lift my lamp beside the golden door!
>
> » Emma Lazarus, "The New Colossus" (1883)

In *Pocho*, the experience of immigration takes place in the early part of the twentieth century, when immigration from Mexico was not restricted in the same ways it is today. Even though the Rubios enter the country without documentation, the construction of "undocumented" did not yet exist. As a result, crossing the border is a much easier and more fluid process for them than it would be for a similar family today. Although it isn't represented as traumatic, the crossing of the U.S.–Mexico border is important because it functions to mark the transition from old world to new.

Unlike the fluidity of the border represented in *Pocho*, the border today is a highly constructed, militarized, and policed space of violence and conflict. Yet *Spanglish* visually and ideologically erases the border. The film provides a sterile version of immigration for its audience, a version that will not offend or disturb a mass audience. A more easily consumed and popular form of cultural production, Hollywood films must cater to a wider audience than novels do to ensure large distribution.[45] As a result, there is a clear absence in *Spanglish* of the troubling conditions of immigration encountered by today's immigrating subjects. The border and all of the ideologies that construct it are missing. There are no walls, no barbed wire, and no border patrol agents making their presence known.

In contrast to the romanticized notion of the "city upon a hill" and Emma Lazarus' soothing words affixed on the pedestal of the Statue of Liberty, "Give me your tired, your poor, your huddled masses," immigrants today find a much different reality upon attempting to enter the United States.[46] In the dominant representation of immigration, how one enters this country is either completely absent or disconnected from the issue of documentation. While a few films have attempted to represent the hardships encountered by immigrants on their journey, most of these representations are found in independent films. Who can forget the harrowing scene of Rosa and Enrique being attacked by rats as they use a sewer tunnel to enter the United States in the film *El Norte*? Or the despair felt by the young boy Carlitos as he is smuggled in the seat of a van in *La Misma Luna*? In contrast, *Spanglish* provides a ridiculous representation of crossing the border that erases the increasing violence against migrating bodies in our post–9/11 moment.

The image of the nation as a place of refuge and enlightenment is predicated on the suppression of stories that do not promote such an ideology. In order for *Spanglish* to adhere to the conventions of the traditional immigrant story, the narrative must continue to perpetuate the notion of the nation as the "city upon a hill." One of the most effective ways of ensuring that this image remains intact is to simply ignore any evidence that contradicts it—a strategy made easy by the magic of Hollywood. Once the decision to leave her and Cristina's home is made, Flor stoically packs them up and they begin their journey. During a scene showing them walking across the desert with nice, rolling luggage, the voice-over informs the audience that their "transportation into the United States was . . . economy class." The euphemism used in describing their entrance into the United States and the comical scene of them lugging their bags behind them as they cross the desert make light of the immigrant experience of entering the country. There is nothing dangerous in the way they cross the desert and no threat of being caught by law enforcement. Through its use of humor, the film alleviates any anxieties the audience might feel in watching the story of undocumented individuals unfold and easily conforms to the conventions of the traditional immigrant narrative.

The fact that Flor and her daughter enter the country illegally and are undocumented is never addressed, and the film would have its audience believe that being undocumented is not a real problem for immigrants. Flor is able to find employment easily and Cristina enters school with no problem. They never show any fear of being deported. The film weaves a fantasy of acceptance for the viewer that is completely divorced from the reality of undocumented workers, who face countless dangers crossing the desert, the threat of physical violence at the hands of law-enforcement individuals and vigilantes, and the constant threat of deportation once they arrive. Flor and Cristina just get absorbed into the fabric of the nation—no questions asked.

While the film was released before the rise of the current anti-immigrant movement, the precarious conditions under which undocumented people must cross the border were nonetheless very much a reality when it came out. In 2002 alone, the U.S. Border Patrol reported that 320 individuals died as a result of dehydration, sun exposure, and other bodily injury that resulted from their attempts to cross into the United States from Mexico (Lydersen 156). This was just two years before the film was released. Since then, the situation has only become worse. On its website, Humane Borders uses medical examiners' reports and border patrol information to map out the 2,269 deaths that occurred in southern California and Arizona between October 1, 1999, and March 28, 2012. These numbers, however, do not account for unreported deaths and undiscovered bodies. The difficulties faced by so many undocumented immigrants are completely absent in the film.

Even though the scene of Flor and Cristina crossing the desert appears for just a few seconds on the screen, the symbolism and implicit message speak volumes. These are not the dangerous bodies represented as invading the country, but instead are two beautiful additions to the nation, "good" immigrants despite their unconventional, "economy class" arrival. In order for their narrative to fit comfortably within the traditional conventions of the genre, the audience has to forget their immigration status. The film positions them as just another set of immigrants searching for a better life and upward mobility based on their hard work. The film would have its audience believe the protagonists' undocumented status is forgotten as soon as they cross the desert and make their way to California. In this traditional immigrant narrative, the phase of contact can only include challenges that can be resolved—being undocumented is a reality that cannot be easily fixed.

Language, Rhetoric, and Making Domestic Work Sparkle

The first statutory requirement of English ability for naturalized citizenship appeared in 1906. The rationale for the statute was that a requirement of ability to speak English would improve the "quality" of naturalized citizens. The Commission on Naturalization of 1905 expressed the prevailing view: "[T]he proposition is incontrovertible that no man is a desirable citizen of the United States who does not know the English language."

» Juan F. Perea, "American Languages, Cultural Pluralism, and Official English" (568)

As in *Pocho*, the individuals with whom the immigrant protagonist comes into contact are important in the development of the traditional immigration narrative. In the second phase of this narrative, the immigrant subject understands the new world through the various interactions s/he has. The community the protagonist enters into tends to get represented as either helping to Americanize the protagonist or foiling the protagonist's attempts at becoming a national subject. Richard Rubio finds support with his neighborhood friends, but feels only misunderstood by the greater community. The supporting characters in *Spanglish* help Flor and her daughter make their assimilation process easier, welcoming them into their family, educating them in the ways of Americans, and helping Flor acquire an understanding of the language.[47] Unlike Richard's racist teachers, the Claskys provide an audience with an image of tolerance for difference that comfortably fits within the rhetoric of liberal democracy and multiculturalism. This image is heavily constructed through linguistic strategies that obfuscate structures of inequality and differences in power.

As a cultural text interested in creating commonalities between two very different families, it is no surprise that in *Spanglish*, the relationship between Flor and her employers is couched in the discourse of family. While Deborah Clasky is represented as eccentric and often selfish, her treatment of Flor and her daughter is based on a maternalistic model of white superiority and benevolence that the audience is encouraged to view as well intentioned. When she hires Flor, Deborah tells her, "Welcome to the family," as if by becoming their housekeeper, Flor has become part of the Clasky family.[48] By employing the rhetoric of the domestic worker as family, Deborah attempts to erase the economic power she holds over Flor and to position herself as the liberal employer who doesn't exploit her employee, whose generosity transcends the class and racial lines between them. In fact, Flor becomes a surrogate mother to Deborah's children, furthering the film's attempts at situating her as part of the Clasky family. Even while there are several instances where Deborah's power over Flor is clearly evidenced, the film attempts to reconcile these narrative fissures through the rhetoric of belonging. Instead of positioning Deborah as an employer abusing her power, she is represented as a well-meaning, benevolent employer who is trying to make it easier for Flor to assimilate into the world Deborah's family occupies. Deborah Clasky's insistence on positioning Flor as part of her family also functions as a metaphor for the nation. The Claskys' unquestioned acceptance of these two immigrant women represents the larger idea of the nation's embracing of "good" immigrants. However, just like the ideology of a meritocratic America is predicated on the rhetoric of inclusiveness (one that attempts to obfuscate a stratified and exclusive, xenophobic society), the rhetoric of family tries to conceal the power relation between the immigrant and her employer.

As employer, Deborah has the power in the relationship and the privilege of constructing a narrative around her own needs and demands. Deborah's privilege is made obvious when the family decides to rent a summer home in Malibu, and she assumes that Flor will go with them. Deborah never asks Flor if she can move in with them, she just announces, "I've rented this house for the summer and she needs to sleep at the house because of the bus schedule." When Flor declines, Deborah responds, "I'm sorry my friend, this is what I need. I don't want to lose you, but . . ." The implicit threat of being dismissed stands in sharp contrast to Deborah's referring to Flor as her "friend," making clear the position Flor is in as her employee and how easily she can be replaced. Flor is left with little choice but to acquiesce to Deborah's demands, understanding her disposability. While the scene displays Deborah's manipulation of Flor, it is quickly forgotten and no comment or critique is made of Flor and Cristina's displacement. Thus, Deborah's actions are justified by the film's treatment of the upper-class world to which Flor and her daughter are exposed—a world they would probably never have had the privilege of experiencing firsthand if it hadn't been for Deborah's "generosity" in sharing her summer home.[49]

In immigrant narratives, one of the trials that the immigrant protagonist faces and must overcome is prejudice based on difference. In *Pocho*, Richard sees prejudice as more of an individual action, not part of an entire system, allowing the perpetuation of the image of the nation as a true democracy. While the novel allows for multiple examples of prejudice to permeate the text, *Spanglish* provides a much more idyllic representation of modern relationships between immigrants and current citizens. The paradigmatic narrative undergoes a major revision in this modern interpretation—shifting from an emphasis on overcoming prejudice to a representation of a "post-racial" and "post-class" America, where race and class prejudice no longer impact the immigrant experience. In the film, Flor and her daughter do not face discrimination based on their lower-class position. In fact, the only time class is referenced is in connection to Flor's shift in work from the public-service sector to domestic labor—which the film assures us pays much more than other forms of service work. The erasure of race in the film is in part facilitated by the protagonist's light skin—Flor might speak with an accent, but her racialized body is light enough to allow for some racial ambiguity. Class and racism are subjects gently ignored in *Spanglish*, allowing the viewer to believe these constructions don't really affect the life of the contemporary immigrant worker.

Racism and the immigrant protagonist's social location are not the only aspects that receive a makeover. The type of labor represented also goes through a revision that makes it easy for an audience to accept. Following the tradition of the popular immigrant narrative, the film uses labor as part of the experience of the immigrant protagonist in the contact phase. However, unlike the labor described in *Pocho*, the work the female protagonist performs in *Spanglish* is not arduous and is sanitized for the screen. The film's romanticization of domestic labor makes it seem like a realistic opportunity to achieve economic success and eventually the American Dream; it is portrayed as a rung on the ladder to upward mobility.

The film romanticizes the role of the domestic worker and the labor involved in the occupation. In fact, Flor has so much time on her hands that she decides to send away for a language program to learn English. As an immigrant, language becomes extremely important to her because, as Juan F. Perea observes, "language is both our principal means of communication and a social symbol, malleable and capable of manipulation for the achievement of social or political goals" (571). Flor walks around with headphones on, practicing her pronunciation of English words. We see her lying on the beach listening to lessons, watching them on TV with Evelyn, or practicing as she plays catch with the Clasky dog. By romanticizing her labor, the film ensures that the audience remains comfortable with Flor's occupation, making it easy to accept the practice of hiring domestic workers and making invisible the exploitation that most often accompanies the employment of the domestic laborer. It works to erase the moral ambiguity around domestic labor for the audience. The film, instead, conforms to the conventions of the immigrant narrative by ensuring Flor's eventual assimilation through her acquisition of the language and by keeping her from being seen performing what an audience would see as demeaning work. Her labor, or lack thereof, leads to her acquisition of English and ultimately frames her as a "desirable" immigrant—civically and sexually.

Contact and Romance—A Question of Gender

They should name a gender after you . . . you are drop dead crazy gorgeous.

» John, in *Spanglish*

While *Pocho* stresses the importance of Richard's quest for the American Dream, the female protagonist of *Spanglish* gets a different treatment. In the film, the immigrant's femininity becomes a major focus in the development of the story. Unlike the male protagonist, whose success must come through the rejection of the old world—by separating from his family and asserting his masculinity as an individual—

the female protagonist becomes part of the new world through her relationship with a white love interest, an assertion of her femininity as a dependent. The female immigrant is represented as being reliant on the male national citizen for transformation from immigrant subject into a potentially naturalized citizen and, as a result, becomes sexualized in order to appeal to the male gaze of her love interest. Individuality and self-reliance remain markers of masculinity, while femininity is infantilized and equated with dependence. Flor doesn't earn her position in the new world through hard work, like Richard. The sexualization of the domestic worker that occurs in the film helps to advance the plotline of the immigrant narrative as the protagonist is fully accepted by her American employer as an equal and her assimilation into the nation appears to become ensured through the romantic relationship. While Flor's story does not culminate in marriage to John, their romance does help constitute her as a desirable immigrant worthy of incorporation into the nation.

In *Spanglish*, the character of Flor is portrayed as a strong and proud Latina. It is not her strength or her hard work, however, that defines her as a "good" immigrant, but her beauty that makes her truly desirable—in multiple ways. The film attempts to overlook Flor's "otherness" to focus on her incredible looks, which are, of course, further emphasized by her exoticness.[50] Everywhere Flor goes, her looks garner attention. Men try to pick her up in several scenes, and the first thing Deborah Clasky utters to her is, "You're gorgeous." In every scene, Flor's beauty is present, from the flowing of her hair in the wind, to her dazzling smile, to her curve-revealing clothing.[51] In the DVD packaging blurb, she is described as "a breathtaking new housekeeper." The viewer never forgets that while Flor might be a domestic worker, her beauty transcends her status; in effect, her looks overcome her class position. To allow the viewer to forget her class status, Flor is never shown performing arduous domestic labor. There are no scenes of her cleaning toilets, wiping windows, or mopping floors. All she does is walk around looking beautiful, solving jigsaw puzzles, straightening up newspapers, and putting board games away. Her beauty is her currency, and it is what allows her to connect with her white male employer.

The emphasis placed on Flor's body advances the romantic plotline of the narrative as the film attempts to create a relationship between John and Flor that transcends the racial, cultural, and economic differences between them. With Deborah coming across as a narcissistic and hysterical woman, it is easy for the film to bring together John and Flor in what is supposed to be a relationship based on deep respect for each other's parenting struggles. The sexual tension between them grows as they spend more time in the Malibu beach house, the attraction facilitated by Flor's new understanding of English. During a late-night discussion about their daughters, Flor tells John, "I never know a man who can put himself in my place like you do." The audience can see that John is distracted by the spectacle of Flor standing in the wind, her clothes molding to her body. The focus of the camera invites the audience to view her body through John's white male gaze. During their conversation, he mentions that it must be hard to be a widow, an assumption he makes because, he says, "I thought that would be the only way a guy would leave you." The setting of the scene—a beautiful night on the beach—creates a feeling of intimacy, with solitary beings casting furtive glances at each other. The tension between them is so strong that Flor scurries off, almost as if she is frightened by the emotions that connect them. Their attraction is finally acknowledged on a night when both of them have had enough of Deborah's treatment.[52]

The romantic dance between Flor and John culminates in a scene that emphasizes Flor's physical desirability while confirming her moral standing as a good mother and worthy immigrant. The pivotal scene in the film occurs in John's empty restaurant, as the two finally confront their feelings. Flor is dressed beautifully, in a simple outfit that accentuates her body, while her long hair is soft and flowing, styled to frame her face. As if on a date, John cooks for her, preparing a meal that literally makes Flor moan with pleasure. As they sit across from each other, John confesses how beautiful he thinks she is: "They should name a gender after you. Looking at you doesn't do it. Staring is the only way that makes any sense. And trying not to blink so you don't miss anything. All of that, and you're you . . . It's just that you are drop dead crazy gorgeous." Flor's beauty leaves John at a loss for words. Again, the beauty of the domestic worker blurs the employer/employee line between them. His sentiments are followed by a tender kiss as the confession continues, "Ever since that conversation that night at the beach, if I knew you were in a room, I just wouldn't go in there." Even though he is extremely attracted to Flor, John has until this point chosen to avoid her in order to try to avoid the feelings he has for her. The scene shifts and they are now sitting on the floor, leaning on each other. Flor's dress strap has slipped off her shoulder and they share longing glances as she tells him, "There are some mistakes you cannot risk when you have children." As they stand, Flor looks at John one last time, utters "I love you," and flees the restaurant.

The decision to resist their attraction functions to position both Flor and John as ideal: she the ideal immigrant, he the ideal citizen. Because her labor gets minimized, it is important for the film to place such emphasis on their morality and to dramatize the unyielded-to tension between them. In her discussion of modern forms of melodrama, Linda Williams argues, "If emotional and moral registers are sounded, if a work invites us to feel sympathy for the virtues of beset victims, if the narrative trajectory is ultimately concerned with a retrieval and staging of virtue through adversity and suffering, then the operative mode is melodrama" (15). Because Flor's labor does not demonstrate her ability to overcome adversity, the film must prove her worthiness through an emphasis of her character. The recognition of her virtue in the face of temptation further genders her immigrant narrative while perpetuating the image of the Latina immigrant as exotic and physically desirable. In addition, John comes to represent the perfect model citizen of the "city upon a hill," providing the audience with what Williams points out is "the entertainment needs of a modern, rationalist, democratic, capitalist, industrial, and now post-industrial society seeking moral legibility under new conditions of moral ambiguity" (23). The film offers a narrative solution that erases any ambiguity the audience might feel about the relationship between John and Flor and her status as his immigrant employee.

However, in attempting to re-create the romance trope of the star-crossed lovers, the film's representation of the connection between Flor and John disregards the difference in power that is at the center of their employee/employer relationship. It also perpetuates the racist stereotype that represents Latina domestic workers as "hot" and available. While they might not have led to a sexual relationship, John's feelings toward Flor are not unwelcome. In the end, Flor turns out to be the stereotypical sexy maid who becomes the object of her employer's desire.

The Happy Ending

Unlike *Pocho*, which gestures toward the achievement of the American Dream, *Spanglish* resolves the narrative with a requisite happily-ever-after ending that follows the model of resolution in the traditional immigrant narrative. After the restaurant scene, where she admits that she loves John but then runs away, Flor quits her job with the Claskys and pulls Cristina out of the private school. Cristina is devastated, but she is so smart that she does not need the advantages the elite academy provided for her. The final scene returns to the Princeton admissions office where Cristina's letter is being read. Her voice-over informs the audience that Flor's hard work has paid off and Cristina is about to finish high school. In her letter, she tells the Princeton admissions committee,

> *I've been overwhelmed by your encouragement to apply to your university and your list of scholarships available to me. Though, as I hope this essay shows, your acceptance, while it would thrill me, will not define me. My identity rests firmly and happily on one fact: I am my mother's daughter. Thank you, Cristina Moreno.*

The film wraps everything up in a neat package for the audience. Cristina has obviously succeeded in her studies and Flor has done a wonderful job raising and providing for her daughter. Regardless of what happened with the Claskys, Flor is ultimately successful in affording her daughter the opportunity to achieve the American Dream, in this case by being recruited and presumably accepted for admission to an Ivy League university. In the end, the movie romanticizes not only the relationship between John and Flor, but also the mother-daughter relationship between Flor and Cristina, in an effort to give the audience a happy Hollywood ending. Cristina ends up living the dream of assimilation through education perpetuated in the dominant immigrant narrative, a dream made possible, we are led to believe, through Flor's hard work, dedication, and her decision to immigrate.

The idea that Cristina is on her way to getting an elite education at one of the most competitive universities in the country is divorced from the difficult economic reality under which most children of domestic workers fall.[53] The fact that Cristina is undocumented makes the simple "assimilation through education" story line even more problematic. As countless numbers of undocumented students know, immigration status remains a major obstacle in the path to receiving an education. The undocumented status of a minor is connected to the status of the parent, and cannot simply be separated. No matter how smart a student is or how hard she works, her undocumented status limits her access to higher education and makes it impossible to follow the simply constructed ideology of upward assimilation through education. From their inability to receive federal financial aid to their lack of the proof of citizenship or legal residency required by many universities, undocumented students face numerous—and sometimes insurmountable—obstacles in their quest for a college education.

A Dream Deferred

The defeat of the federal DREAM Act is a vivid reminder of the fact that it does not matter how well one plays by the rules, the undocumented status of students cannot be transcended by their hard work or education.[54] In her 2007 testimony at the UCLA Center for Labor Research and Education conference, the student Carla tells the panel,

> I no longer remember the struggle of crossing the border between Mexico and the United States, a struggle made by my parents for our future. The simple fact that I do not have documents turns me into a thing. I am no longer human. I live a life of fear; fear that at times I try to hide, fear that torments me at night, the fear of deportation, discrimination, and dehumanization. This is what I constantly feel. (Undocumented Students 7)

Carla vocalizes the dehumanization that being labeled "undocumented" creates—a reality completely absent in *Spanglish*.[55] Unlike the Hollywood ending for Cristina in the film, young people like Carla are left out of the construction of the American Dream. Her testimony highlights the fabricated nature of this pervasive ideology.

While the DREAM Act is an important piece of legislation that would decriminalize countless young people, at its heart remains the rhetoric of achieving the American Dream through hard work and perseverance.[56] Even as the act makes visible the exclusion of a population from the dream, it employs the same classic immigrant narrative. The inherent contradiction is glossed over in a strategy that seeks to invoke the notion of worthiness of citizenship. The fact that the rhetoric of the American Dream and the construction of worth continue to hold such ideological power is a testament to the enduring myth of the United States as the "promised land." The popularity of the traditional immigrant narrative seen in the early twentieth century has not waned. The narrative commonality between *Pocho* and *Spanglish* speaks to the ease with which the paradigmatic immigrant narrative transcends genres and time periods. The film and novel follow the conventional narrative schema and promote the ideology of the United States as the "shining city upon on a hill" where hard work and perseverance pay off. Each one ends with a satisfying narrative that gestures toward the achievement of success. The characters are all on a path to upward mobility, a mobility that will allow them to transcend their immigrant background. This traditional narrative, however, is not all encompassing. The following chapter expands the discussion of the Latin@ immigrant narrative by focusing on texts that challenge the linear structure of the narrative and reject the simple resolution of the immigrant story. Some of these narratives, like the testimonies of the twelve undocumented students at the conference about the DREAM Acts, are compelling stories of dreams deferred.

CHAPTER TWO

Cleaning Up After the National Family, and What a Mess They Make

Am I going after the American Dream? No, I'm not. It's nice to dream, but here we have to live in the reality of who we truly are.

» Judith, in *Maid in America*

In the 2004 documentary *Maid in America*, director Anayansi Prado follows the lives of Judith, Eva, and Telma, three immigrant domestic workers in Los Angeles. Through the film, the audience is witness to the difficulties the women face as they try to make their lives and the lives of their loved ones better. In a departure from the kind of dominant immigrant narratives outlined in the previous chapter, the stories in Prado's film illustrate much more complicated narratives of immigration, stories that do not comfortably fit into a model of upward mobility and assimilation. Instead, the documentary provides us with an example of an oppositional cultural text that challenges the invisibility of Latina domestic workers and rejects the simplistic rhetoric of the pursuit of the American Dream. The women in the film do not come across as naïve, ignorant, or criminal. They are intelligent women who perform a necessary, but often unnoticed, labor in hopes of bettering their lives. However, not all of this is hope based on abstract notions of the American Dream. In the epigraph above, Judith makes it very clear that for her, the American Dream is just that, a dream that does not exist in her reality. As the film demonstrates, these women remain in the margins—and lack the privilege of becoming part of the nation—because of their immigrant status, their class standing, and their racialized bodies.

The power of the traditional immigrant narrative lies in its ability to repress difference, and so it is through the insertion of difference that counternarratives challenge the schema's ideological authority. By making the work and struggles of domestic workers observable, Chicana/Latina cultural productions defy the usual marginalization of this group of female workers, whose labor and bodies are most often rendered invisible. Prado's *Maid in America*, along with Lucha

Corpi's novel *Cactus Blood*, Milcha Sánchez-Scott's play *Latina*, and Lisa Loomer's play *Living Out*, presents alternative narratives of immigration and labor that favor the point of view of domestic workers whose stories do not easily fit within the discourse of the hegemonic immigrant story. The narratives offered by these Chicana/Latina cultural producers provide powerful accounts of real people and depictions of fictional characters that dispute the stereotypical representation of domestic workers as silent servants, maternal nannies, or hypersexual bodies. While the genres of these four works differ, read together they present us with a new way of looking at immigrant laboring bodies and encourage us to reexamine traditional narratives of immigration and to think differently about the American Dream.

Through their emphasis on contesting the rhetoric of family, rejecting the ideology of meritocracy, and challenging the romanticization of the domestic worker, the four texts in this chapter dismantle the simplistic rhetoric favored by the more popular cultural productions circulated by Hollywood and mass-media outlets. The portrayal of domestic labor and immigration in the following texts is not clean and clear cut, but messy and complicated, and it cannot be easily subsumed into the bootstraps model of success promoted by the traditional immigrant narrative. The texts in this chapter offer a Latina genealogy of immigrant narratives that excavate experiences of immigration that have remained outside of the construction of the popular immigrant narrative. They track some of the important changes that have taken place in the process of Latin@ immigration due to the changing composition of immigrants, a rise in xenophobic sentiments and rhetoric, an increase in anti-immigrant legislation, and the militarization of the border between Mexico and the United States. These stories foreground histories of systemic violence and economic oppression that cannot be reconciled under a nationalistic schema of upward mobility and meritocracy. They propose accounts of immigration that disrupt and displace notions of national belonging while offering realistic narratives of labor and mobility.

Gender, Labor, and Immigration—A Legacy of Exploitation

> Most histories of immigrants in the United States begin as experiences of migratory men disguised as genderless humans.
>
> » Donna Gabaccia, *From the Other Side* (xi)[1]

In the past, the popular representation of immigrants has been a masculine one. More recent cultural productions, however, challenge archaic mainstream notions of the immigration journey to expand our understanding of who immigrates now, and they complicate our interpretation of why and how immigration takes place. No longer is the image of the lonely male immigrant entering the country the reality.[2] In its stead we have a rapidly growing number of women—of various ages—entering a transnational workforce and a growing number of cultural productions that represent this new trend and help shape how we understand it. Cultural productions are not created in a bubble, separate from the historical moment in which they are formed. Instead we can think of cultural texts—which include traditional literary texts along with other narrative texts like performance art, theater, film, and visual art—as being in dialogue with the ideologies that surround them. As such, it becomes important to understand the ways in which contemporary cultural producers are engaging with the changes in immigration. As the number of female immigrants rises, it becomes vital to document their presence in research and scholarship and to represent them in cultural productions.

It is easy to see why the representation of immigrants has tended to favor masculine narratives, as male workers were once the predominant imported labor. At different times, capitalist enterprises in the United States have depended on a racialized immigrant body to supply cheap labor. From Chinese and Mexican immigrants brought in to build the national railroad system to Japanese and Filipino immigrants working the agricultural fields of Hawaii, American corporate interests have been very successful in the recruitment of immigrants.[3] For decades, the type of desired laboring body was a masculine one. What made male immigrant workers so desirable to capital was the fact that they were framed as transitory laboring bodies—bodies that could simply be shipped back to their countries of origin once their labor was no longer needed.[4] Their disposability was directly connected to their racialized bodies, bodies that could not conform to the racial construction of whiteness so necessary in the creation of an acceptable national subject. The example of the Bracero Program, begun in 1942, illustrates the nation's desire for a foreign labor force that can be imported and exported based on the changing needs of capital with little regard to the lives of immigrants or the effects that their displacement has on the communities they leave behind.[5] The attractiveness of a temporary immigrant labor force is not one relegated to our past. President George W. Bush's proposed guest-worker program, which was intended to legalize the labor of undocumented immigrants to protect the labor needs of U.S. employers, included the caveat that workers would return to their countries of origin after a maximum six years.[6] The legacy of worker programs like the Bracero

Program remains not only in terms of constructions of immigrant bodies as transitory, but also in the perpetuation of an image of immigrant workers as predominantly male.

Because of the spatial construction of the private as female and the public as male, women have had a more complicated—and sometimes contradictory—relationship to the nation as immigrants and laborers. On the one hand, the ideology of domesticity, which functioned to position women as belonging in the domestic space of the home, helped construct female immigrants as a threat—especially immigrants of color. Unlike male immigrants, they could not easily be constructed as "birds of passage" since the gendered division of space aligned women with the creation and maintenance of the home. Exacerbating the problem, the reproductive capabilities of women of color immigrants threatened to undermine the notion of a homogenous white citizenry.[7] In performing their prescribed gender roles, female immigrants represented a disruption in the state's ability to ensure the expulsion of laboring bodies whose "otherness" was undesirable.[8] On the other hand, the same ideology of domesticity functioned to situate female immigrant laborers as desirable domestic workers. The belief in women's innate ability to run a home and care for others helped frame women immigrants as suitable for domestic service—especially as native-born women left the occupation, creating a need for new laborers.[9] In addition, the gendered architecture of domestic labor and its low status made it one of the easiest labor sectors for immigrant women to enter. Throughout the late nineteenth and early twentieth centuries, domestic labor "was the single most important class of women's gainful employment . . . [and] as a low-status occupation without any educational, experiential, or skill requisites for entry . . . [domestic service] was work performed disproportionately by immigrants and blacks" (Katzman 44). The historical connection between domestic labor and immigration to the United States persists today, but on a much larger scale.

The U.S. middle and upper middle classes' reliance on the labor of immigrant domestic workers that David M. Katzman documents in *Seven Days a Week* is one that we can now see manifested in a transnational system of labor importation and exportation. Unlike the informal connections that guided immigrant women into the domestic-service sector in the late nineteenth and early twentieth centuries, the current system is much more organized and formally structured. For example, the dependence of global cities in many countries on the service labor provided by immigrant women has led to the creation of such programs as the Sri Lankan government's training workshops for women who are being exported to work as domestics.[10] Sri Lanka is not special in its reliance on the transnational movement of its laboring female citizenry. The practice of contracting workers from the periphery to the core has grown dramatically throughout the world. The United Nations Population Fund's "State of World Population 2006: A Passage to Hope: Women and International Migration" notes that "Singapore and the Philippines, for example, are home to an astounding 600 and 1,000 agencies (respectively) devoted to the recruitment or deployment of overseas workers, many of whom are domestic workers" (54). In these cases, the states are exporting their female workforce for the benefit of their national economies. Female residents have been reduced to the status of newest profitable export, and their labor is now helping support not just the families they leave behind, but the nations dependent on their remittances.

To understand the economic role immigrant women are now playing in the global economy, all we have to do is look at the changes in transnational movement documented by immigration scholars. In their study of population movement, Stephen Castles and Mark J. Miller explain,

> In the past, most labor migrations and many refugee movements were male dominated . . . Since the 1960s, women have played a major role in labor migration. Today women workers form the majority in movements as diverse as those of Cape Verdians to Italy, Filipinos to the Middle East and Thais to Japan. (5)

Our neighbors to the south offer a closer example of the changing gender of migration. By 1990, the number of Latin American and Caribbean women migrating was the same as men; this was the first geographic group of female immigrants to reach parity with male immigrants (Zlotnik). In their introduction to *Global Woman: Nannies, Maids, and Sex Workers in the New Economy*, Barbara Ehrenreich and Arlie Russell Hochschild report that half of the migrants leaving Mexico for all destinations are women, and that "throughout the 1990s women outnumbered men among migrants to the United States" (6). By 2006, more than 60 percent of the estimated $20 billion in remittance money received by Mexico was being sent by women (Frontera NorteSur).

The growing body of scholarship on women and migration is beginning to rectify years of neglect. Because patriarchal structures, like the family wage system, have traditionally positioned men as the wage earners in the family, more attention has been paid to men's roles in the global economy. The practice of rendering women's work as merely "supplementary" has led to the continual erasure of their contribution to national economies. It does not help that much of the work performed by immigrant women is contained within occupations traditionally seen as "feminine," which reinforces gendered structures of labor. In its "State of World Population 2006," the United Nations Population Fund reports that while male immigrants often occupy high-skilled jobs, women "are often restricted to tradition- ally `female' occupations—such as domestic work, work in the ser- vice sectors (waitressing etc.), and sex work." The labor of immigrant women is devalued and their financial participation in transnational financial systems diminished. The work of scholars like Saskia Sassen, Rhacel Salazar Parreñas, Susan Martin, Evelyn Nakano Glenn, and Pierrette Hondagneu-Sotelo has introduced the history of women and immigration into mainstream scholarship. By inserting gender into an analysis of bodies, mobility, and capital, this scholarship inter- venes in a history of exclusion and excavates the valuable contribu- tions women make to (inter)national economies.

The work of uncovering women's histories of migration helps to decenter the masculine experience of immigration as the universal model and transforms how we think about the movement of laboring bodies. While women might not have migrated in the same numbers as men historically, they did traverse national boundaries and in- fluence the creation of immigrant communities in the United States. Their experiences, however, have not been documented.[11] These have been subjugated knowledges, ever present but rarely acknowledged. The history of female immigrants has been discounted under a sys- tem of analysis that favors the masculine in a gender-biased perspec- tive. Women's immigration experiences are rendered too "specific" and therefore dismissed under a theoretical lens that positions the male immigrant experience as universal. The privileging of male voices in narratives of immigration continues to perpetuate the ideol- ogy of men as creators of history and women as observers. Under such a gendered framework, women's stories get relegated to the arena of the supplementary, enhancing our historical knowledge but not necessarily creating it. In a similar practice of exclusion, the complex stories of immigration offered by women of color writers continue to be marginalized in contemporary cultural productions.

The fact that Chicana/Latina immigrant stories do not fit comfort- ably into the form of the hegemonic immigrant narrative has worked to further secure their position in the periphery. From this space of ex- clusion, Chicana/Latina cultural producers create narratives that rep- resent the local, the differential, the knowledge found in communities neglected by the mainstream. For Michel Foucault, the combination of "buried scholarly knowledge" with the knowledges "disqualified by the hierarchy of erudition and science" offers a powerful histori- cal understanding of struggles and the possibility to reveal injustices faced by oppressed groups (8). It is this combination that Foucault argues has led to the critique of systems of power, institutions, and discourses. By combining the uncovered historical scholarship on women with an analysis of marginalized narratives of immigration, we can begin the process of excavating a Latina immigrant geneal-ogy. The literary genealogy created by the Latina cultural producers I analyze in this chapter disrupts popular notions of assimilation and meritocracy and challenges the mainstream media's representation of immigration and Latina working bodies.

Creating a New Genealogy of Resistance

In contrast to historic masculinist claims to cross-border unity between Mexico and México de afuera, women's testimonies reveal a distinct female imaginary operating in the border space.

» Alicia Schmidt Camacho, "Migrant Melancholia" (833)

In the conventional immigrant story, the impetus for immigration is an important element in the narrative structure because of the ways in which it represents the nation as a meritocracy and situates the United States as the "land of opportunity." While the dominant nar-rative allows for differing motivations for immigrating, the structure ultimately limits difference to that which can be subsumed under an ideology that continues to construct the United States as a space where the American Dream can come true. The following texts, how-ever, echo the maid Judith's rejection of the dream ideology expressed in the epigraph to this chapter. They represent the reason for immi-gration as not necessarily based on the optimism of achieving eco-nomic success or the pursuit of the American Dream, but instead as a basic quest for survival. In a global economy marked by austerity measures and foreign-imposed economic policies, the texts empha-size the lack of choice many female immigrants find themselves fac-ing. These cultural productions represent women's histories of trans-national movement and insert the danger and violence that remains absent in popular tales of immigration, in the process creating what Schmidt Camacho refers to as a "distinct female imaginary" ("Mi-grant Melancholia" 833). These narratives also choose to highlight the negotiation of the spaces of liminality that exist between the time that immigrants leave their countries of origin and the time they en-ter the United States.

In what follows, I offer an analysis of four diverse texts created by Latina cultural workers that help make up a genealogy of opposi-tion. The oldest of these texts is Milcha Sánchez-Scott's play *Latina*.

The play provides an important historical point from which to begin the excavation of subjugated knowledges of labor and immigration. First performed in Los Angeles in 1980, the text bears witness to the changing composition of immigrants in California due to escalating violence in Central America and challenges the misrepresentation of domestic labor. *Latina's* critique of exploitative labor practices was not new and is part of a longer legacy of activist theater that illuminates the unjust treatment of Latin@ immigrants.[12] What makes the play an important starting point for the building of this specific genealogy is its central focus on the lives of women rarely seen represented on stage and the historical moment in which it was created. The play is set in a domestic agency, where the lives of various women intersect. The Felix Sanchez Domestic Agency caters to a white population of middle-class housewives in Los Angeles looking for cheap domestic labor. The action in *Latina* takes place in one day and gives the audience a glimpse into the difficult lives the characters lead. With the exception of the Chicana receptionist, Sarita, all of the employees of the agency are immigrant domestic workers, most of them undocumented. The play challenges the erasure of the border and its dangers through its representation of the difficulties encountered by immigrant women as they attempt to enter the United States.

Published fifteen years later, in 1995, Lucha Corpi's mystery novel *Cactus Blood* places at the center of the narrative the character of Carlota Navarro, a Mexican woman who immigrated to the United States as a young teenager and was employed as a domestic worker for the Stephens family.[13] While the format of the novel is a rather traditional rendering of the mystery genre, Corpi's text does not follow the conventions of the immigrant schema nor the more linear structure of a typical novel. The action of the story revolves around the protagonist, Chicana detective Gloria Damasco, attempting to discover the cause of death of Sony Mares, a Chicano poet and former United Farm Worker activist. Gloria's investigation of Sony's death leads her to Carlota, who is at first considered a possible suspect. Corpi's narrative, however, goes beyond the basic disentangling of a mystery. As the novel progresses, Carlota's immigrant story reveals that she is in fact a survivor of rape and pesticide poisoning. Unlike the immigrant narrative formula followed by the masculine hegemonic tale, Carlota's story is not always told through her perspective and lacks the linear structure popular in coming-of-age stories. The plotline's focus on the investigation into Sony's death functions as an impetus for uncovering the multiple histories of oppression, which intersect in Carlota's body. Her narrative directly challenges the notion that an immigrant's life becomes significantly improved with her movement to the United States.

The documentary *Maid in America* increases the scope of the immigrant narrative beyond written literary texts. Released in 2004 and originally broadcast on the PBS series Independent Lens, Anayansi Prado's film was Impacto Studio's first production.[14] The documentary, whose descriptive tagline reads, "A documentary about the Latinas who clean your homes and help take care of your children," follows the lives of three Latina immigrants who work in Los Angeles: Judith, from Guatemala; Eva, from Mexico; and Telma, from El Salvador.[15] The film documents the types of labor these women perform while encouraging its audience to see these immigrants as more than just cheap labor. By incorporating a documentary into this genealogy of opposition, we can expand the parameters of the construction of the immigrant narrative. Prado's documentation of these women's stories also presents a filmic re-imagining of the immigrant narrative and allows for the voices of real women to intervene and challenge their representation in popular media.

The concluding text, Lisa Loomer's theatrical production *Living Out*, brings us back to the beginning.[16] While *Living Out* premiered almost twenty-five years after *Latina*, many of the issues raised by Sánchez-Scott are also present in Loomer's play, indicating the lack of progress that immigrant domestic workers have made. The theatrical genre of the text provides a visual representation of various issues and allows for a multiplicity of voices to be featured.[17] The play has a cast of characters that includes several domestic workers and their employers. The main protagonists are Ana Hernandez, a Salvadoran nanny, and her employer, Nancy Robin. While the violent homeland conflicts that Sánchez-Scott's characters were fleeing have diminished in scope, the militarization of the U.S.–Mexico border area, combined with anti-immigration sentiments and the rise of protonational groups, has created an environment of layered hostility that makes living in the United States a much more precarious project. In addition to remaining undetected, undocumented workers must learn to navigate a system of laws intended to keep them marginalized and subjugated. *Living Out*'s critique of our current immigration system and the continued exploitation of domestic workers highlights the ways in which some experiences with immigration have changed and some have remained the same. Combined with the previous texts, Loomer's play points to the resilience the dominant narrative continues to enjoy but also illustrates the possibilities of the erosion of this popular narrative.

Challenging the Invisible

> From the Conquest to the present, women have been targeted in gender-specific ways during militarized conflict.
>
> » Sylvanna Falcón, "Rape as a Weapon of War" (31)[18]

In the novel *Cactus Blood*, Carlota's story inserts into the immigrant narrative genre an account of the danger and gender violence present in the project of transnational movement. Gloria first discovers part of Carlota's story by mistake, coming across a taped interview of Carlota that is part of a compilation titled *The Chicana Experience*, which consists of interviews of Chicanas who had participated in the Chicano Movement in the sixties and seventies—an element in the narrative that comes into play later in the novel. The title of the compilation is important as it directly situates Carlota's narrative as part of a larger, collective Chicana history. In this interview, Carlota recalls her journey from Michoacán, Mexico, to Fresno, California, after the deaths of her parents:

> With enough food and water to last me two days and a few pesos in my coin purse, I left my village, walked twenty kilometers to Morelia, and boarded the bus that would take me across the U.S.–Mexico border, where, on a dirt road a few miles from El Centro, California, Dr. Stephens waited for me. The doctor handed Chuchita's uncle an envelope, led me to the car, and helped me into the trunk. (45)

The narrative introduces a border-crossing journey that begins in the interior of Mexico and is rife with danger, especially for a young girl of only fourteen. With her parents' deaths and no other family to take care of her, Carlota has no choice but to leave her hometown and her country in order to support herself. The fact that Carlota leaves for the United States already having a job points to the connections that exist between the core and the periphery in the contracting of labor. It is important to point out that Carlota's words allude to some sort of transaction that takes place between her friend Chuchita's uncle and her future employer, Dr. Stephens.[19] For all intents and purposes, Carlota is purchased by Dr. Stephens, a transaction that lies beyond any narrative convention. Though an individual action, the money exchange that takes place is illustrative of a transnational labor market where gendered bodies are bought and sold.

As a young girl without a family, Carlota is in an extremely vulnerable position that leaves her open to exploitation. Carlota's gender and her youth challenge the stereotype still prevalent in the mid-1990s of the immigrant as an adult male, while her story also rejects the mold of the traditional narrative of departure. She does not leave Mexico dreaming of a better life, or believing in the American Dream, but leaves having no other option. Her border crossing, however, is predicated on a system of labor that depends on the importation of working bodies. The need for cheap domestic labor ensures that trans-actions like the one between Dr. Stephens and Chuchita's uncle con-tinue to exist, thus her experience reflects that of twenty-first-century immigrants who are caught up in a complicated web of mobile labor and capital, except that now, the role of individuals in "facilitating" transnational movement has given way to a larger system of trade in human labor. The role of exporting women to meet the needs of trans-national capital has been taken up by national governments, part of a process that Saskia Sassen has theorized as "counter-geographies of globalization." For Sassen, these "counter-geographies" consist of cross-border circuits of migration that are "profit- or revenue-making circuits developed on the backs of the truly disadvantaged" and in-clude the illegal trafficking in people and cross-border migrations of documented and undocumented individuals ("Women's Burden" 1). Without a familial network of support, Carlota is left on her own, dependent on a national economy that cannot absorb her labor. The state, no longer responsible for her physical presence in the nation, benefits from her migration and her entrance into a cross-border cir-cuit of labor. Carlota is just one more Mexican working abroad.[20]

Corpi's text demonstrates an understanding of migration processes that rejects the rhetoric of immigration for simple upward mobility. Instead, the novel offers a narrative of movement complicated by geopolitical policies of population movement and control. The need for such a young person to leave her country of origin is predicated on a country's inability to absorb its citizens into a domestic labor market. Women and girls like Carlota enter cross-border circuits of labor that have become a major source of revenue for countries of origin. These women, however, are often unwanted by both the host countries and their countries of origin. The representation of Carlo-ta's entrance into the host nation in the trunk of a car illustrates the contradictory position of undocumented immigrants, whose labor is desired but whose presence remains unwanted. Her introduction to the nation falls outside of the parameters of the traditional narra-tive as her story embodies the uncertain condition of immigration and rejects the positioning of the United States as the beacon of de-mocracy. The text critiques both the host and the home nation and a system of border enforcement that places bodies like Carlota's in precarious situations.

Carlota's introduction to the United States is not welcoming. There is no Statue of Liberty to embrace her; no shining beacon of hope awaits her. Instead, her entrance into the nation in the trunk of a car is a dark and frightening one, a foreshadowing of the difficulties she will soon face. Even after crossing the border, Carlota is forced to remain in the trunk to avoid being caught by the border patrol. Her recorded voice haltingly recalls:

> It must have been about six in the evening . . . But it was still so hot in-[. . .]-side the car trunk, that every mouthful of air I inhaled felt like an exhalation from the Devil's breath . . . Inside Dr. Mark Stephens's car trunk, not knowing which was worse, dying or being caught by la migra and sent back to Mexico. (44–45)

The trunk of the car threatens to become a metal tomb. Unlike cultural productions that downplay or ignore the physical trauma of crossing the border, Corpi's novel makes a conscious attempt to represent the horrific situations faced by undocumented immigrants who try to enter the United States—struggles that remain marginalized in popular discourse of border security. In the trunk, Carlota not only experiences appalling physical conditions but must also face the fear and anxiety of being caught by *la migra*. As the trunk opens and she is helped out, she remembers that "two hands held me up gently, and I knew they couldn't be the hands of a border patrolman or a sheriff's deputy" (46). The way in which she is held up without being mistreated is an indicator for Carlota that she has not been caught.[21] Carlota's wariness points to the violence experienced by undocumented immigrants at the hands of U.S. law-enforcement officials.[22] Her reaction is informed by an alternative system of knowledge and information shared amongst an immigrating community—an insight into state-sanctioned hostility and aggression ignored by mainstream media outlets. Corpi employs her character's experience of border crossing to comment on the role that violence plays in the policing of the border.

In our current moment of globalization and increased migration, core nations use the policing of national borders as a means to control the immigration of people from the periphery. The legislating of construction of border walls and fences is but one example of the attention placed on regulating national boundaries. In 2005, the U.S. Congress approved a high-tech border-fence project intended to monitor the border with Mexico through surveillance technology.[23] The bill authorizing the construction of a seven hundred–mile fence along the U.S.–Mexico border, originally estimated to cost more than $1.2 billion, was signed into law in 2006 by President George W. Bush (Hsu; Koch).[24] At the state level, the passage of legislation like SB 1070 in Arizona illustrates the growing anti-immigrant sentiment permeating our current national discourse. Neither state nor federal legislative measures take into account the rise in unofficial border-policing activities organized by civilian groups like the Minutemen and the Border Fence Project.[25] At the center of these plans and policies is the fear of immigrant bodies rushing the border.

The popular discourse of border violence is one of erasure, one that erases violence against immigrants in general and women specifically. In her article "Senseless Deaths and Holding the Line," border scholar Cynthia L. Bejarano argues that

> border violence is conceptualized as the fear of terrorism, undocumented immigrants, and drug smugglers that are rushing the Border: All three are metamorphosed into one massive threat to border security. All other types of violence remain an afterthought: The rape and sexual assault of women trying to cross the border, the robbing and beating of undocumented immigrants, and even the forced trafficking of human beings to work in agricultural fields, construction sites, or domestic work fall outside standard conceptual frameworks of border violence. (269)

Bejarano's argument makes a compelling case for the acknowledgment of the limitations inherent in an analysis of immigration and border violence that remains divorced from larger economic policies and globalization.[26] She critiques the fact that border violence that confronts individuals, especially those whose existence and reality remain marginalized, is only rendered visible when it affects the state. It is this invisibility that *Cactus Blood* challenges with its emphasis on Carlota's narrative of immigration. Through her story of movement and border crossing, the text inserts a history of violence that often remains buried under official state narratives. While Carlota's entry into the United States might seem less violent than those of people who confront physical force, the psychological trauma caused by the fear of detection and the physical trauma of being locked in the trunk of the car are forms of violence. The popular rhetoric used in discussions of border security obscures an increasingly violent process of immigration. Gendered counternarratives, including those found in cultural productions, reveal the effects that border enforcement has on transnational workers.

An earlier intervention in the hegemonic framing of the immigrant experience is found in Sánchez-Scott's theatrical production *Latina*. The play's representation of crossing the border is starkly different from the popular narrative of immigration, whose structure limits the acknowledgment of problematic constructions of national boundaries. For example, in *Spanglish*, the image of Flor and her daughter walking across the desert pulling rolling suitcases represents a sterilized version of entering the nation, a version easily accepted by an audience. The ludicrous scene obfuscates the difficulties faced by undocumented immigrants, especially women, in their attempts to cross the border. *Latina* rejects this erasure and pays specific attention to the role that gender plays in the immigration experiences of women, who face the threat of multiple forms of violence on their journey to the United States. The stage directions draw attention to the hardships that one woman attempting to cross the border, Elsa (identified as New Girl), faces on her journey to the United States:

> At one point we see NEW GIRL paying off a policeman. Another moment a woman steals her shawl. Then a man accosts her at knife point and tries to rape her, but she escapes. Next, she is giving money to a slick city coyote, dressed in American type work clothes, who takes her to the end of the tunnel where it is night . . . We see a large barbed wire fence . . . They both hit the ground and crawl on hands and knees to the barbed wire fence. She crawls through . . . She stands up on the other side and looks back. There is triumph in the music with a moment of Peruvian flute. (85)

Once she leaves her village, Elsa is no longer under the protection of her community and, like many real immigrants, is confronted with a corrupt justice system and the constant threat of physical danger. As a woman, however, Elsa is even more susceptible to peril, because as another immigrant, Lola, explains, "The policeman on the road wants his mordida. What the police don't get, the bandits take. Better for them if it's a woman. Then they try to get paid in other ways or sometimes they just kill the people" (107). As a woman, Elsa faces not only the threat of rape at the hands of the coyotes and other men she encounters, but also the possibility of being killed.[27] The play informs the reader or viewer that she is successful in escaping the would-be rapist, but also alludes to the fact that many other women are not so lucky.

Sánchez-Scott's text highlights a history of border violence and migration danger and introduces the role that gender plays in the transnational movement of laboring bodies. Performed and set at the beginning of the 1980s, the play is situated at a time when conflict and struggle were widespread throughout Latin America. Guatemala was in the midst of a bloody civil war, while violence and state repression were growing in El Salvador and Nicaragua. A young woman like Elsa would have been one of a growing number of immigrants making their way to the U.S.–Mexico border at that time.[28] The dangers she experienced might be unknown to a U.S. theater audience, but would be common knowledge amongst immigrant communities. The inclusion of this subjugated knowledge in *Latina* illustrates the role that the informal dissemination of alternative knowledge has played in the process of immigration for decades.

Like *Cactus Blood*, *Latina* inserts an immigrant experience of violence that disrupts the hegemonic narrative and illustrates the importance that gender plays in the transnational movement of peoples. Lola's sentiment "better for them if it's a woman" underscores the existence of female narratives of immigration and the use of rape in terrorizing women who embark on the border-crossing journey. The individual aggression faced by these women becomes a form of state-sanctioned brutality when the violence is ignored or dismissed, especially in the case of corrupt government officials. Today's official and unofficial policing of the border have made traveling to and crossing into the United States a much more dangerous project than in the past.

While Elsa succeeds in reaching the United States, the triumphant music that plays as she crosses the border is ironic. Being incorporated into the United States is much harder than adding Peruvian flute to the musical score. Unlike the happy endings of Hollywood movies, Elsa's success in crossing the border does not last, as she is faced with the difficulties of being an undocumented worker. In Los Angeles, Elsa, like the other women of the domestic agency, lives in constant fear of *la migra*. For her, the journey of coming to the United States, the "land of opportunity," becomes the challenge of remaining in the country, an aspect of immigration that does not exist within the hegemonic immigrant narrative. When discussing the fear of detection, Elsa's fellow worker La Chata describes her anger and the fact that *la migra* makes her "feel hunted, like an animal" (106). The character of La Chata voices the dehumanizing aspects of being an undocumented worker. Their constant fear of being deported makes La Chata see *la migra* as the hunter while she and the other women are the prey.

The fear of deportation is just one of many threats that undocumented immigrants face. Bejarano's understanding of the range of border violence is especially useful when considering the danger that detection poses for undocumented immigrants, specifically women. If we think of border violence as affecting those individuals who make the journey to and through the border, instead of relying on a notion of border violence as simply border security, we can expand the scope of analysis to include the violence perpetrated on immigrant women after they enter the United States. La Chata's sentiment of feeling hunted by *la migra* is not just about the fear of being detected, but also about the fear of what happens once one is arrested. In her work on Immigration and Naturalization Service (INS) raids, activist and lawyer Renee Saucedo concludes, "Generally, INS raids, arrests, and detentions are characterized by abuse, physical violence, and humiliation. These are all the things that immigrant women have to face and are terrorized by almost every day" (135). The fear of terrorism associated with this type of border violence is an individual and communal one.

The constant threat of detection works to control bodies beyond the physically demarcated border. Saucedo argues that the INS raids perform the ideological function of keeping undocumented women oppressed. These visible exhibitions of power work to "intimidate immigrant women so they won't ask for the services they're entitled to, morally and legally. They use intimidating tactics so that immigrant women will be afraid to complain or assert their rights. They are trying to subjugate women into submission so they won't fight back" (137). The strategies that keep undocumented women silent and invisible must also be considered within the context of a wider ideology of gender that seeks to keep women in subordinate positions. In her critique of the role of the Mexican government in the feminicides of Juárez, the murders of hundreds of women there beginning in 1994, Rosa Linda Fregoso argues that critiques of globalization and sexual violence fail to account "for the ways in which global manifestations of power differ from as much as they intensify earlier and more traditional forms of patriarchy within the nation-state" (18). Female immigrant workers have already disrupted gender roles through their immigration and labor; the threat of deportation exposes them to ongoing gendered violence.[29]

Even though Carlota in *Cactus Blood* and the women in *Latina* have succeeded in entering the country, their undocumented status will not allow them any sense of security, and they continue to live in fear of detection and deportation. The instability of their presence in the United States stands in stark contrast to the traditional narrative of the immigrant who works hard and establishes a stable new home in this country. The homes the women have created for themselves are precariously balanced on their ability to remain undetected, a challenge exacerbated by the ways in which they are visibly marked by their race.[30] In the prevailing narrative, the immigrant does not face the constant danger of deportation or the threat of being identified as undocumented based solely on the color of his/her skin. The constant state of liminality in which undocumented immigrants must exist and function does not fit comfortably into the three narratives stages of the traditional immigrant schema. Their immigration status not only excludes them from the mainstream, but also adversely affects their experiences as workers.

Labor and the Family

We just love her. She's like one of the family.

» Alice Childress, *Like One of the Family* (1)[31]

The role of labor is an important aspect of narratives of immigration, and the stories analyzed here continue the tradition of highlighting the experiences of work and the structure of the workplace. Like the traditional male narrative, which emphasizes how hard the young male protagonist works to support his family, the texts by the Chicanas/Latinas discussed in this chapter situate their protagonists as breadwinners, but in these texts, those breadwinners are women. The women in these texts are not like the female characters in *Pocho*, who must depend on the men of the family to support them and whose labor is restricted to the home. Instead, these fictional women offer a representation of participants in the countergeographies of globalization; they embody what Sassen refers to as the "feminization of survival." Due in part to the growing number of female immigrants and the dependence on their labor by their countries of origin, documenting the gendered realities of immigration in our current moment is critical. By offering representations of Latina immigrants working in transnational systems of labor, these authors intervene in a system of knowledge that dismisses immigrant women and their stories as inconsequential or too specific to be of real importance. They demonstrate how the entrance of women into a transnational labor system has gendered the processes of immigration.

The characters created by these Chicana/Latina writers are also starkly different from the female domestic workers represented in films, who are almost nonexistent or whose labor is "cleaned up." Instead, we get representations of domestic workers who are exploited and who are subjected to unfair labor practices, racism, and violence. Also important is the fact that the immigrant domestic worker must labor in a space that relies heavily on patriarchal gender roles. As sociologist Mary Romero argues, "The ideology of domesticity connects women's identities to their roles as wives and mothers" (99). In effect, their labor is predicated on a construction of femininity that naturalizes care work and imposes it on women. In *Forced to Care*, Evelyn Nakano Glenn argues that "the social organization of care has been rooted in diverse forms of coercion" and that such an organization has made it the responsibility of women to care for their families (5). This social organization has also led to a tracking of "poor, racial minority, and immigrant women into positions entailing caring for others" (5). For Nakano Glenn, women are obligated to perform care work based on kinship, gender, and race/class. As such, immigrant women are bound by this "triple status duty to care" (5). Unlike the individual male protagonist of *Pocho*, the women represented in the following texts cannot escape responsibility for family, both their own and the ones for which they work.

In *Spanglish*, Deborah Clasky's "Welcome to the family" greeting to Flor is an attempt to make audiences comfortable with the employer/employee relationship. Through the euphemism of "the family," employers attempt to naturalize the hierarchy existing between the employer and the employee. By including the rhetoric of family into the immigrant narrative, cultural productions can further that naturalization process while creating a representation of domestic labor that eliminates exploitation. The rhetoric of the family is a complicated linguistic strategy that, while appearing to be inclusive, is actually a strategy of negation. Under such a rhetorical move, the economic relationship that exists between the employer and the employee is denied and the exploitation of the worker is rendered invisible. Employing such rhetoric romanticizes the labor of the domestic worker. All four of the cultural productions discussed in this chapter challenge the obfuscation of the economic relationship between employer and employee that dominates the rhetoric of family. The texts draw attention to the difference between care work as physical labor and care work as uncompensated emotional labor—especially in the complicated relationship between care workers and children.

While the word "nanny" often conjures up images of Mary Poppins–like characters or "Supernanny" Jo Frost, with their crisp British accents (read as cultured), the reality for immigrant Latina nannies is much different.[32] Unlike the type of nanny one hires through an elite nanny service, these nannies are most often paid much less and expected to perform labor beyond caring for children. Oftentimes, nanny work involves the type of labor expected of traditional domestic workers, like cleaning, laundry, cooking, etc. In some households, the "nanny" is responsible for the welfare of the entire household and not just the child. In her study on immigrant workers and domestic labor, sociologist Pierrette Hondagneu-Sotelo found that "racial inequality increases the likelihood that employers will require the same employee both to care for children and to take full charge of the housekeeping. While white 'American' nannies are generally not expected to do housecleaning, Latinas regularly are" (148). As a personnel recruiter told Hondagneu-Sotelo, when he explains to employers the difference race plays in dictating work duties, he emphasizes that "an American nanny . . . is very different from a Latina nanny/housekeeper, and he must instruct employers that they cannot expect white American nannies to clean" (148). While the distinction between domestic worker and nanny functions when discussing white employees, the collapsing of duties that occurs in the employment of immigrant Latina nannies situates their work as a form of domestic labor.

The normalization of unpaid care work and the ease with which domestic workers are exploited is mapped out in Corpi's *Cactus Blood*. At first, it seems like Carlota's story is a happy one. Once she reaches Fresno, she works for the Stephens family and begins to take English classes, making new friends like Josie Baldomar. She declares,

> Since I had left my village in Mexico, I hadn't been as happy as I was during the following year, living with the Stephenses in Fresno. I cleaned their house, cooked for them, did their laundry, and cared for their garden. I also took care of their six- and nine-year-old daughters on weekdays, and made sure they did their homework when they came home from school. (47)

Carlota's description of her labor points to the ways in which she functions not only as a full-time housekeeper and cook, but also as a child-care provider and gardener. Carlota, a young girl of fourteen, is performing the tasks of three different individuals. Moreover, as an underage undocumented immigrant, Carlota is completely at her employers' mercy. Since she has no family of her own, it is easy for Carlota's employers to fold her into the fabric of the home and make her feel "like one of the family." Being a part of the family, however, is directly predicated on the worker's ability to perform both physical and emotional labor. In her research on migrant domestic workers, Bridget Anderson finds that one of the advantages of constructing a worker as part of the family lies in "the erasure of the worker's own family," a process made easier if the worker is undocumented (125). With the inability to care for one's own family or rely on them for support, undocumented domestic workers are left in a more vulnerable position and exposed to a higher level of exploitation. Carlota's character represents the difficulties encountered by undocumented immigrants whose immigration status and lack of familial networks are used to manipulate them within the confines of the private space of the home. This is not to say, however, that when a worker's network of support is present, conflict and manipulation are necessarily absent.

In *Latina*, the characters of Mrs. Levine and Ms. Harris use the agency to hire child-care providers, affording the play the opportunity to present an alternative to the simplistic representation of the Latina domestic worker, as the loving nanny, a stereotype that obfuscates the economics of care work. By having the women use the Felix Sanchez Domestic Agency in looking for someone to care for their children, *Latina* makes clear the connection that exists between paid domestic work and the unpaid emotional labor that takes place in the care of actual human beings. The women they employ are expected to perform the duties of two separate jobs, those of a domestic worker and those of a nanny, without being paid for both, thus reflecting the findings of Hondagneu-Sotelo, who found that "most

Americans who hire a domestic worker to come into their homes on a daily basis do so in order to meet their needs for *both* housecleaning and child care" (38). Romero reports that sometimes, "domestics are seen as 'protomothers': they are expected to perform the emotional labor of 'mothering' both the women employers and their families" and that employers assume that domestic workers will be naturally nurturing (137). The strategy of collapsing care work, emotional labor, and domestic work is dependent on a construction of gender that positions women as "naturally" belonging in the home and situates domestic work as an extension of a woman's innate abilities. The play, however, goes to great lengths to illustrate the economic aspect of care work and, in the process, challenges the ideology that naturalizes the care work performed by the women in the agency.

One of the most multifaceted representations of care work is found in Prado's documentary *Maid in America*. While the film captures the warm relationship between Telma and the Marburys, her employers, there is always a reminder of the employer/employee distinction that exists between them. Telma clearly loves Mickey Marbury, the young boy she cares for, but she is also honest in defining the nature of their relationship: "I tell the boy, you are my rent. I grab him and hug him and tell him, you are my rent and my food." Such acknowledgment takes nothing away from her affection, but it does make clear the fact that, as a worker, she is dependent on caring for her young charge in order to earn a living. Even though she is always aware of the economic relationship between herself and Mickey, Telma cannot help but love the young boy she is helping raise, and it is this part of care work that does not get figured into the economic equation: "Since I treat him with love, he sees me as his mom." There is a cost, however, to the emotional labor Telma performs. She tells us that "when you take care of a baby you have him with you all day . . . You start to love them as if they were your own children. But always in the back of your mind you are thinking, 'When he grows up, I am going to have to leave him. He won't need me anymore.'" Unlike the mother-child relationship, which is not so easily severed, Telma's relationship with Mickey will come to an end when he enters school full time and her services are no longer needed. It is a hard emotional cost to pay. When discussing her future plans, she tells the camera, "I'm not working as a nanny anymore. You get too attached . . . to the children. I'm not taking care of kids again."

Telma's story is important because of its representation of the complexities of paid care work and the historical connection it makes between domestic labor, immigration, and women of color. The Marburys are fair and thoughtful employers who truly value the work

Telma performs for them. They pay her what they can, because for them, the person who cares for your child "deserves your best."[33] The Marburys' understanding of the worth of Telma's labor comes from an understanding of their own family history. Mr. Marbury tells the audience, "As a black family, coming from where we come from—I'm from the South, and I know that, you know, my folks, 'my people,' did a lot of domestic work. They were the previous domestic workers. I know that my grandmother, my mother's mother, that she used to work in somebody else's house—iron their clothes, do that kind of thing for them." His words are framed by old pictures of black domestic workers/nannies, in a montage that ends with a picture of Telma and Mickey. Prado's interview with Mr. Marbury situates Telma's labor within a long history of women of color and domestic labor.

The rise of the global city and the growing number of women immigrants has shifted the supply of available workers and positioned immigrant women as the desirable labor pool. Just as African American women replaced European immigrants in the domestic-service sector after World War II, Latina immigrants are now replacing African American women in the occupation.[34] The previous shift in the demand for service work and the supply of domestic workers was based on the changes that industrialization brought to the domestic space.[35] The current shift is also based on a transformation of the labor system, this time to one established on globalization projects and transnational networks of labor exchange. The processes might be different, but in both phases, immigration and race have played essential roles in structuring the domestic-service sector. Under a racially structured system of wages, the labor of women of color is constructed as less valuable and is further devalued with the introduction of immigration status. For the viewer, Mr. Marbury's family history functions as a microcosm, reflecting the changes in the occupation—in a few generations, his family went from performing domestic labor to hiring domestic workers. While Mr. Marbury sees the domestic labor of his ancestors as the steps they took to a better life, Telma's immigrant status makes it more difficult to position her labor as ensuring upward mobility. While it might have been challenging for Mr. Marbury's family to become upwardly mobile because of class and racial barriers, the added complexities of being an immigrant further complicate the process of using domestic labor as a stepping-stone to a better life. The anti-immigrant rhetoric so popular in the mainstream has ensured that Latina immigrants like Telma remain in the periphery of the construction of citizenship—always foreign and highly suspicious—regardless of their un/authorized status.

Maid in America underscores that while Telma might be working under better conditions than Mr. Marbury's ancestors, she is still being charged with a type of work that defies easy definition. Telma is paid for the everyday physical care of Mickey, but her emotional labor cannot be adequately measured and compensated—a situation familiar to many Latina nannies. The fact that she will leave the family once Mickey gets a bit older betrays the rhetoric of family. Like Telma, the audience is unable to forget that she is an employee, no matter how much she loves Mickey. The rhetoric of love cannot erase the economic reality of their relationship. Instead, the documentary employs Telma's narrative to complicate our understanding of care work and to historically situate the invisible work of women of color in raising the nation's children.

Rejecting the Romance Plot

All social orders hierarchically organized into relations of domination and subordination create particular subject positions within which the subordinated can legitimately function. These subject positions, once self-consciously recognized by their inhabitants, can become transfigured into effective sites of resistance to an oppressive ordering of power relations.

» Chela Sandoval, *Methodology of the Oppressed* (54)

One of the most troubling trends in the visual representation of domestic workers is the need to cast them as the romantic interest of the employer. It seems to be one of the easiest ways to ensure the upward mobility of the protagonist. The plot of the romance between the employer and employee, à la *Jane Eyre*, provides the narrative with an uncomplicated way of ensuring a happy resolution that will please a mass audience. This narrative is dangerous because it ignores the level of power an employer wields over the domestic worker, and, more importantly, it erases a history of violence perpetrated on domestic workers of all racial backgrounds in the privacy of the domestic space.[36] The sexualization of the domestic worker that occurs in films like *Spanglish* helps to advance the plotline of the immigrant narrative as the protagonist is fully accepted by her American employer as an equal and her assimilation into the core is guaranteed through the romantic relationship. Such a plot device also obfuscates the domination and subordination present in the employer/employee hierarchy and impedes the possibility for a consciousness of resistance that Chela Sandoval envisions as transformative.

The romanticization of the employer-employee relationship popular in prevailing narratives of immigration in film stands in stark contrast to the dangerous conditions represented by Sánchez-Scott's *Latina* and Corpi's *Cactus Blood*. The construction of the Latina body as available and willing, a dangerous subtext of the commercial representations, is summarily rejected by the Chicana texts. Through their deconstruction of the economic relationship and their attention to the inherent imbalance of power between the female domestic worker and her male employer, Corpi and Sánchez-Scott rip off the dreamy lens through which romantic narratives attempt to represent such a relationship. Instead, their works interpolate multiple examples of the violence to which domestic workers are subjected—a violence that remains invisible in the mainstream. They remind us of the risk the enclosed space of the home holds for women in general, and the more vulnerable domestic worker specifically. The narratives demonstrate what is at stake in the project of representing racialized gendered bodies.

From the beginning of its introduction of domestic labor, *Latina* makes visible its critique of the type of representation that has reduced Latina workers to sexual objects. It is no coincidence that the opening shot of the domestic agency shows two dummies in the window—dummies meant to signify the kind of worker available for hire. The stage directions describe the two dummies: *"one in a white uniform holding a pink baby dummy, the white dummy looks very maternal like a Madonna, the second dummy is in a short black uniform with a white frilly apron, holding a feather duster. She looks like a naughty French maid"* (86). The display in the window re-creates the virgin/whore dichotomy and reinforces the popular conception of domestic workers either as natural caregivers or as sexually available objects. The window sells the image of the worker as either the loving Latina nanny or the sexy Latina lover, stereotypes that hold consequences for the women identified as Latinas.[37] In both instances, the Latina body is represented as being able to meet the needs of her employer—either in the nursery or in the bedroom. The care work expected of the Latina domestic worker is now expanded to include sexual services. The construction of domestic workers as natural caregivers, combined with racist ideologies of brown women's sexuality, functions to position Latina bodies as hypersexual, more sexual than white women's bodies and therefore ready, willing, and able.

Although she is an actor and was born in the United States, the character of Sarita in *Latina* is subject to the same process of sexualization as the immigrant domestic workers. Even though she has taken extra care to dress in a way she believes will not mark her as a domestic worker, just standing by the domestic agency where she works as a receptionist and being Chicana mark her in the eyes of the men in passing cars.

MALE VOICES: [1st] *(off stage)* Oh, oh, oh, *(loud kissing sounds)* baby. [2nd] Oh, Señorita, I am in love. [3rd] Hot tamale! Hey little beaner. [2nd] What a cute little maid! [3rd] Hey Señorita! Hey little maid—you sure are pretty. You want to come to my casa? *(SARITA at first looks embarrassed, then bored. She has been through this before and knows how to stop it. She puts a stupid expression on her face, picks her nose and says . . .)*

SARITA: *(Like goofy [sic].)* Yuk, Yuk. *(Loud sounds of car peeling off.)* (86–87)

Sarita's disidentification with the immigrant Latinas who work as domestics for the agency is a personal strategy that fails when confronted by the overarching institutionalized stereotypes that construct Latina bodies as hypersexual. The sexual harassment of Sarita by the three men in the car is an example of the intersecting ideologies of race, class, and gender that make it acceptable to objectify women of color, especially domestic workers. The fact that she is Latina, and the men's misidentification and their unwillingness to see her as anything other than a domestic worker, makes her accessible to their male gaze and leads to their verbal assault. Their referring to her as a "hot tamale" and a "little beaner" makes the racism inherent in their sexualization of Sarita clear, and in their calling her "a cute little maid," the men's classism comes through. It makes no difference that Sarita is not employed by any of these men; sexist, classist, and racist ideologies about domestic workers pose a threat to any woman identified as one. The fact that the stage directions make reference to Sarita's experience with this type of treatment points to the widespread attitude the men exhibit.

In her career as an actor, Sarita is hindered by the commonly held stereotypes about Latinas, and the roles she lands fall strictly within the construction of Latinas as inhabitants of the "barrio." However, unlike the victims she has portrayed on television, Sarita is not a passive victim in real life.[38] She has learned that the only way to effectively resist such advances is not through open confrontation or pretending it isn't happening, but through the employment of strategies such as dumbing herself down. Such strategies ensure that she will avoid further harassment by men, but while comical in this case, Sarita has had to find ways of dealing with the threat present in such verbal assaults. While the harassment might be verbal, it is still dangerous, and an open confrontation of the car's sexist and racist inhabitants could lead to an escalation to physical violence. Sarita might not be an immigrant, but her gendered and racialized body, positioned in front of the agency, is read as available and she is subject to the same type of treatment as the immigrant women she helps place. The fact that the harassment occurs on the street illustrates the ways in which the bodies of Latina women are constructed as on display both in the public and private spheres.

On stage, Sarita undermines the stereotypes that dictate the roles Latinas are restricted to playing in commercial productions. She becomes a much more complicated character than the image she is reduced to by casting agents or the men on the street. As a working-class woman of color, Sarita has had to learn strategies of resistance and deflection to protect herself. When discussing the different technologies of the oppressed, Sandoval identifies one of them as the "process of challenging dominant ideological forms through their deconstruction" (82). In refusing to position Sarita as existing within the construction of the virgin/whore dichotomy and by providing her character with strategies of resistance, Sánchez-Scott deconstructs and challenges these stereotypes. By following the description of the dummies in the window with the harassment of Sarita, the play also makes visible the connection between the construction of images and the bodies those images represent.

Corpi's text provides a much more chilling representation of the threat of violence under which some domestic workers labor. As a female domestic worker, Carlota is vulnerable to more than one form of exploitation. Carlota is uncomfortable with Dr. Stephens' physical displays of affection and with how he gazes upon her body. As her employer, Dr. Stephens has power over Carlota, a power that grows exponentially with her undocumented status. Because she is undocumented and underage, quitting and finding new employment is not a viable option for Carlota. Her situation is made worse by her dependence on the Stephenses for lodging. Alone and with no family to turn to, all she can do is smile and "avoid his gaze" (50). Pretending it isn't happening, however, does not protect Carlota for long, and one day Dr. Stephens corners her while his family is out of town. As he comes toward her, Carlota is terrified of what is about to happen:

> A chill ran up my spine, but I didn't move. I wasn't sure what I should do. First, he put his hot, sweaty palm on my face. Suddenly, he tried to force my lips and teeth open, to stick his tongue into my mouth. I was determined not to let him do it. I turned my face away, my revulsion for him beginning to stir around inside my stomach . . . I began to push him away, but he overpowered me and pushed me down on the ground . . . Fighting him off made my tears rush out. Oblivious to my cries and pleas, he began to suck and bite my lips harder and harder . . . Die. I would rather die. No. Live! Contradictory thoughts crossed my mind, back and forth . . . Nothing was going to stop him, I realized helplessly . . . The burning pain inside me and my rage made me scream. Despair and impotence took over, making me wish for sudden death. (50–51; my ellipses)

Corpi's description of Carlota's rape is a brutal account of the abuse of power that can occur in the relationship between employer and employee. Unlike the films that choose to romanticize the connection between the domestic worker and her male employer, this novel offers a much more critical assessment of that association. As a fourteen-year-old girl with no legal protection, Carlota is in a precarious position that leaves her vulnerable to abuse at her employer's hands. Being a Mexican immigrant marks Carlota's brown body as accessible to her white employer. Not only is the doctor in a privileged class position, but, as a white man, his race ensures him an even greater level of power over Carlota.[39]

When discussing the long history of violence against people of color in the United States and the Americas, Chicana historian Antonia Castañeda explains that this legacy of violent domination "is rooted in sexual and other violence against women. The first political acts of domination were acts of rape and sexual aggression against women" (313). She goes on to argue that "the legacy of the Americas is violence and exploitation based on sex, gender, race, sexuality, class, culture, and physical condition—based on the power and privilege to exploit and oppress others that each of those elements confer on us" (317). The rape of Carlota's brown, immigrant, poor, and female body represents a long history of violence against women of color by those who are positioned as superior in multiple hierarchies. Through Carlota's narrative, Corpi reveals to her reader how intersecting forms of oppression continue to impact the lives of women like Carlota, women whose stories help make up the compilation of interviews called *The Chicana Experience*. She exposes the violence naturalized by the romance narratives of popular culture. The rape of the young Carlota is an atrocious experience that strongly challenges the ways in which domestic workers are viewed in many texts and represents the dangers that portrayals of these women as sexually available pose to women whose labor is confined behind closed doors.

After the rape, Carlota leaves the only home she has known since immigrating. She walks many miles through pesticide-coated fields to get to her friend Josie Baldorama. As a rape victim, Carlota attempts to erase the physical imprint of Dr. Stephens from her body by viciously scrubbing herself and washing away any outside evidence of the rape. In the process, she makes her skin extra sensitive, allowing the pesticides to more easily enter her body. María Baldorama, Josie's mother, recalls,

> After the rape, Carlota was very sick for days on end. At dawn, the day after the rape, Josie brought her to me, vomiting, convulsing, screaming. Her skin was red, partly because she had scrubbed herself so hard, but there was more. Carlota didn't know it then, but the fields she went through on her way to Josie's house had been sprayed with the Devil's blood. (85)

Carlota's body becomes contaminated not only through the rape, but also through the poisons used in the fields. Her body ends up embodying the abuse of both the domestic worker and the migrant worker who is forced to work in noxious fields. Not only does Carlota become the victim of rape and pesticide poisoning, she also comes under scrutiny from law enforcement when Dr. Stephens dies the day after the rape.

> Two Fresno homicide detectives came snooping around, asking us questions about Carlota . . . Mrs. Stephens herself came to Josie's house the day after her husband died . . . she wanted to talk with Carlota . . . Mrs. Stephens told Josie that she wanted to beg Carlota not to tell anyone about the rape, for her daughters' sake . . . Ironically, that day was Carlota's fifteenth birthday. (85)

All of a sudden, Carlota goes from being a rape survivor to being a possible murderer. Even after Dr. Stephens' death is attributed to his weak heart, Carlota is still wanted by the authorities for being undocumented. In the eyes of the law, she is a criminal, not a victim. As an undocumented worker, Carlota would have no access to justice for her rape, but her immigration status also denied her the medical care she needed: "Josie wanted to take her to a hospital, but Carlota had no papers; she had come into the country illegally" (87).[40] Because of the doctor's violent attack, Carlota is sentenced to a life of pain and suffering—the lasting physical consequence of pesticide poisoning.

The violence perpetrated on the bodies of women like Carlota is made possible under a patriarchal system that differentiates between the worth of women's bodies based not just on race and class, but also on immigration status. The rape of women of color is nothing new, but the growing criminalization of—and hostility to—immigrant women from the south has intensified the racist and xenophobic patriarchal structure already in place. When we situate the rape of immigrant women as part of the border violence that Bejarano discusses in her work, it becomes possible to see how the precarious processes of crossing the border do not end once a woman enters the nation. In the same way in which the domestic space of the nation is not a safe space for immigrant women of color, the domestic space of the home remains a place where violence is always a possibility for them as well. The criminalization of the undocumented body further helps to victimize women who would resist or challenge attacks on their bodies.

In her discussion of national security and rape, Sylvanna Falcón argues that one reason militarized-border rape can be categorized as a form of national-security rape is that "the absence of legal documents positions undocumented women as 'illegal' and as having committed a crime. Thus, law-abiding citizens need 'protection' from these criminals; the existence of undocumented women causes national *in*security, and they are so criminalized that their bodily integrity does not matter to the state" ("'National Security'" 121). For the state, the bodies of women like Carlota are not worth protecting, especially if it means taking sides against someone who is constructed as a law-abiding citizen. The rhetoric of border violence espoused by state agencies and mass media renders the violence against immigrant women invisible, especially when that violence is not specifically located on the border. Corpi's text, however, intervenes in this erasure and offers a chilling representation of the threat many immigrant women face.

Even though Carlota goes on to become a vocal advocate for the banning of pesticide spraying in fields, she is never able to get well herself and must live with the consequences of running through the fields after the rape. Corpi's text does not allow romantic narratives of domestic workers who fall in love with their employers to stand unchallenged. Carlota's story illustrates the dangers that exist in the domestic employee's line of work and the abuse of power that is a lived reality for many. The very different representations of the sexualization of the domestic worker in *Latina* and in *Cactus Blood* reject the romance plot popular in the immigrant narrative portrayed in films. The two texts make clear the role that the intersection of characters' gender, race, class, and immigration status plays in positioning immigrant domestic workers, and they refuse to provide experiences in the narrative that can be easily reconciled in the path toward resolution.

No Happy Ending

There are believed to be 11 million undocumented immigrants in the United States. We're not always who you think we are. Some pick your strawberries or care for your children. Some are in high school or college. And some, it turns out, write news articles you might read. I grew up here. This is my home. Yet even though I think of myself as an American and consider America my country, my country doesn't think of me as one of its own.

» Jose Antonio Vargas, "My Life as an Undocumented Immigrant"[41]

The ideology of the American Dream and its connection to the immigrant story dictates that immigrant narratives provide a resolution that perpetuates the myth of success—a narrative strategy employed by the texts in the previous chapter. For Richard in *Pocho*, his rejection of his family and his decision to enlist in the Navy ensure his participation in the nation through his military service. *Spanglish*

also concludes with the requisite happy ending, with Cristina apply-
ing for college admission. The cultural productions discussed in this
chapter reject the neat and tidy narrative closure promoted by films
like *Spanglish*. In Corpi's *Cactus Blood*, Carlota suffers the fate of having to live a life riddled with illness. While the detective story ends
with the uncovering of the mystery and the resolution of the crime,
Carlota's experiences in the contact phase of the immigrant narrative have been so dramatic that they are ultimately insurmountable.
In the end, Carlota must return to her country of origin, the "home"
she hasn't seen for most of her adult life, to die in peace. Even in
death, Carlota's body cannot rest in the soil of the nation that has so
summarily rejected her. The narrative rejects the old world/new world
binary and instead reasserts the connection between the core and
the periphery that the immigrant domestic worker has maintained
through her many years in the United States.

In *Maid in America*, Eva is the one woman most invested in the idea
of the American Dream. Unlike Telma and Judith, Eva speaks to the
camera in English and proudly displays the multiple certificates she
has been awarded for her various studies. Holding a BA in account-
ing from a Mexican university, however, has not easily translated
into success in the United States. Her faith in the meritocratic principles inherent in the ideology of upward mobility motivates Eva to
pursue another level of eduation through night school. For one brief
moment, the audience witnesses Eva's success as she finds employment as a tax preparer. It seems that her story proves the possibility
of achieving the American Dream through hard work and perseverance. Even the description of Eva on Impacto Films' website lauds her
accomplishments: "Staying motivated and positive regardless of your
job or living situation is not easy. It sure hasn't been for Eva. But she is
a perfect example of how determination, perseverance and a positive
attitude can help overcome any obstacles" ("*Maid in America*: The
Women"). However, Eva's story is more complicated. In a follow-up
with the three women that Prado conducted in 2005, we find out that
Eva's dream job was only temporary. Prado reports in a PBS interview,
"Unfortunately, Eva hasn't found work as a tax accountant again . . .
She's working three days a week cleaning houses; she doesn't want to
be tied down to working all week. She's currently taking a break from
night school."[42] No matter how hard she has worked or how positive
her attitude has been, Eva's status as an immigrant worker cannot be
overcome simply by following the myth of meritocracy.

Prado's documentary also captures the pain experienced by Judith
as a mother caught in the web of a global system of labor. The audience is witness to her struggles as she tries to raise her newborn

in Los Angeles while her older children remain in Guatemala. The film visually documents the two different worlds connected through Judith's labor. While she works in the United States, half of her income returns to Guatemala to contribute to the cost of raising her four young daughters, whom she left behind with her mother and sister. Judith laments the separation and her inability to raise her children together. The danger of bringing her daughters to the United States and her mother's worsening health force Judith to return to Guatemala. Prado's camera records the reunion between mother and daughters. The audience witnesses Judith's emotional promise, "I won't leave you," as the cost of their separation becomes visible.[43] The documentary captures the transnational connections created by the immigrant labor of women like Judith and the impossible disconnect between old and new world. The film offers an immigrant narrative based on multiple movements across national boundaries and a link between host country and country of origin that is not easily broken.

The text that most directly challenges the narrative containment of the immigrant story convention is Sánchez-Scott's *Latina*. In part, *Latina* becomes the story of Sarita's burgeoning solidarity with her fellow Latinas, and her confrontation with one of the employers, Mrs. Camden, brings to the forefront the types of attitudes many employers have toward women of color domestic workers and the resistance of domestic workers to being objectified. Faced with Mrs. Camden's racist and classist insults to Lola and the other women of the agency, Sarita is forced to take a stand and choose between solidarity with the women or acquiescence to employers like Mrs. Camden. In a traditional narrative, Sarita's newfound consciousness would provide for a happy ending. Her championing of the women would be seen as the triumph of the "little guy" against the rich and greedy bully, a popular trope in commercial productions. In reality, however, the immigration status of the women and their lack of economic and political power make a happy ending impossible. Right after the women assert themselves and Sarita is accepted as one of them, the INS raids the agency.[44] The women are rounded up and, we assume, deported. The conclusion of the play reveals the very precarious position under which undocumented immigrant women live. As strong as Lola might be in the face of exploitation, she has no power in dealing with *la migra*, and she becomes just another immigrant expelled from the country. The play concludes with a realistically grim ending, rejecting the kind of ideological closure on which the resolution of the immigrant narrative is typically predicated.

The More Things Change . . .

> Deportations without due process; detention without access to lawyers; separation of families; and racial profiling are some of the ways that immigration policies and practices violate immigrants' and citizens' human rights.
>
> » Tanya Maria Golash-Boza, *Immigration Nation* (159)

Since *Latina* first premiered in 1980, the process of immigration and the conditions under which immigrants live and work have only grown more complicated. In addition to the militarization of the border, the increased internal enforcement of immigration policies (through raids, detention, and deportation) has deeply impacted immigrant communities.[45] The public spectacle of U.S. Immigration and Customs Enforcement raids has raised the fear of detection for those who lack the official documentation securing their presence in the nation. Similar to the way in which the media played a pivotal role in the mobilization of Mexicans and Mexican Americans during the 1930s repatriation campaign, the vast dissemination of images from current raids has led to a rise in the movement of undocumented migrant communities and has relegated them further into the margins.[46] These images also function to visually criminalize all immigrants to a mainstream audience and to advance the myth of the dangerous immigrant. Conspicuously absent from this public image is the reality of the human-rights violations encountered by detained immigrants listed in Golash-Boza's statement in the epigraph that opens this section. No longer are the tactics of wearing the right clothes or anglicizing one's name enough to avoid detection.

Loomer's *Living Out* inserts a form of local knowledge that demonstrates the strategies that workers like Salvadoran nanny Ana Hernandez employ today to avoid detection and remain employed. During one of their discussions in the park, Ana explains to Sandra and Zoila, her fellow Latina nannies, how she procured a driver's license while being undocumented. When Zoila questions the type of person who would lie, Ana simply states, "A person who wants a better job!" (51). Loomer's play illustrates the ingenuity of individuals in creating strategies of survival and resistance and the informal network of communication that allows for these strategies to circulate. At the same time, the play critiques a system that continues to rely on the labor of undocumented immigrants while making these workers unwelcome. The need for employment forces individuals to find ways to navigate structures put in place to ensure that undocumented individuals remain in the margins. In fact, the inability of undocumented workers to follow common laws, which have no bearing on immigration, actually forces individuals to break laws, therefore further criminalizing them. *Living Out* was written and performed more than two decades after *Latina* and, while the marginalization of Latina immigrants and the fear of being caught remain ever present, Loomer's play captures the added challenges that avoiding detection pose for undocumented migrants. In the post–9/11 era, the structural changes to immigration policies dictate new strategies for survival—Ana's character highlights the necessity for marginalized communities to circulate local knowledge in opposition to draconian national policies. In addition to contributing to a longer literary dialogue on the conditions of undocumented women and tracing some of the changes resulting from the restructuring of immigration-enforcement agencies, the play also offers a heartbreaking representation of the sacrifices made by women who attempt to balance work and family and the higher cost immigrant women pay in this effort.

For many immigrants, the reason for migration is the need to support family members in their countries of origin. As a result of the mass migration of laboring bodies, the practice of sending money home has become a major source of income for countries of origin. Not only do these remittances help support the families left behind, but they also aid in the overall economy of the home country. In the conventional immigrant narrative, part of the tension between the old world and the new is resolved by leaving the old world behind for a new and better life in the new world. The dependence of those left behind on the labor of an immigrant worker, however, makes such a solution nearly impossible for those who choose to remain connected with their families. In contrast to commercial productions, which ignore the question of parenting, *Living Out* focuses attention on the difficulties encountered by immigrant mothers who are forced to leave their children behind.

Loomer's emphasis on the issue of motherhood in *Living Out* maps out the struggles of people raising children in a transnational system of mobile labor. The main plotline of the play centers on the story of Ana and her employer, Nancy. As the nanny for Nancy's daughter, Jenna, Ana is representative of working immigrant mothers who have children of their own, but spend most of their day caring for someone else's children. The audience learns that Ana has two children, Santiago, who lives with her and her husband, Bobby, and Tomás, the son left behind with his great-grandmother in El Salvador. The action of the play follows Ana's quest to raise the money necessary to hire an immigration attorney to help reunite Tomás with his family. Unlike the racist and classist employers represented in *Latina*, Ana's employers, Nancy and Richard Robin, are representative of a modern-day couple torn by the necessity to hire a child-care provider.[47] The Robins are a sympathetic couple struggling with Nancy's re-entry into the workplace after the birth of their daughter. *Living Out* captures the difficulty of trying to juggle motherhood and career, a process aided by the ability to hire assistance. While Nancy and Richard are well-meaning employers, they too fall victim to common ideologies regarding immigrant workers, including the belief that immigrant women are untrustworthy and unreliable.[48] Even though Nancy is represented as much more progressive than other employers, she is still guilty of employing the rhetoric of family to manipulate Ana. The ease with which she is able to rely on a discourse of familial belonging reveals the pervasiveness of such a rhetorical tool in the employer/employee relationship between parents and nannies.

While both Nancy and Ana are working mothers, only one of them has the power to disguise their economic relationship within the discourse of friendship and family. Nancy selectively employs such a vocabulary on occasion when asking Ana to go beyond the time boundaries established for her work. One day, because Richard has to work late, Nancy begs Ana to watch Jenna longer, offering her extra money for staying late. While offering to pay overtime illustrates Nancy's regard for Ana's labor, her insistence that Ana work overtime, even after being told no, shows her disregard for Ana's personal life.

> **NANCY:** I wouldn't ask if I didn't really need your help, Ana. What if we say sixty dollars for the four hours—?
> **ANA:** It's not the money!
> **NANCY:** Well, could you possibly just do me a—favor? Just this one time? (*Touches her hand.*) As a . . . a friend? (56)

When extra money fails in getting Ana to agree, Nancy employs the rhetoric of friendship to guilt her into staying late. After she agrees, Nancy takes the strategy further, telling her, "'Listen, Ana, whatever they [her kids] need . . .' (*Takes her hand.*) 'I mean, you're really part of the family now'" (57). While Nancy is understandably upset over her need to make an important business meeting, her manipulation of Ana reveals the power she holds as Ana's employer. The language of family employed by Nancy fails in light of this manipulation.

The moment the Robins are no longer dependent on Ana for her labor is the point at which the need to keep up the pretense of being family is gone. The rhetoric of family is a versatile one that can be invoked by employers when convenient and dismissed when the employee's labor is no longer required. When Richard decides to take a better-paying job for a corporation in order to facilitate Nancy's exit from the labor force, Ana is simply let go. While this was a difficult decision for the couple, Richard and Nancy enjoy the privilege of choosing to become a one-income household and they have the power to eject Ana from their "family." Their choice to dismiss Ana exposes the fact that their relationship is not based on familial ties, but on an economic dependency. The home might be a place of belonging for the family, but for the Latina nanny, the home remains the space of labor. As a site of labor, the household remains a precarious space for a domestic worker, one from which she can be rejected, regardless of the emotional labor performed and regardless of the employer's use of the rhetoric of "family." Loomer's play illustrates that a domestic worker's position in an employer's house remains as unstable as it was when Sánchez-Scott's play premiered. Like *Latina*, *Living Out* rejects the happy ending required in popular productions and leaves the audience with an uncomfortable narrative that defies an easy resolution.

The conclusion of *Living Out* reveals the vital roles that citizenship and class privilege play in the project of parenting. While Nancy and Richard settle their differences and reach an agreement that will ultimately benefit Jenna, Ana and Bobby are not so lucky. The audience discovers that while Ana was caring for Jenna, Ana's own son, Santiago, suffered an asthma attack. The lack of quality health care at the local clinic leads to the young boy's death. Unlike the rhetoric of *Spanglish*, which tries to presume some kind of commonality based on parenthood, *Living Out* elucidates the difference in what is at stake for each of the families. The stage directions make this very clear: "*([Richard and Nancy] look at each other, smile, and go off to Jenna's room, hand in hand. Bobby enters in the scene transition and sits on the bed which is now his and Ana's)*" (63). The scene in which Richard decides to work for Halliburton to make it possible for Nancy to stay home is followed by the heartbreaking scene of Bobby getting ready to go to work. Ana sits on the bed facing away from him. He is trying to make plans to return to El Salvador and bring back Tomás.

ANA: Gracias. But I think he's better down there. With my grandmother.
BOBBY: Ana—
ANA: It's better.
BOBBY: A grandmother is not a mother—
ANA: Sometimes . . . a mother is not a mother, Bobby.
BOBBY: Ana, please! Don't turn away from me!—because—it wasn't your fault.
ANA: If I'd picked him up . . . If I'd been there. Like a mother. Like any mother. I never saw him play soccer, Bobby! Did he play good? Did he look for me? Tell me, Bobby! 'Cause I never saw him play!
BOBBY: Ana—I'm telling you and you got to listen—because Santi was my son too! (*Cries.*) My son! Mi hijo. M'entiendes? And I'm telling you . . . Let him rest. (*Through*

tears.) He's . . . sleeping with the angeles, Ana. Just like you always telling him! Tell him. Dile, amor—
ANA: Duérmete . . . Duérmete con los angeles, mijo . . . (*He holds her, lets her cry. Then he sits her down on the bed.*) (64-65; suspension points in original)

The anguish expressed by both Ana and Bobby at the loss of their child forces the audience to acknowledge the differences in what is at stake for the two families. While Nancy can afford to leave the workforce to become a full-time mother, Ana never has that privilege. Her need to reunite her family and provide her children with a good home is impossible without her wages contributing to the family income. The play gestures toward the similarities between the two women, but the tragedy at the end works to remind the audience that there are some differences that similarities cannot overcome. Loomer's text also demonstrates the challenges faced by immigrant women who must labor in transnational spaces to ensure the economic survival of those left behind. These connections remaining in place across national boundaries make separation from the country of origin a much more complicated process. The countergeographies of globalization have made parenting a much more complex and difficult practice for many immigrants.

‡

The plays, the novel, and the documentary analyzed in this chapter expand the meaning of immigration and offer complex representations of contemporary immigrant narratives. The cultural texts challenge the belief that once an immigrant enters the nation, her connection to her previous nation must be severed. In its stead, we are given stories of global familial connections and the challenges of raising children in multiple national spaces. The complicated nature of these relationships and the often unmanageable distances between immigrants and countries of origin make happy endings, like reunions, impossible. As the global dependence on service workers continues to grow, so does the number of women who must leave their families to ensure their economic survival. Their stories offer important interventions in a narrative that makes their experiences invisible.

In light of our growing dependence on the labor of immigrant women, the need for more complex representations of domestic labor and gendered bodies is more important than ever. The texts analyzed in this chapter provide an intricate representation of gendered laboring bodies whose immigrant status impacts their daily existence. Most of those representations are fictional, but this does not mean the challenges represented are mere creations of the cultural producer. The texts introduce an alternative version of domestic work, one that is grounded in immigrant realities, one that is not easily consumed. Instead, we are confronted with images meant to create discomfort and raise consciousness. Reading two plays—separated by more than two decades—alongside a novel and a documentary might seem like an unlikely grouping of texts, but by placing them in dialogue, we can expand our notions of what constitutes an immigrant narrative. Unlike the schema of the conventional immigrant narrative, these various stories do not attempt to simply provide a tale of success through hard work or upward assimilation. For the subjects of these works, the hard work, perseverance, and personal sacrifices that have been made have not provided them with the success the ideology of the American Dream promotes. Instead, the cultural productions by the Chicana/Latina writers employ the structure of the genre to offer new narratives of immigration, which expand the conventions of the genre and propose a more complex understanding of contemporary immigration and global networks of labor. They do so through multiple strategies and formats, but ultimately, all four texts stand in direct challenge to the happily-ever-after ending so popular with commercial productions. They insert local knowledges into dominant global structures, creating a new Latina genealogy of an immigrant literature of resistance and opposition.

CHAPTER THREE

Laboring Bodies, Laboring Spaces in the Hospitality Industry

> When women put on a housekeeper uniform, they become invisible. The grittier aspects of hotel work—the work of scrubbing toilets, changing sheets, and encountering guests alone behind closed doors—are the hidden foundation on which an atmosphere of luxury and comfort are built.
>
> » "Housekeepers Are Organizing for Safe and Secure Workplaces"

The beloved story of Cinderella teaches us that if one is beautiful, kind, cheerful, and a hard worker, a prince will notice us, sweep us off our feet, and carry us off to his castle. In this traditional storybook romance, being a servant is temporary, just the first stage in a happily-ever-after story.[1] The reality, however, is quite different. Being a service worker most often means being invisible, a dehumanizing experience. After all, Cinderella is imperceptible in her servant's rags—seen only by her stepfamily. Her visibility is predicated on a makeover that erases her labor and invites the prince's gaze—a heteronormative gaze of desire for beauty. For real domestic workers, however, visibility is much more complicated since they are confined within the enclosed space of the home/hotel room. On May 15, 2011, Dominique Strauss-Kahn, the managing director of the International Monetary Fund, was arrested for the sexual assault of thirty-two-year-old Nafissatou Diallo, a member of the housekeeping staff of the upscale Sofitel New York hotel.[2] All of a sudden, an immigrant woman of color, single mother, and hotel worker became the topic of international conversations.[3] Questions began to circulate, with people asking why would a successful and powerful man like Strauss-Kahn attack a hotel worker and jeopardize his chance to run for the French presidency?[4] Even though the district attorney's office chose not to file charges against Strauss-Kahn, Diallo's story destabilized the use of romance to make sexual violence and the threat of such violence against housekeeping staff members invisible.[5] The criminal charges might have been dismissed, but the international attention remains important because it made visible a laboring space that is most often invisible. After all, the bodies of domestic workers in the hospitality industry, and the conditions under which they are expected to work, do not normally make the front page of the *New York Times*.

While housekeeping workers might be more visible than domestic workers who labor within the home, the domestic labor performed in the public space of the hotel room, motel hallway, or corporate office most often gets relegated to the racialized, gendered, and classed margins. In Ken Loach's film *Bread and Roses* (2000), Ruben tells fellow janitor Maya, "Did I tell you my theory about these uniforms? They make us invisible." Ruben's remark draws attention to the ways in which laboring bodies are dismissed and ignored, even when they are physically present and visible. Yet, with the rise of global cities and the increasing demand for service workers to meet the labor needs of these transnational economic spaces, the strategy of disregarding these workers is being challenged on multiple fronts.[6] The growing number of service workers has led to a mobilization in union efforts. While popular cultural productions continue to ignore or romanticize and exoticize Latina workers in public domestic work, the rise of oppositional narratives of labor and immigration provide us with alternative representations and offer an analysis of work, gender, and immigration that cannot be simply subsumed under the ideologies of the dominant immigrant narrative.

In this chapter, I expand the conversation about domestic labor to include the complex laboring spaces growing within an interconnected system of global cities. Through the popular trope of the romance plot, Wes Anderson's *Bottle Rocket* (1996) and Wayne Wang's *Maid in Manhattan* (2002) capture, on film, the labor that takes place in the public space of the hotel/motel industry. While Wang's film in particular offers an example of how traditional narratives continue to perpetuate notions of meritocracy, such representations fall apart when confronted with the works of Ken Loach, Marisela Norte, and Esmeralda Santiago. These alternative narratives of laboring bodies incorporate the stories of those workers who remain in the periphery, and whose stories and knowledge are dismissed by the mainstream. While not Latino-created, Loach's *Bread and Roses* expands the discussion of domestic labor in the public space while documenting the resistance of workers to exploitative labor practices.[7] Norte's spokenword piece "Act of the Faithless" (1991) and Santiago's *América's Dream* (1997) offer accounts of domestic labor and immigration that challenge an audience's assumptions about the labor of the hotel industry and draw connections between an individual's country of origin and the United States. By concentrating their focus on the realities of work in a transnational context, the three alternative stories reject the common practice of constructing the Latina worker's body as exotic, erotic, and sexually available. Through their oppositional stories, Norte's and Santiago's texts also provide examples of the types of emergent narratives creating a new Latina immigrant genealogy.

Similar to the ways in which the traditional immigrant narrative grew in popularity with the rise of European immigration to the United States, new immigrant narratives are a product of our current historical moment. The changing patterns in the global movement of people are created by an economic system that relies heavily on cheap labor across a range of fields, including care work, service labor, and construction. Contemporary cultural productions engage with the changes occurring within a transnational labor network, especially the rise of immigrants in urban spaces, or what Saskia Sassen refers to as "global cities." For Sassen, the new phenomenon of migration to global cities is predicated on the ways in which technology has altered the physical landscape of migration and transnational networks of communication. She argues,

> The technological transformation of the work process, the shift of manufacturing to less-developed areas domestically and abroad, in part made possible by the technological transformation of the work process, and the ascendance of the financial sector in management, have all contributed to the consolidation of a new kind of economic center—the global city from where the world economy is managed and serviced. (Mobility 127)

Sassen's global city has specific labor needs. There is a need not only for financial managers and other high-income/professional workers, but also for low-income workers to provide services for the inhabitants of these global cities.[8] From dry-cleaning businesses to restaurants, low-wage labor is required to meet the needs of a white-collar workforce managing the economic interests of global industries and transnational governing bodies.[9] Hotels and office buildings that cater to these economic centers rely heavily on immigrant labor for services, including domestic workers.[10] The labor of domestic workers not only occurs in the privacy of the domestic sphere of the home, but is a more visible component of international business and trade. After all, someone has to clean up after the busy agents of global cities. The lives of the workers who help run global cities from the margins, however, continue to exist outside of the parameters of the conventional immigrant story.

Labor on the Border

> *I don't belong here and neither do you.*
> *I'm just passing through here, remember?*
> *I'm not from here and neither are you.*

» Marisela Norte, "Act of the Faithless"

An important aspect of the traditional immigrant narrative is its emphasis on the permanent movement to and settlement of the immigrant subject in the new country. In 1991, Marisela Norte, known as the "Poet Laureate of Boyle Heights," released a CD spoken-word collection, *NORTE/word*, that is a collage of stories based on her reflections and observations riding public transportation in Los Angeles.[11] In 2008, Norte published the performance pieces as a written text, but I limit my discussion of the text here to the recorded performance because of its original format and because of the impact of the spoken word.[12] As in poetry, spoken-word texts are concise and compact. They tell a story in a few short lines, giving us some symbolic expressive details but also leaving gaps for our own imagination to fill. Popular in urban areas and with communities of color, the genre allows for the circulation of thoughts and ideas from a place within the margins, outside of the mainstream world of traditional poetry. Following in the tradition of *corridos* and other forms of oral storytelling, spoken word creates a space for the circulation of oppositional narratives and marginalized voices.[13]

Norte's "Act of the Faithless" disrupts the organizing logic of the traditional narrative by representing a type of circular migration that falls outside of the constructed parameters of the popular immigrant story. It discusses the life of her uncle's girlfriend, whom Norte refers to as her aunt, a worker employed by an El Paso Holiday Inn. Unlike the domestic workers who relocate to the United States, Norte's aunt has a work permit that allows her to cross the border to El Paso, Texas, to work while still residing in Juárez, Mexico, just across the border. Norte's narrative makes the connection between the long history of immigrant domestic labor in El Paso and the growing number of hotels now dependent on immigrant workers. In the piece, the aunt has brought a young Norte to the worksite with her, and this experience gives the latter, as well as the audience, an idea of the kind of life her aunt leads as a member of the housekeeping staff while, at the same time, ensuring that Norte's audience questions notions of border crossing.

One of the most popular ideologies constructed around immigration suggests that individuals migrate to the United States to achieve much better lives. While the ideology of the American Dream plays an important role in the conventions of the immigrant narrative, Norte's spoken-word piece challenges the assumption that crossing the border means social mobility. In discussing her aunt, Norte makes the statement, "El Paso, mal paso que te das al cruzar la frontera" (El Paso, the bad step you take when you cross the border). The play on words is used to signify the reality that crossing the border into El Paso (which translates as "the step"), for the aunt and other workers, is a bad move. There is no glorification of crossing the border and no romantic illusions of what awaits them on the other side. In El Paso, the aunt is reduced to an invisible worker, one of many, who cleans up after tourists in a hotel. The hotel that employs her becomes a symbol of the concrete class differences that exist between the house-keeping worker and the individuals who enjoy the fruit of her labors. She cleans the honeymoon suite daily, knowing that she and El Cura (Norte's uncle) will never have access to it. Twenty stories up, she cleans windows that overlook a city, El Paso, that does not claim her as one of its own. She takes Norte up to the pool area, where she tells her,

> "If there is no one up there, you can take your shoes off and put your feet in the water." . . . she whispers, "But if someone's up there, I can't let you do that. They'll know that you are not from here. Que tú no eres de aquí, mija."

The aunt's words to Norte help reinforce the reality of the alienation that occurs between the worker and the results of her labor. They also work to explain how race is intimately connected to the aunt's status as a worker. As women of color, Norte and her aunt are visibly excluded from the amenities of the hotel, and their skin color identifies them as "other." Her aunt reminds her, "I don't belong here and neither do you." Although Norte is from Los Angeles, her status as "other" and as a nonpaying guest excludes her from belonging there. Even if Norte were a paying guest, as a woman of color, she would still be positioned outside of the construct of what a hotel patron is supposed to look like. She doesn't have to be wearing a uniform for her racial/class difference to mark her as "not from here," to remind her, in her aunt's words, "que tu no eres de aqui mija." The uttering of the phrase in both languages underscores the fact that she remains an outsider.

Norte's text is also important in that it illustrates the historical connection between the city of El Paso and immigrant domestic workers. The practice of employing women of color as domestic workers and nannies is a popular one that dates back to the colonization of the Southwest, first by Spanish, then by Mexican, and finally by white

American settlers. In the twentieth century, El Paso so heavily relied on domestic workers from Juárez that white women there created their own organization in 1954, the Association for Legalized Domestics.[14] The organization's primary aim was to get help from the INS in importing Juárez women to perform domestic labor. It proposed a "bracero maid" program with a specific contract for one year's service (Ruiz 274–275). The program never materialized, but the fact that this organization existed and pushed for its inception illustrates the reliance of the El Paso middle class on domestic workers.[15]

Today, domestic workers are not just crossing the border from Juárez but also emigrating in much larger numbers from the interior of Mexico and other parts of Latin America.[16] Unable to find employment in Mexican border cities, many workers look to cities on the U.S. side of the border.[17] The growing dependence on immigrant bodies for labor in the transnational space of the hotel offers immigrant workers the option of performing their labor outside of the domestic space of private homes. Norte's aunt is one of the many workers who traverse the border for employment, but unlike workers in popular representations of immigration, her aunt remains strongly connected to her home, refusing to sever her connection with Juárez. Norte's narrative gestures toward a circular pattern of migration not commonly represented. As Jennifer A. González and Michelle Habell-Pallán point out, the text illustrates how constructed borders "drawn between national and economic communities are negotiated by women who live and work across national boundaries."

The significance of Norte's text also lies in the representation of immigrant domestic labor outside of the traditional sphere of the home. The labor taking place in the performance piece is situated in the much more global context of a hotel that caters to a tourist clientele and traveling corporate employees. The gender, class, and racial hierarchies present in the domestic space are reproduced in the public space of the hotel industry. The major employers of immigrant domestic workers are no longer just middle-class families or upper-class white women, but now include transnational hotel chains, like Holiday Inn. What remains in place is a patriarchal system of labor that continues to position women of color as part of a larger, racialized servant class, which continues to meet the ever-evolving needs of capital.[18]

Brincando el Charco—Migration from Puerto Rico

> Our stay in the United States, permanent or not, is a curiously continuous experience that produces cultural anxiety precisely because of its ambiguities. American citizens by birth, with almost two-thirds of their numbers on the mainland, Puerto Ricans can make el charco as large or small as they want.
>
> » Frances Negrón-Muntaner, "When I Was a Puerto Rican Lesbian: Meditations on Brincando el charco" (512)[19]

The circular migration pattern witnessed in Norte's spoken-word piece is not the only geographically situated migratory cycle commonly ignored by popular productions. The journey of Latin@s between Puerto Rico and the U.S. mainland is another form of movement that is often overlooked. At first glance, it would seem incongruous to employ the lens of the immigrant narrative when analyzing *América's Dream* and *Maid in Manhattan*. After all, both of the protagonists of these texts are Puerto Rican or of Puerto Rican descent and have American citizenship. I am in no way attempting to collapse the differences between Latin@ populations in the United States in trying to make such an argument, but am wondering whether it's possible to read migrant narratives through the lens of the immigrant narrative. I would argue that it is, especially when dealing with the Puerto Rican Latina's racialized body and her conditional position as citizen of the nation.

Unlike the more clearly defined citizenship status of Latina immigrants from Latin America, Puerto Rican Latinas have inherited a complex construction of citizenship connected to the island's conditional incorporation into the nation after the Spanish-American War in 1898. Puerto Ricans were initially granted citizenship under the 1917 Jones Act, but the passage of the act did not imply equal protection. In fact, in 1922 the Supreme Court decided in *Balzac v. People of Porto Rico* that "the Jones Act did not make Puerto Rico a part of the United States and that the protection of the U.S. Constitution did not fully extend to the island" (Pérez y González 29-30). While the Jones Act granted citizenship to Puerto Ricans, the Supreme Court case made it clear that Puerto Rico and its inhabitants were not part of the nation and therefore lay outside of its construction. One of the most important factors in the limits imposed on Puerto Rican citizenship can be traced back to ideologies of race and difference popular during the late nineteenth and early twentieth centuries. As scholars like Ronald Fernandez have pointed out, the Spanish background of Puerto Ricans and the presence of an African racial makeup led to Puerto Ricans' being constructed as different, as "inferior offspring of an already mid-level race" and therefore "unfit for democracy"

(Fernandez 13). Today, Puerto Rico is still identified by its political commonwealth status and defined by the racial history of difference conjured by its position as a modern colony. While the Puerto Rican Latina's citizenship provides a certain level of protection from unfair labor practices and completely eliminates the fear of deportation, it does not make her immune to the nation's racial and gender hierarchy that continues to place women of color at the bottom of the social ladder. The cultural and linguistic differences between the Puerto Rican community and the mainstream white population also mark the Puerto Rican migrant as "other" or "outsider," and, as such, she must confront the same racist and sexist U.S. society encountered by her immigrant sisters from Latin America.

In her text *Puerto Ricans in the United States*, María Pérez y González makes the argument that, in defining the movements of Puerto Ricans to and within the United States, both the terms "migrant" and "immigrant" apply because while Puerto Ricans might have U.S. citizenship, which allows them to move freely between the island and the mainland, the island is not an incorporated part of the United States. For Pérez y González, "Puerto Ricans who have relocated to the United States since the Spanish-American War in 1898 to the present time, can be considered immigrants because they are relocating from one country to another; although Puerto Rico is not a sovereign nation, that does not negate the fact that it is a country" (33–34). While some might question labeling Puerto Rico as a "country," the fact that it is a colony does allow for consideration of an ambivalent status for the relocated Puerto Rican. The im/migration of a Puerto Rican individual is very different than the migration of someone from one state to another.[20] Even though a person from a dynamic urban space in Southern California would experience a certain level of culture shock in moving to a small New England town, the language and overall customs would remain basically the same. Puerto Ricans who im/migrate to the U.S. mainland encounter a much more pronounced sense of culture shock. Even though Puerto Ricans are constructed as citizens, Puerto Rican culture—including its food and traditions—is different. In Puerto Rico, Spanish remains the island's predominant language, marking another important difference between a state-to-state migration and the im/migration between Puerto Rico and the mainland.[21]

The posited dual position of Puerto Ricans as both immigrants and migrants allows for the reading of Puerto Rican narratives of migration through the lens of the immigrant narrative. In fact, several stories of migration by Puerto Rican authors follow the structure of the traditional immigration narrative. For example, Esmeralda Santiago's first book, *When I Was Puerto Rican*, follows the paradigm of the more popular story found in *Pocho*. Even though Santiago pays closer attention to the issue of gender, her protagonist moves from being a subject of the periphery to a full citizen of the nation through education, as occurs in Villarreal's text. While her first novel is much more traditionally structured, Santiago's *América's Dream* offers a more interesting text for analysis because of the movement of her protagonist from Puerto Rico to New York, and between the laboring spaces of the home and the hotel. Like Norte's "Act of the Faithless," *América's Dream* illustrates a circulation pattern of working bodies that most often go unnoticed. The film *Maid in Manhattan* and Santiago's novel are both narratives of migration, but they offer differing representations of what it means to be a Latina and to labor as a housekeeping worker in the hotel industry.

In the film *Maid in Manhattan*, director Wayne Wang updates and racializes the classic Cinderella story to provide audiences with a contemporary fairy tale that casts Jennifer Lopez as the modern-day rags-to-riches heroine.[22] Released in 2002, the story revolves around Marisa Ventura, played by Lopez, a Puerto Rican single mother who works as a maid at The Beresford, an upper-echelon hotel in Manhattan, to provide for her son, Ty. The hotel is important as it functions as a metaphor for the global city, complete with a transnational clientele and an im/migrant labor force. The hotel is a space where multiple political and economic interests converge, where the movers and shakers of the world interact with each other and make connections. It is a site where Marisa, a working-class Latina from the Bronx, has the opportunity to interact with wealthy individuals who would have no reason to cross the class line into her neighborhood. Through her position at the hotel, Marisa comes into contact with and eventually falls in love with Chris Marshall, an idealistic politician played by Ralph Fiennes.[23] The film revolves around the love story between Marisa and Chris, but also includes the story line of Marisa's ambition to step into a management position at the hotel.[24]

While Marisa was born and raised in the Bronx and is represented as a savvy New Yorker, the film reproduces the conventions of the hegemonic narrative through its emphasis on immigration and social mobility. The film frames Marisa's story as the story of assimilation and success made possible by her parents' immigration. In the traditional narrative, it is often the second generation, rather than the immigrant first generation, that is able to achieve success through the hard work of the parents. In the conventional paradigm, the first-generation immigrant negotiates the old world and the new world, a challenge not necessarily encountered by the children of the immigrant subject. The simple resolution of the popular narrative in suggesting the immigrant subject's ability to assimilate sets the ground-work for the success of the next generation, and further implies that the second generation's firm foothold in the nation is guaranteed. In Wang's film, Marisa comes to embody the success of the second generation. Not only is she fully assimilated, but the film's emphasis on Ty's schooling and Marisa's investment in his intellectual growth perpetuates the ideology of meritocracy, the achievement of success through hard work and education.

The casting of Jennifer Lopez as the protagonist in the film further emphasizes the importance of reading the narrative through the lens of the dominant immigrant story. As a visual text, there is a strong significance in who visually represents the characters of the story on the screen. Unlike books, where the reader can create a mental image of the protagonist, films provide the viewer with a concrete representation of the characters, so the selection of an actor to be cast in the role of the protagonist is an important decision. The fact that Lopez plays the lead in the film is significant because of what Lopez represents to the audience.[25] Even though her racial background has allowed Lopez to play a wide array of ethnically and racially diverse characters, her music and interviews have emphasized her identity as a Nuyorican artist.[26] The audience would most likely be aware of her background and the fact that she herself is supposed to be the embodiment of the American Dream.[27] As the daughter of parents who migrated from Puerto Rico, Lopez has achieved the success envisioned by countless im/migrants.[28] Lopez has, in fact, become the poster child for the successful Latina. By casting Lopez as Marisa, the film visually promotes, on more than one level, the ideology of success and assimilation through hard work.

The film takes off where the traditional immigrant story ends, but continues with the ideologies of upward mobility so important to the initial narrative of immigration. Wang's movie makes a clear distinction between Marisa and her mother, Veronica Ventura. While Marisa occasionally uses phrases and words in Spanish, her English is unaccented. Veronica, however, speaks the language with a heavy accent, which, along with the color of her skin, marks her as different. The more traditional immigrant narrative is based on the binary between old-world and new-world ideologies and the eventual embracing of new-world ideas, especially those of democracy. Just as conventional narratives like *Pocho* position mothers as the symbol for old-world thoughts and values, the film situates Marisa's mother as representing archaic ideas about class and social position. It is Marisa's job to reject her mother's ideas in order to fully live up to her potential as an American citizen. While one can argue that the divergence in views between the mother and daughter is based on the generation gap, differences in generation do not fully explain Marisa's investment in the ideology of the American Dream or her mother's inability to embrace the myth of equality on which the dream is based. Veronica's disapproval of her daughter's career ambitions and dating above her class status point to a more complex ideological difference in the characters' construction of the nation.

Domestic Labor in the Hotel

Women in most societies are presumed to be naturally capable at cleaning, washing, cooking, and serving. Since tourism companies need precisely those jobs done, they can keep labor costs low if they can define those jobs as women's work. In the Caribbean in the early 1980s, 75 percent of tourism workers were women.

» Cynthia Enloe, *Bananas, Beaches, and Bases* (34)

As I have argued in previous chapters, how labor is represented in cultural productions is an important aspect of the type of ideological narrative being promoted. Even though *Maid in Manhattan* provides the audience with a typical Hollywood story line, it does offer a critique of the strategies employed in making workers and the type of labor they perform invisible. From the very beginning of the story, the film makes it clear that the purpose of the staff is to serve the needs of the hotel's elite clientele. During a scene that at first seems unimportant, the manager of the domestic staff, Paula Burns, played by actress Frances Conroy, instructs the new domestic workers, "A Beresford maid is expedient. A Beresford maid is thorough. A Beresford maid serves with a smile. And above all, a Beresford maid strives to be invisible." Her words are visually emphasized by a sign on the wall that reads "Strive to be Invisible."[29] Burns' speech illustrates the contradictions under which these domestic workers must labor. For the hotel, the ideal maid works hard, fast, and with a pleasant disposition, but at the same time, is supposed to remain unseen. She is supposed to embody the image of the happy domestic whose presence is hardly felt and rarely acknowledged. The irony of such a contradiction is not lost on the domestic workers, as Clarise, Marisa's coworker, sarcastically mutters, "Maybe we can disappear altogether." The politics of whose bodies are worth noticing is based on a hierarchy that privileges certain bodies over others. While some bodies are meant to be seen (e.g., front-desk workers, concierge, etc.), the bodies performing the dirty work, cleaning up after paying customers, must be hidden away.

Like Norte's "Act of the Faithless," the film critiques Marisa's invisibility to hotel guests—a convenient erasure of her presence until she is needed to serve. In one scene, a hotel guest, Caroline Lane, begins her request to Marisa with the condescending, "I know this isn't your job and I'd never normally ask . . ." When Marisa attempts to inform her that it is the concierge's job to run errands for guests, Caroline politely insists that Marisa get her the stockings she needs, while also unpacking her wardrobe and returning clothes to the hotel shop. Caroline not only expects Marisa to do as she wishes, she constantly addresses her as "Maria."[30] While Caroline's polite condescension is grating to Marisa, it is nothing compared to the hostility she experiences at the hands of Caroline's friend, Rachel Hoffberg. Rachel snaps orders at Marisa in broken Spanish and takes pleasure in referencing her as "the maid." She assumes that Marisa "barely speaks English" and speaks down to her. Rachel's assumption that Marisa does not speak English gestures toward the film's acknowledgment that the major part of the housekeeping labor in the hotel industry is, in fact, performed by immigrant workers. The racism displayed by the two white women is downplayed, however, through the film's emphasis on the ridiculousness of the characters.

The outlandish and outrageous behavior of the characters situates their racism as the actions of individuals, rather than portraying structural or institutional racism. Caroline and Rachel are so outlandish that it's easy for the audience to dismiss them as elitist versions of Cinderella's evil stepsisters. (Also, in fitting with the Cinderella story line, Caroline becomes romantically interested in Chris Marshall, the white prince of the story.) It is important that Marisa is able to assert herself, especially in reacting to Rachel's treatment. While remaining polite, she makes biting comments aimed at Rachel and "accidentally" snaps her with the sheets while making the bed. The audience is entertained by Marisa's acts of resistance and the fact that there are no consequences for her actions. The scene is humorous and this effectively glosses over the abusive treatment of domestic workers. It also reduces racism to the individual level, positioning it as a trial easily overcome and therefore more effortlessly subsumed under the dominant narrative of immigration. The film's attempt to critique the invisibility of domestic workers falls short because of its superficial treatment of structural inequalities.

In true Hollywood fashion, the labor Marisa and the other members of the housekeeping staff perform is visually contained to tasks that ensure an audience remains comfortable while watching them. Again, the audience has to be presented with an image of labor that can easily be reconciled under the rhetoric of work performed as a way of gaining upward mobility. During their working hours, the labor we see performed includes Marisa and her best friend Stephanie laughing as they make a bed together and Marisa running errands for demanding guests like Caroline Lane. In another scene, the housekeeping staff is stocking their cleaning carts with supplies while Stephanie, Clarise, and Barb are playing around. Laughing, they tell Marisa, "We need more fun in our lives . . . You only live once." The women Marisa works with are represented as happy maids who laugh while they work and find ways of making their labor fun.[31] They act as Marisa's comic foils. In turn, Marisa is represented as being more serious than her fellow workers, but this doesn't necessarily mean the audience actually sees her performing difficult work. In fact, we see Marisa performing rather pleasant duties, such as putting together lovely sprigs of lavender for pillows to make beds more inviting for the guests, a scene similar to Flor's flower arranging in *Spanglish*. Like Flor, Marisa is never seen actually cleaning up after the hotel guests in a way that would make the audience completely disidentify with her, or would interfere with her position as the love interest in the film.[32] The audience doesn't see how dirty, dangerous, and degrading housekeeping jobs actually are.

Unlike *Maid in Manhattan*, which often attempts to alleviate through humor the tension around racism, sexism, and the danger/discomfort of the housekeeping worker, Norte's "Act of the Faithless" and Santiago's *América's Dream* provide much more biting critiques of the ways in which housekeeping staff are treated by those they serve. Norte's narrative highlights the invisibility of her aunt, but also observes the ways in which the housekeeping worker is treated when her presence is acknowledged. While cleaning the area around the pool, Norte and her aunt come across a couple that has fallen asleep by the pool. Norte looks at the couple and thinks the man looks dead. The man, however, awakes and sees Norte's aunt cleaning up.

> *"Excuse me, uh, Señorita. Can you come here por favor?" . . . He waves an empty glass at her . . . Señorita, the name stings like the sun. My aunt smiles at him and cusses him out real good in Spanish under her breath. She puts the sunglasses on and leads me back to the elevator . . . The man in the chair is still trying to get her attention. "Maria, uh, Maria?" Only I can't hear it anymore. Only his lips are moving. I tug on her arm, I point at the man now gone silent.*

The tourist assumes that because she is a hotel employee, Norte's aunt is there to serve him. While he may not know who she is, he assumes she only speaks Spanish and attempts to get her attention through the few Spanish phrases he knows.[33] Although he doesn't say it in English or Spanish, the way he shakes his glass at her makes clear that he expects her to refill it. The tourist sees her only as a maid, a "Señorita," or worse, as a "Maria," a member of the servant class. By hailing her as a "Maria," the tourist reduces Norte's aunt to a generic stereotype, a maid named Maria, someone who is not an individual, but just a worker there to serve him.[34] These tourists don't have to leave the comfort of their national space to experience their white colonial fantasy—all they need is to be served by racialized/exoticized bodies to help them weave a narrative based on a historically enduring racial hierarchy of servitude. The tourist's treatment of Norte's aunt suggests that immigrant workers are invisible laborers who only become visible when their services—be they physical or ideological—are needed. Her aunt, however, refuses to be defined as just another "Maria" or play along with this racist fantasy.

As an employee of the hotel, Norte's aunt cannot openly react or resist the rudeness of the tourist. She masks her real feelings behind a smile but under her breath, curses him. Norte hears her aunt telling the tourist off "real good" in Spanish, using his inability to speak Spanish to her advantage. By smiling at him, she pretends to acknowledge his superior position, but by placing the sunglasses on her face and walking away, she refuses to acknowledge his request. Through her disregard of the tourist's request, she resists not only labor exploitation, but also the identification of the "Maria" stereotype. In refusing to serve him, she rejects the role of the submissive maid the tourist wants her to play, and asserts her individuality. She also provides a model of resistance for the young Norte to remember.

Another literary representation of a smart Latina laboring in the global space of tourism is found in Santiago's *América's Dream*. The novel follows the story of América Gonzalez, a woman whose life in the tropical island of Vieques is anything but paradisaical. América works full-time as a maid in a hotel, La Casa del Francés, to support herself and her fourteen-year-old daughter, Rosalinda. Correa, América's lover and Rosalinda's father, is married and has another family, so it is up to América to provide for her daughter. While the hotel is not in the same league as The Beresford, it does cater to wealthy tourists, especially white Americans.[35] Along with her mother, Ester, América cleans the rooms of the hotel's guests and occasionally babysits for those who travel with children—offering multiple forms of care work normally contained within the domestic space of the home.[36] While América's im/migrant narrative doesn't technically begin until her move to Bedford, New York, it is her labor in the hotel that brings her in contact with her future employers, Karen and Charlie Leverret. The babysitting she performs for the Leverrets, in turn, acts as a bridge between the domestic labor she performs in the hotel and her eventual employment in the Leverrets' home in New York as nanny to Meghan and Kyle Leverret.[37]

From the first page of the novel, the reader is given a picture of domestic labor in the hotel that is not fun or easy. Santiago introduces América to the reader with a description of her that begins, "On her knees, scrubbing behind a toilet at the only hotel on the island" (1). By opening her novel with the scene of América having to clean up after the guests' bodily functions, a job that would be seen as demeaning, Santiago illustrates the very low position of her protagonist. As she scrubs the uneven tiles, América "catches a nail on the corner of one and tears it to the quick . . . the bright pink crescent of her nail hangs by the cuticle . . . drawing salty blood" (1). The description of her working on her knees without gloves and hurting herself comes right after Santiago writes that América is always humming while she works, and that she is "surprised when tourists tell her how charming it is that she sings as she works" (1). América's humming and singing can be seen as a way for her to break up the monotony of her labor, as a way to mentally escape the physical work she is performing. While the tourists attempt to position her as the stereotype of the happy domestic, by misrecognizing her singing as proof of her contentment with her tasks, the manner in which Santiago juxtaposes América's labor and her injury with América's singing rejects such a representation. Instead, we get a portrayal of domestic work that cannot be easily reconciled under the stereotype of the happy domestic or the beautiful housekeeper.

América's work at the hotel is described as difficult and physically exhausting. The representations of the tasks she performs challenge the labor scenes found in *Maid in Manhattan* and other films. In the films, the absence of hard labor works to advance the plotline of the domestic or housekeeping worker as visually desirable. Unlike the light tasks—placing flowers on pillows or changing sheets—projected in the films, domestic and housekeeping labor is in reality a physically challenging form of work that takes its toll on the body of the worker.[38] Santiago describes how exhausted América feels after her work:

> *She's so tired! The five days of the month in which she allows herself to feel depressed are also the five days in which she feels the exhaustion, the aches and pains caused by hours of lifting, scrubbing, mopping, polishing, bending, and straightening up numerous times as she picks up the clutter tourists leave behind. (80)*

Her need for steady work and an income does not allow her to focus on the effects that her labor has on her body.[39] Only a few days out of the month does América allows herself the luxury of concentrating on the pains and aches caused by her line of work. Santiago's description of América's pain is consistent with what we know about the wear and tear on the bodies of hotel housekeepers. According to UNITE

HERE, the union that represents workers in the hotel, gaming, food service, manufacturing, textiles, distribution, laundry, and airport industries in the United States and Canada, hotel workers have a 40 percent higher injury rate than other service-sector workers. A study conducted by a team of researchers and UNITE HERE found that "with an injury rate of 10.6, Hispanic housekeepers had the highest injury rate of all housekeepers studied. Hispanic housekeepers face a risk of injury almost twice that of white housekeepers" ("Latina Housekeepers Hurt"). There is nothing glamorous or fun in the work Santiago describes. We don't get images of happy housekeepers laughing and joking with each other in the novel. Instead, Santiago provides the reader with a representation of domestic labor as hard work that is performed by poor women who have few options.[40]

In the novel, América performs tasks that an audience would have a hard time seeing Marisa doing on the screen. It's one thing to see Marisa and the other maids making beds and teasing each other over rolls of paper, it would be quite another to actually see them on their knees scrubbing the toilet. América not only has to clean the hotel rooms, she also has to clean up the mess the hotel guests make. On one occasion, the guests of one room leave behind remnants of the previous night's activities: "They have left two condoms on the floor near the bed, all snotty and slimy. She picks them up with a paper towel, rolls the whole thing into a ball. `¡No les da vergüenza!' she mumbles as she dumps the mess into the trash can" (79). The utter lack of respect exhibited by the guests' leaving used condoms on the floor with the understanding that the "maid" would pick them up is just one example of how little the guests think of América and the other women who clean their rooms. América might have to clean up after them, but she expresses her disgust with them and wonders at their lack of shame. Santiago goes on to describe América's bewilderment with American tourists:

> That's one thing she has never understood about Yanquis. They do things like leave their used condoms on the floor, or bloody sanitary pads, unwrapped, in the trash cans. But they throw a fit if there's a hair in the shower drain, of if the toilet is not disinfected. They don't mind exposing other people to their germs, but they don't want to be exposed to anyone else's. (79)

Unlike the representation of the maid as the happy worker who enjoys taking care of others, América's character vocalizes the frustration of the housekeeping worker who is expected to provide a clean space for the hotel guest regardless of the guest's behavior. The fact that the guests so easily leave unsanitary messes behind for América to clean shows their level of entitlement and feelings of superiority.

While they do not want to be exposed to anyone else's germs, they have no problem exposing workers like América to their potentially dangerous body fluids.[41] Their bodies are worth protecting, but the brown working bodies cleaning up after them are not. It is also important to notice that América identifies the tourists as Yanquis, or Americans, because it emphasizes that although she might have American citizenship, she does not see herself as an American, as one of them, in spite of her name.[42] While the disidentification could be a result of the class difference between them, it is more likely due to how tourists view service workers as "other" and the ways in which "American" is racialized as white. América understands how even those guests who see her and acknowledge her presence actually view her as part of the landscape they are consuming through their tourism. She is part of the colonial fantasy weaved by the hotel.

Unlike the representation of invisibility we see in *Maid in Manhattan*, which focuses on the hotel industry's attempts to make guests more comfortable by training their employees to be as inconspicuous as possible, Santiago's novel illustrates the ways in which hotel guests automatically render the housekeeping worker invisible. América recognizes the manner in which the hotel guests perceive her.

> She notices how they look right past and pretend not to see her. She feels herself there, solid as always, but they look through her, as if she were part of the strange landscape . . . Those who do see her, smile guardedly, then slide their gaze away quickly, ashamed, it seems, to have noticed her. (30)

América might not be noticed by them, but she is aware of how they view her. Even though they see right through her, she feels herself "solid as always." By refusing to internalize the hotel guests' practice of rendering her invisible, América rejects becoming part of the landscape. While she might not be able to forcefully assert herself to the tourists by demanding they acknowledge her presence, in emphasizing the ways in which she feels solid, she reaffirms her position as more than just an object to be guiltily gazed upon, or completely ignored. She also denaturalizes the act of rendering one invisible by observing the ways in which the hotel guests "pretend" not to see her. The guest must make the conscious decision to attempt to erase América's presence, be it out of guilt or out of a sense of superiority. Either way, América does not let her erasure go unchallenged. Santiago captures the discomfort felt by hotel guests when confronted with the laboring body responsible for creating their vacation fantasy.

Compared to the type of labor seen in *Maid in Manhattan*, the representation of labor in *América's Dream* is so unpleasant that it cannot be reconciled with the discourse of hard work as a way of achieving success. América's labor resists being categorized alongside glamorized versions of domestic work, as in *Spanglish* and other popular cultural productions. Santiago's novel is also important because of the connection the text makes between the hotel industry, tourism, and imperialism. Unlike the dominant narrative of immigration, which attempts to sever the ties between the old and the new worlds or situates the story of the immigrant subject as beginning at the moment of entrance into the United States, *América's Dream* illustrates the connection that exists between the periphery and the core. Even though in popular discourse Puerto Rico is positioned as a U.S. commonwealth and not a separate country, the United States has exploited Puerto Rico in the same ways in which core countries exploit those in the periphery.[43] Tourism has become the newer form of imperialist exploitation of labor and land resources.[44]

Migration and Colonial Legacies

> Whatever the actual legal framework of Puerto Rico's relationship to the United States may be, there is no turning back to the "fantastic" nation Puerto Ricans have created under a century-long subjection to American colonialism.
>
> » Frances Negrón-Muntaner, "When I Was a Puerto Rican Lesbian" (520)

> Nostalgia for Spanish colonialism is generally invoked without reference to the decimation of the indigenous population or the legacy of chattel slavery.
>
> » Alicia Swords and Ronald Mize, "Beyond Tourist Gazes and Performances" (58)

In *América's Dream*, the binary between old and new worlds is rejected in favor of a representation that positions América's experiences as occurring in a space that is temporally and physically connected. Like Sassen's argument that immigration policy "is shaped by an understanding of immigration as the consequence of the individual actions of emigrants; the receiving country is taken as a passive agent, one not implicated in the process of emigration" (*Globalization* 7), the conventional immigrant narrative perpetuates the idea of im/migration as an individual choice through its new/old world binary. By highlighting the historical connection between the United States and Puerto Rico, Santiago's text rejects that binary and instead emphasizes the colonial relationship that continues to exist today. The text also historically situates the bodies of women of color as participants in a long legacy of service work.[45]

Situated in Vieques, Puerto Rico, the hotel where América is em-

ployed becomes a fitting metaphor for the colonial history of the island and the various imperial projects that have taken place on its
shores. The first owner of the hotel was a Frenchman who had it built
as a house "by the peons [he] inherited with the hacienda," hence the
name La Casa del Francés (77). The Frenchman planned to use the
house and the riches he acquired through the acres of sugarcane surrounding the hacienda to bring home a French wife. Santiago writes
that the Frenchman had "envisioned his bride floating through the
airy rooms . . . without having to mingle with the dark natives whose
work made his fortune possible" (76). After the Frenchman, the hacienda was "passed on to a Venezuelan who visited the casa in the
summers" (77). The house went through various owners until the
American Don Irving, another transplant to the island, "bought the
decaying plantation house and converted it into a hotel" (36). In all
of the house's various stages of ownership, one of América's female
relatives had cleaned the house and been sexually involved with the
owner, beginning with Marguerite, the maid of the Frenchman's wife.
The various foreign owners of the house make visible a history of
powers exploiting the Caribbean for its land and its labor.[46] The fact
that the hacienda goes from being a home built on the labor of the
island's people to a hotel that caters to white tourists illustrates the
continuation of imperialist practices in Puerto Rico.[47] Through the
novel's emphasis on the connection of América's female ancestors to
the hacienda, the colonization of the land as a masculinist project
that is predicated on the labor and body of the island's female population gets further accentuated. While América is no longer one of
the "peons" the Frenchman "inherited," she is part of a continuing
legacy of exploitative labor practices, transnational movement, and
imperialist fantasies.[48]

The status of Puerto Rico as a U.S. territory has not ended the long
line of imperial projects on the island. In fact, tracing the history of
the hacienda from one foreign owner to another, from the original
French owner to Don Irving, works to position the United States as
an imperial power in a long line of colonizers and more modern im-
perialists. He is "the latest in a long history of foreigners to own the
house that is still referred to as La Casa del Francés, The Frenchman's
House" (77). The character Don Irving is portrayed as a nice man,
but as an outsider nonetheless. Even though he is a U.S. citizen, as are
América and her fellow employees, he is still seen as a foreigner and
placed in the same category as the previous owners of the hacienda.
Although he is an outsider, his position as owner allows him to assert
his power over his Puerto Rican workers. It is significant that when
América and the other hotel employees refer to him they use the title

of "Don," not only because it is a term of respect, but also because of the gender, class, and racial distinction the term implies.

As one more foreign owner of the hacienda, Don Irving has converted the old house into another money-making venture by turning it into a hotel. Like other imperial projects, the hotel is intended to benefit Don Irving, not the inhabitants of the island. The reader discovers that Don Irving "has never learned Spanish and speaks as if it didn't matter, as if it were the person he's talking to who has to make sense of what he's saying" (36). While it would seem to make sense that Don Irving would learn to speak Spanish, not only because it is the language his employees speak but also because it is the language of the island, he instead chooses to force his employees to decipher what he means when he speaks to them in English. Don Irving behaves the way a tourist often does, expecting those who serve the tourist to understand his/her language. His disdain for the language of Puerto Ricans speaks loudly of his racism and sense of superiority.

As a hotel owner who must cater to the needs of tourists, Don Irving seems to worry only about communicating with the guests, all of whom speak English. In fact, he is most interested in creating a vision of Puerto Rico for tourists that meets with their image of the island as a colonial tropical paradise. The colonial architecture of the hotel, along with the colorful flowers and singing birds, are just part of the picture. As América observes,

> Don Irving greets his guests on the back porch, seated on a rattan chair with peacock back. He's always dressed in white, looks like something out of a movie, large, white-haired, with a white mustache, a straw sombrero shading hazel eyes under severe white brows. (35)

América's description of Don Irving is reminiscent of the romantic image of the hacienda owner or southern plantation owner who sits on his porch and oversees the labor of his servants. Don Irving positions himself as the hacienda owner whose peons are now the housekeeping workers who clean the hotel. The picture he provides for his guests ensures that they feel as if they have stepped back in time. He feeds into their ideas of what a tropical paradise should look like—a place where the power of whiteness continues to be revered. It doesn't matter that Puerto Rico is considered part of the United States, for Don Irving and his guests, the island and its people continue to be the exotic "other."[49] The hotel offers a nostalgic past for a new transnational tourist industry to enjoy.

The narrative constructed on the racialized bodies of the Puerto Rican "natives" is one that follows América off the island to New York. Unlike the conventional immigrant narrative, Santiago's protagonist cannot simply work hard to make a better life for herself and her daughter. Her classed, gendered, and racialized body renders the privilege of her citizenship invisible and she is reduced to being just one more Latina nanny, overworked and economically exploited. While she might have escaped Correa's physical abuse, América cannot escape a labor structure that systematically positions Latinas on the bottom, even in the "liberal" suburbs of New York.

The Possibilities for Resistance

> Even if one is not an actual immigrant or expatriate, it is still possible to think as one, to imagine and investigate in spite of barriers, and always to move away from the centralizing authorities towards the margins, where you see things that are usually lost on minds that have never traveled beyond the conventional and comfortable.
>
> » Edward Said, *Representations of the Intellectual* (63)

Unlike the sanitized version of domestic labor offered by films like *Maid in Manhattan*, Ken Loach's *Bread and Roses* presents his audience with a critical version of labor and immigration. Released in 2000, the film tells the story of two Mexican immigrant sisters, Maya and Rosa, who work as janitors for Angel Services, a company responsible for the cleaning of multiple high-rise buildings in Los Angeles. Based on the actual "Justice for Janitors" campaign of the early 1990s, *Bread and Roses* fictionalizes the efforts to unionize Angel Service workers in an effort to improve working conditions.[50] The title of the film, a direct reference to the 1912 textile workers strike in Lawrence, Massachusetts, links the unionization efforts of the Justice for Janitors campaign to the long history of labor activism in the United States.[51] By connecting the two labor movements, Loach's film highlights a legacy of worker struggles and resistance.[52]

While janitorial work takes multiple forms, the majority of labor performed falls within the parameters of domestic labor within the public space. The cleaning, dusting, and vacuuming necessary to maintain the global spaces from which the world economy is controlled and managed is similar to the labor performed in the home—just on a much larger scale. Like the invisible work performed in the domestic space, janitorial labor is made imperceptible. Most often, the cleaning of office buildings occurs under the cover of darkness, after all of the white-collar workers and high-powered executives have left the building. By working at night, janitorial staff can remain concealed, the faceless bodies who clean but whose labor goes unacknowledged. Unlike traditional domestic labor, janitorial labor is not gendered as "women's work" to the same extent and it is common to find men performing the same tasks most often relegated to female domestic workers. While both men and women are employed by Angel Services, because the narrative follows Rosa and Maya more closely, women perform most of the labor documented on the screen. As a result, Loach's film offers an example of a cultural production that resists the stereotypical representation of immigrant domestic workers and instead offers a narrative that privileges the alternative voices of immigrant workers and gestures toward the possibilities of resistance in global spaces of labor.[53]

At the center of *Bread and Roses* is Maya, a newly arrived undocumented immigrant from Mexico. When the audience meets Maya, she is running across the desert, along with other immigrants, trying to avoid being detained by the border patrol. From the beginning of the film, Loach visually highlights the danger faced by undocumented immigrants, ensuring his audience will not underestimate the severity of crossing the U.S.–Mexico border. The director's choice to have Maya face rape at the hands of the coyotes also illustrates the threat of sexual violence faced by immigrants. When Maya's sister, Rosa, is unable to give the coyotes the full payment for smuggling her into Los Angeles, they abscond with Maya in the van and flip a coin to decide who will leave with her. The ease with which they dismiss her resistance and callously flip for her demonstrates that this form of violence is a common practice for the coyotes. The opening sequence of the film expands our visual understanding of what border violence means for those who exist outside of the official narrative of border violence offered by the state.[54] The fact that Maya's would-be rapist takes her to his apartment in Los Angeles also increases the parameters of border violence beyond the immediate border area. Maya's immigrant narrative underscores the inability of the dominant immigrant story to capture the complexities of global migrations under militarized zones of danger and conflict.

While the rise of global cities has been predicated on the needs of transnational capital, these spaces of labor also offer possible sites of resistance. The system that depends on immigrant workers for cheap labor is the same system that makes it possible for workers to come into contact with each other. Loach's *Bread and Roses* documents the ability of immigrant workers to come together, regardless of differing backgrounds, to resist economic exploitation. The film fictionalizes the story of the Justice for Janitors campaign, but it represents some of the important aspects of the real movement, including the role that women and immigrants played in the success of the campaign.

Unlike the more isolated domestic work that takes place in the home, the labor performed in the public space of office buildings allows for the possibility to create networks of connections amongst workers. In "Helots No More," the authors point out that "the peculiar conditions of building service work created a sense of occupational community: working at night, when few others did, the janitors form a somewhat isolated group [. . .] Thus, 'even though LA is famous for no community . . . we found a community of janitors'" (Waldinger et al. 21). The authors also argue that "the presence of a critical mass of class conscious immigrant workers" was one of the key ingredients in the Justice for Janitors campaign. The workers that make up this transnational labor force came together to fight a global system of labor exploitation. The campaign was predicated on an understanding of the changes that the global city had created in the industry. In her study of Justice for Janitors, Cynthia Cranford points out that the union moved away from the traditional organization of entire cities in favor of dividing Los Angeles into "'mini-cities' of concentrated commercial real estate" to more effectively recruit members ("Gendered Resistance" 317). The strategy helped organize the large number of Latin@ immigrants, many undocumented, who were recruited by non-union cleaning companies. In organizing these immigrant workers, women were a key element in the success of the unionizing effort.

In the film, it is Maya's ability to discuss with her fellow workers the advantages of unionizing that leads to their mobilization. While the union leader, Sam, might be a white, male organizer, it is clear from the beginning that he would have been unsuccessful without Maya's assistance. Loach's representation of a strong female presence in the union is consistent with the role that Cranford argues women played in the Justice for Janitors campaign, which organized women from the very beginning. For Cranford, the union's organizing practice of making unionism a "family affair" more closely suited the reality of immigrant families than would other kinds of unionizing strategies. By organizing through this framework, the union facilitated women's participation by incorporating families "into the protests so that both women and men could participate in the major union activit[ies] . . . Since children required care, their presence at the protests meant that caregiving was brought into a very public realm where it could be visibly connected with union politics" ("Constructing Union Motherhood" 368). While women are still constructed as being responsible for care duties, by reframing their organizing strategies as a form of "union motherhood," the campaign engaged women workers and connected motherhood "to explicitly political union leadership" ("Constructing Union Motherhood" 375). Through its framing of Maya as a powerful organizer, the film offers viewers an alternative representation of immigrant domestic labor, in the transnational space of the global office building, that makes visible labor exploitation but also the possibilities for worker resistance. In the process, the immigrant narrative advanced by the film rejects the simple conventions of the traditional story and challenges an audience's belief in the myth of meritocracy.

The Romance Plot Revisited

As we saw in chapter 1, when dealing with women, Hollywood films are guilty of reducing the immigrant experience to a storybook romance—most often casting white men in the role of Prince Charming. By adhering to the conventions of the romance, such a narrative provides the audience with an easily developed story line that ends with the happy ending, and *Maid in Manhattan* is no different. The relationship between Marisa and Chris is very similar to that between the domestic worker and employer in other popular films. Even though Chris is not her employer, as a paying hotel guest, he does have a relative amount of power over Marisa. After all, the domestic worker is there to serve the needs of the guest. What makes *Maid in Manhattan* different from *Spanglish* is the fact that when Chris first encounters Marisa, he doesn't know she is a maid. Marisa is clothed in an all-white Dolce & Gabbana pantsuit that makes her hypervisible, unlike the maid's uniform, which renders her invisible.[55] As when Cinderella meets the prince, Marisa is basically in wealthy white-woman drag when she meets Chris, and he mistakes her for a hotel guest of possible "Mediterranean" descent. Chris' misidentification of her working-class, Puerto Rican background makes her socially and racially acceptable (exotic, but not dangerously so) for his attraction/attention.[56]

The culmination of their love affair begins at a wealthy fundraiser meant to replicate a ball—the pivotal moment of meeting between Cinderella and her prince—and ends in Chris' hotel room. With the help of her staff-member friends, Marisa goes from being a hotel maid to a modern-day princess, decked out in a beautiful designer gown, glorious shoes, and a Harry Winston wreath of diamonds. While the idea that a housekeeping employee would be allowed to borrow such valuable merchandise seems completely absurd, it is easy for the viewer to accept Marisa's change from domestic worker to socialite because Jennifer Lopez has become known as a fashionista and her framing on the screen in designer gown and jewels is a familiar image. Like Cinderella, Marisa goes to the ball, dances with the prince, and runs out. The modern-day story, however, doesn't have Marisa leave the dance, but has her end up in Chris' room for a romantic rendezvous that consummates their physical relationship and ensures the audience a glimpse at Lopez' body. Marisa is hesitant to sleep with Chris, not because of lack of desire, but because of the threat the relationship holds for her career advancement. In fact, Lionel, the head butler training her for the management program, urges her to end her flirtation with Chris, at least until she becomes a manager. The beginning of the hotel scene positions Marisa on the bed, her hair flowing loose behind her, looking more exotic that in any previous scene. As she looks up to Chris, her face is illuminated by what we assume is the moonlight coming through the window. The positioning of Chris standing over Marisa, looking down on her, locates him within a larger visual discourse of white male superiority and perpetuates the ideology of Latina bodies as sexually willing and available. The viewer is encouraged to forget Marisa's initial hesitation and instead accept the conquering of her body by the powerful white politician. Beyond the dangerous erasure of the unequal power in their relationship, the fact that their affair culminates in his hotel room goes completely uncomplicated in the film.

While the romance between Chris and Marisa is extremely problematic, their sexual encounter does more than advance the plotline—it erases a real threat of violence. The convention of the romance plot employed in the development of the relationship between Marisa and Chris negates the danger that the hotel room poses for housekeepers. *New York Times* labor and workplace reporter Steven Greenhouse notes that "housekeepers and hotel security experts say that housekeepers have long had to deal with various sexual affronts from male guests, including explicit comments, groping, guests who expose themselves and even attempted rape."[57] The precarious nature of the enclosed space of the hotel room is in no way suggested. Instead, the hotel room is idealized as a space of romance and desire where colonial fantasies can be made reality. The racialized, working-class body of the housekeeper is the place where such fantasies get played out.

The romance plot perpetuated in mainstream films like *Maid in Manhattan* is not unique. While the level of disbelief required to consume the romance in the film is much higher than in other films, the practice of using this tired plotline remains extremely popular. Though it was a commercial failure, Wes Anderson's first film, *Bottle Rocket* (1996), is considered a critical success that helped start his career as a filmmaker and Owen Wilson's career as a writer/actor. The film, a quirky story of an outcast group of friends, utilizes Anderson's brand of humor to follow the (mis)adventures of Dignan (Owen Wilson), Anthony (Luke Wilson), and Bob (Robert Musgrave).[58] While

117

the three young men make up the protagonists of the film, secondary characters play an important role in the development of the main characters. Dignan is obsessed with Mr. Henry, Bob lives in the shadow of his brother, Future Man, and Anthony falls in love with Inez, played by Mexican actor Lumi Cavazos.[59] In the film, the character of Inez is a member of the housekeeping staff of the motel the three misfits end up hiding out in after robbing a bookstore. Anthony, who has recently checked himself out of a mental institution, falls for Inez the first time he sees her.[60]

The audience first sees Inez through Anthony's perspective. We witness his emergence from the depths of the motel's pool and watch as Inez captures his attention.[61] Though she is wearing just a simple white uniform, with straight hair and little makeup, Inez' beauty enthralls Anthony. The camera renders Inez' working body visible and positions it as desirable through its emphasis on her body's framing. We watch as the wind blows her hair and teasingly twirls the edges of her uniform, a thin garment that hints at the body beneath the fabric.[62] She moves slowly, allowing Anthony, who is riveted by her, a full view of her body. In an interesting costume choice, Inez is shown cleaning the motel rooms in her bare feet. The scene might be humorous, but the message that gets relayed is serious. Inez is represented as pretty and simple, but also "different." The camera's focus on her bare feet, and the subsequent shot of her sandals lying useless on her cart, offers the audience the opportunity to view Inez as "natural"—which could also be read as premodern—a stark contrast to the women with whom Anthony normally associates.[63] The fact that she doesn't speak English and Anthony doesn't speak Spanish doesn't stand in the way of their romantic entanglement. She offers Anthony, and the viewer, a perfect love interest—someone who doesn't speak the language and won't complicate his criminal predicament. It would be easy to dismiss the representation of Inez simply as part of a cast of characters who cannot be taken seriously, but the framing of her body in the scene that introduces her sets Inez up as the traditional embodiment of the sexually desirable and available Latina housekeeper.[64]

The romantic relationship that develops between Anthony and Inez is predicated on subtle stereotypical notions of Latina sexuality. While the romance between them is represented as more endearing than exploitative, the film's emphasis on her physicality continues the perpetuation of the stereotype of the sexy Latina maid. The song that plays on the radio during Inez' introduction, "Prendeme la vela," functions as an audio clue to illustrate her otherness. The Latin beat with its Afro-Peruvian rhythm works to exoticize Inez beyond the visual. While the sexualization of Inez is not as gratuitous as that found in other cultural representations, the film's choice to base Anthony's affection for Inez exclusively on physical attraction reduces her to the stereotype of just another sexy Latina body. His "love" for her has little to do with who Inez is as a human being, as all he, and the audience, knows about her is that she is from Paraguay and she works as a domestic worker at the motel. For Anthony, however, this is enough to fall in love with her. The character of Inez is relegated to the margins of the story, reduced to the object of desire in a stereotypical romance plot that helps advance the white male's character development.

In the film, the sexualization of the immigrant Latina body is used not only to perpetuate the requisite love story, but also to restore heteronormativity. Inez' body works to navigate any uncomfortable sexual tension that might exist between Anthony and his close male friends—whether that tension is visible in the film or inserted by audience members. The relationship between Dignan, Anthony, and Bob is based on their inability to operate within their community, giving rise to the need to create their own space of belonging.[65] Their dysfunctional relationships are, in part, based on their failure to perform normative masculinity.[66] Anthony's inability to cope with the world, which is what initially leads to his hospitalization, and his constant following of Dignan lead to Inez' observing that he is "like paper flying" with no real substance or direction. All of the characters are seen as lacking the strength and power that are stereotypically associated with dominant white masculinity. By sleeping with Inez, Anthony performs heteronormativity and distances himself from Bob's and Dignan's flawed masculinity. Through Inez' body, heteronormativity is restored and Anthony's masculinity is reinforced. It becomes easier for heterosexual male audience members to identify with Anthony as he is set apart from Bob and Dignan through his relationship with Inez. The romance makes Anthony a more relatable character while making Inez a desirable one. Once Inez declares her love for Anthony, fulfilling the terms of the heterosexual contract, she disappears from the story.

There seems to be an inability or unwillingness of films to focus attention on Latina domestic workers without succumbing to the employment of a romance plot. Audiences have become comfortable with the stereotype of the sexy Latina maid commonly employed in cultural productions, which makes the perpetuation of such a character a popular practice. It is easier for audiences to consume an image with which they are familiar, and so films will often employ such images to expand their appeal. While Bread and Roses provides a much more complex and progressive representation of domestic labor in the transnational space of the global city, it too weaves a heteronormative romance around its female protagonist. In the film, Maya becomes romantically involved with Sam, the union organizer. Their relationship gives the film the opportunity to humanize both Maya and Sam, while offering an audience the possibility of a happy ending. However, the relationship between them cannot survive the realities of Maya's undocumented status.

While it is important to be critical of the ways in which the romance plot in *Bottle Rocket* functions to perpetuate heteronormativity, it is also significant to acknowledge the role that character development plays in the ultimate image created for an audience. The difference between the representation of Maya in *Bread and Roses* and that of Inez in *Bottle Rocket* or Marisa in *Maid in Manhattan* lies in the level of sexualization and racial "othering" that takes place. While Inez and Marisa become characters whose physical appearance lies at the heart of their character development, Loach chooses to incorporate a romance plotline into the narrative but represents Maya as a strong, intelligent, and determined character, allowing her to be seen as more than just the beautiful love interest.[67] Her escape from the coyote, her dedication to the unionization of Angel Services' workers, and her willingness to sacrifice herself for Ruben's future allow an audience to view her as much more than just a desirable Latina body. Unlike other representations of Latina workers, Maya is never the focus of the type of voyeuristic lens that would frame her body as sexy and "other." While she is beautiful on-screen, her body is never put on display in provocative clothing or placed in "wind shots" with her hair flowing romantically behind her. The relationship that forms between Maya and Sam is predicated on what is represented as an equal level of respect of both individuals. Maya admires Sam's dedication and work with the union, and Sam is impressed by Maya's willingness to fight for the rights of her fellow workers.

Another important difference between the representation of the romance plot in *Bread and Roses* and in more popular films is the construction of Latino masculinity within that trope. The positioning of the heterosexual white male as the object of love for the beautiful Latina worker is predicated on the vilification/erasure of a Latino masculinity. In both *Spanglish* and *Maid in Manhattan*, Latino masculinity is rendered undesirable. The Latino men with whom Flor and Marisa had previously been romantically involved are represented as failed husbands and fathers, men who abandon their families to pursue their own selfish interests. *Bread and Roses* offers an alternative to the image of the deviant Latino male through the character of Ruben. In the film, Ruben offers Maya an optional love interest to Sam. He is represented as ambitious, smart, and caring. While he chooses to protect his own interests over those of the union, the film represents the decision as a difficult one and avoids an image of the Latino male as less moral or courageous than the white male love interest. Even when faced with Maya's rejection, he is not reduced to the violent, angry, or macho construction of the stereotypical image of Latino masculinity.

Happily Ever After?

The range of texts in this chapter provides differing endings and resolutions to the female characters' stories. The conclusion of *Maid in Manhattan* fits in well with the stage of resolution in the traditional narrative of immigration. After Marisa's masquerade as a hotel guest is discovered and she is fired, she is forced to confront her mother and the ideas she represents. In the scene that represents Marisa's rejection of her mother's beliefs, the elder Ventura confronts Marisa and asks, "What were you thinking going out with someone like that?" The assumption in Veronica's question is that Marisa is not good enough to date a man of Chris' position. Marisa refuses to allow Veronica's question to go unchallenged, retorting, "People like you make people like him some kind of God. Why, because he's rich? White? He has things we don't have . . . that we don't want to dream about? It must really burn you that I think I have the right to go out with him." Her mother's reply of "You don't" cements the differences between the mother and daughter. Marisa gets represented as someone who does not believe in the hierarchies between rich and poor, or brown and white. Instead, she embodies the promise of a meritocracy that allows one to dream about a better future. She chooses to believe as Lionel does, that serving people does not define her. Lionel's last piece of advice, "What defines us is how well we rise after falling," provides Marisa with an alternative way of thinking about herself and her labor. Lionel's words, "To serve people takes dignity and intelligence. But remember, they are only people with money. And although we serve them, we are not their servants," also provide the audience with an easy resolution to any discomfort they might have about domestic labor. By emphasizing the individual's actions in persevering, the speech also conforms to the ideology of success being based on the individual and not on the existing structures of inequality that make a true meritocracy a myth. In contrast to Lionel and Marisa, Veronica becomes the embodiment of old-world ideas of rigid boundaries and unattainable goals.

Veronica is upset not only because she feels Marisa was dating above her station, but also because she cannot understand Marisa's ambition. Veronica's frustration with Marisa is based on her inability to fully believe in the possibility of dreaming for a better life, as she herself has been unsuccessful in assimilating. By separating herself from her mother's influence and doubt—by silencing her voice—Marisa, the film shows the audience, can use her abilities as a good worker to move up the socioeconomic ladder. The main difference between mother and daughter comes down to the fact that Veronica is not invested in the ideology of the American Dream and the movie ultimately represents her assimilation as a failure. As in the popular immigrant narrative, it is up to the second generation, or Marisa, to achieve that dream. Ironically, Veronica's doubts are much more realistic than Marisa's ambitions. In fact, Peréz y González writes that for Puerto Rican im/migrants, "what they expected in terms of decent, good-paying jobs, affordable housing, and education did not materialize for many of them" (64).

Maid in Manhattan's conclusion resolves all of the conflicts experienced by Marisa in ways that ensure the audience is comfortable. Because of its heavy emphasis on the Cinderella story, the only ending that would appease an audience would be the reconciliation between the two lovers. As the embodiment of true American ideals, Chris has no problem in accepting Marisa as a domestic worker. The film represents their love as a fairy tale; it is so strong that it can overcome all of the obstacles and barriers between them. Unlike Cinderella, who gets carried off to the prince's castle, Marisa becomes successful not just in love but also in her career. The last scenes of the film depict Marisa on the cover of trade magazines, illustrating her success. To make the ending even happier, not only has Marisa become a member of management, she has inspired other workers to do the same. The film promotes the myth of meritocracy and upward assimilation through hard work and perseverance. Marisa's mother is represented as unable to fully assimilate because she lacks faith in the American Dream. As her daughter, however, Marisa comes to embody the successful national citizen by embracing the new-world ideas of the country and participating in white heteronormativity through her romantic relationship with the ideal male citizen.

Based on the title of the novel and the end of the narrative, it would seem that *América's Dream* also resolves the conflicts encountered by the migrant protagonist. However, the novel does not provide the happy ending we see in *Maid in Manhattan*. In leaving Puerto Rico, América and her mother arranged to keep the location of her employers' home a secret to keep her violent lover, Correa, from finding her. After writing to their daughter, however, Correa discovers the town América is living in and comes to take her back to Puerto

Rico. When América resists, Correa brutally assaults her and almost kills her. After surviving the attack, América is fired by the Leverrets and returns to work in the hotel industry. Even before Correa's brutal attack, América's life was difficult, with the unreasonable demands placed upon her by the Leverrets and their refusal to pay her the wages she deserved. Instead of her life getting better in the mainland United States, América works as hard as she did in Puerto Rico and sees no improvement in her or her family's quality of life.

The title of the novel is not a reference to the achievement of the American Dream, but instead alludes to América's ability to free herself from the very abusive relationship in which she was trapped. She does not escape the drudgery of work, and her relationship with Rosalinda continues to be a complicated one. Unlike the ideology promoted by the dominant immigrant narrative, in which the immigrant subject severs her connection to her home, América remains connected to Puerto Rico through her relationship with her mother, who refuses to move to New York, gesturing to that circulatory migration pattern that is a big part of Puerto Rican identity. While América allows herself to become romantically involved with Darío, a Nuyorican friend of Paulina's family, he is not represented as a Prince Charming who will rescue her. Instead, he is cab driver, a gentle father of two, and a recovering drug addict.[68] In the end, América rescues herself by fighting back and offers a powerful story of struggle and survival—a much richer story of movement/migration.

In "Act of the Faithless," Norte leaves her audience without a satisfactory conclusion to the narrative. Instead of completing the important phase of resolution, as in the conventional immigrant narrative, "Act of the Faithless" ends with Norte's aunt's silent resistance to the tourist's hailing and her words, "'There is too much to see,' she said, 'too much to remember.'" The melancholic tone to her words, combined with her inability to openly resist the white male's degradation, negates a simple narrative ending. We know that on the other side of the border, more labor awaits, this time in a household ruled by Norte's uncle. And for Maya in *Bread and Roses*, the success of the union does not translate into a happy ending. In an effort to provide Ruben with the money for his tuition payment, Maya robs a store. Her sacrifice for her friend ends up leading to her deportation. While her fellow workers rejoice at their victory, Maya is ejected from the nation, forced to return to Mexico. Her immigrant narrative, like her sister's, lacks a happy ending.[69] The challenges facing undocumented immigrants cannot be easily resolved. In *Bread and Roses*, the audience is left with contradictory feelings and an unhappy ending.

‡

For domestic workers, visibility is a complicated issue, mediated through intersecting ideologies of race, class, and gender. Being invisible is dehumanizing, but becoming visible is not always a good thing—especially when that visibility is based on objectification; after all, "movies teach . . . they form, in short, a powerful public textbook . . . long after school education has ended, we continue learning through the media" (Cortés 91). While the Dominique Strauss-Kahn case monopolized media attention, another prominent international businessman was being arrested in New York for the sexual harassment of a hotel housekeeper. On May 3, 2011, Mahmoud Abdel-Salam Omar, former chairman of the Bank of Alexandria and the Egyptian American Bank, was charged with the sexual abuse, unlawful imprisonment, forcible touching, and harassment of a Pierre Hotel housekeeper. After pleading guilty to a misdemeanor sexual abuse charge, Omar was sentenced to one year of probation and five days of community service (Katz and Debusmann). He now faces a multi-million-dollar civil lawsuit, but Omar was not required to serve any jail time or register as a sex offender. The apparent leniency of his sentence illustrates the ease with which violence against a gendered, racialized, and classed body is dismissed and only marginally made visible when a powerful man is at the center of the story. These high-profile cases have, however, increased the public's awareness of the occupational hazards of hotel housekeeping. The capacity of clientele to harass and abuse housekeepers within the space of the hotel industry is finally getting some attention. While hotel workers and administrators have long known of the dangers faced by housekeepers, the ability to openly discuss their safety has led to several industry changes.[70] What remains unchanged, however, is the mainstream image of domestic workers as sexually available.

The proliferation of sexy Latina bodies on the big and small screen has advanced an image of Latina sexuality that is detrimental to im/migrant women of color. It reduces individuals to sexual objects and represents Latina domestic workers as willing participants in their exploitation. After all, don't all Latina domestic workers want their own fairy tale ending? Isn't the easiest way to get it by marrying their own Prince Charming? The danger of films like *Maid in Manhattan* and *Bottle Rocket* lies in their perpetuation of the stereotypical image of Latina domestic workers as sexually willing and available—a problematic image that carries with it assumptions about im/migrant Latina bodies. These visual cultural productions also dismiss the economic exploitation of domestic labor through their representation of housekeeping labor as simple or enjoyable or temporary. Like other popular texts, *Maid in Manhattan* closely follows the conventional narrative of immigration that functions as a structure of containment. The narratives by Norte and Santiago, however, pose challenges to those representations by advancing complex portrayals of immigration and domestic labor. These representations resist being submerged under the rhetoric of assimilation or upward mobility. They offer examples of a new Latina genealogy of immigrant literature that strongly challenges the erasure or romanticization of domestic work and refutes the dangerous stereotype of the sexy Latina woman. While the limited circulation enjoyed by these oppositional narratives restricts the scope of this intervention, their mere existence is a powerful testament to the strength of subjugated voices. The resistance created through the words of Norte and Santiago is further developed and built upon by the visual oppositional narratives discussed in the next chapter.

Trovoy Alex Walker holds a sign featuring an image of Citlali at the UNITE HERE day of action at the Grand Hyatt Hotel in San Antonio on July 21, 2011. (Photograph by Adela Arellano, copyright © 2011. Courtesy of Adela Arellano and Trovoy Alex Walker.)

CHAPTER FOUR

Calling All Superheroes
Recasting the Immigrant Subject

No chingen con mi Raza.

» Citlali, La Chicana Superhero[1]

On July 21, 2011, a group of workers, community activists, and union organizers came together in a demonstration outside of the Grand Hyatt Hotel in downtown San Antonio. Part of a national day of action organized by the labor union UNITE HERE, the demonstration sought to focus attention on the working conditions of hotel housekeepers and on what UNITE HERE said were the Hyatt Hotel chain's unfair labor practices.[2] To publicly challenge the hotel's treatment of its employees, protesters braved the high temperatures and scorching sun to march together, carrying signs and chanting slogans rooted in a long history of labor activism. Above the sea of red "UNITE HERE!" T-shirts hung a brightly colored banner calling for economic justice. The banner, a work of art designed by Chicana artist Debora Kuetzpal Vasquez and painted by community volunteers, featured on one end a hotel housekeeper and on the other Citlali, La Chicana Superhero, a character created by Vasquez. Citlali appears in various websites and installations, including the web magazine *Lucha Vista Magazine*. The words "Hyatt, our community demands justice for mujeres trabajadoras"—placed between these two imposing mestiza figures—loomed over the demonstrators. The banner offered up an image of strength and community solidarity and made central the bodies of "mujeres trabajadoras" (women workers). More than words, Vasquez' piece connected the rights of hotel workers with larger issues of economic justice through the incorporation of her imagined superhero.

The importance of Citlali's appearance at the action lies in the intervention offered by the creation of alternative myths and narratives to challenge the invisibility of worker exploitation. As a defender of the rights of Chican@s, Citlali represents the strategy of creating new narratives when state constructions of justice fail communities of color. Through the banner's emphasis on the figures of Citlali and the housekeeper, workers' rights become part of a larger discourse of human rights. The strategy of deploying the figure of a superhero, one who battles injustice and oppression, highlights the inability of the state to protect its workers. In solidarity with the "mujeres tra-bajadoras" of the Hyatt, Citlali is taking care of those community members the nation has ignored in the interests of capital. While she might be protecting the disenfranchised, Citlali, whose name means "star" in Nahuatl, does not follow the traditional model of white masculinity popular in the construction of the superhero fig-ure. The re-imagining of the superhero as a woman of color posi-tions agency as existing within the community.[3] Her appearance on the side of the workers and activists also calls into question the authority of the police or other hegemonic state agents to define justice.[4] Her non-normative, classed, racialized body is used to high-light the multiple modes of oppression intersecting and operating in the exploitation of "mujeres trabajadoras."

Offering a narrative of opposition, Vasquez' banner counters the lack of positive representations in mainstream media that continues to affect the ways in which audiences imagine domestic workers and their labor. It is hard to admire individuals who are always positioned

Workers raise a banner designed by Debora Kuetzpal Vasquez reading "Hyatt, our community demands justice for mujeres trabajadoras" at the UNITE HERE day of action July 21, 2011, at the Grand Hyatt Hotel in San Antonio. (Photograph by Adela Arellano, copyright © 2011. Courtesy of Adela Arellano.)

as inferior or take seriously anyone who is reduced to the butt of jokes or simply a sexually alluring body. In large part, the move to resist the problematic representation of women, labor, and immigration has involved the act of altering preconceived ideas through the creation of more complex images of domestic workers. Through their representation of domestic workers as fully human individuals who must deal with the precarious position of being immigrants, cultural producers resist the traditional immigrant narrative that simplifies and sanitizes our understanding of immigration. Vasquez' Citlali is representative of a new strategy of resistance being deployed by cultural producers. This strategy involves the appropriation and revision of the traditional heroic figure and relies heavily on the visual to offer alternative representations of immigrant workers.

The current use of the trope of heroes is a powerful strategy in combating the invisibility of labor structures and in the creation of counternarratives of immigration. The adoption of the trope in service of uncovering subjugated knowledges provides yet another example of the oppositional possibilities in projects of deconstruction and resignification. In her photograph series *Superheroes*, Dulce Pinzón re-imagines what the figure of the superhero can mean and incorporates the notion of alternative/secret identities into a photo series that makes visible a transnational labor market dependent on remittances. Similarly, in her documentary *Maid in America*, Anayansi Prado portrays the use of a domestic-worker superhero, "Super Doméstica," by the Coalition for Humane Immigrant Rights of Los Angeles (CHIRLA) to inform workers of their rights. Playing with the image of the glamorous spy, Laura Alvarez' digital series *Double Agent Sirvienta* uses the figure of the double agent to critique multiple structures of power from the position of a spy/computer hacker. Alvarez' character Double Agent Sirvienta, or DAS, uses her cover of domestic worker and its accompanying invisibility to infiltrate multiple spaces and becomes a modern hero in the struggle against oppression. All three contemporary cultural productions illustrate the use of multiple visual genres and modern technology in creating stories of immigration and labor that reject the racist, sexist, classist, and xenophobic ideologies operating in current debates around immigration. As such, the subjects of Pinzón's, Prado's, and Alvarez' work reject the traditional immigrant narrative's schema of assimilation and resolution and instead embrace a multiplicity that complicates an audience's understanding of labor and the processes of transnational movement.

A Quest for "Truth, Justice, and the American Way"

> A superhero is a man or woman with powers that are either massive extensions of human strengths and capabilities, or fundamentally different in kind, which she or he uses to fight for truth, justice and the protection of the innocent. A substantial minority of people without powers as such share a commitment to the superhero mission, so they are generally regarded as superheroes in spite of their absence of such powers.
>
> » Roz Kaveney, Superheroes! (4)

One of the most popular and enduring types of character in cultural productions remains the figure of the superhero. From comic books, to television series, to multi-million-dollar Hollywood films, superheroes are important actors in the creation and perpetuation of a specific national imaginary. These are the individuals who, while flawed, always use their powers to fight for the innocent.[5] They might be tortured souls, grappling with their roles as defenders of justice or attempting to find a way of fitting into the mainstream. Regardless of their own personal angst, superheroes ultimately save the day and help a mainstream audience continue to believe in the idea that good will always triumph over evil. Like the organizational logic of the traditional immigrant narrative, the mainstream superhero genre relies on simplistic notions of merit and a binary construction of good versus bad.[6] They offer an audience a comfortable lens through which to frame questions of justice and fairness.

Americans began their long-lasting love affair with superheroes in the 1930s. The creation of the DC Universe, a product of National Allied Publications, offered readers a universe inhabited by lasting characters such as Superman (1938), Batman (1939), and Wonder Woman (1941).[7] These figures fought for the side of good and triumphed over evil, making the world a better place. The fact that comic book heroes were being created in the middle of the World War II upheaval is no coincidence. Historian Les Daniels points out that, as products of their time, superheroes were very much a part of the war ideology propagated during those tumultuous years. He puts forth the argument that "the idea of the superhero, who gave up his ordinary life and put on a uniform to battle the bad guys, had special resonance during wartime; costumed characters became one of the emblems of the age. In a sense they were America" (64). Comic book heroes gave their audience a version of a homogenous America, a simplistic construction that fit comfortably within the government propaganda of the time. The rise of the superhero figure during such a tumultuous historical moment helped an audience define itself within a global stage of violence and the unexplainable horror of the world war. The narrative of the superhero functioned to ideologically construct the United States as the defender of the world, a more modern imagining of the "beacon of democracy." Like the hegemonic immigrant narrative, the construction of this unified "America" precipitated the exclusion of those not fitting within this nationalist imagery.

The image propagated by the traditional superhero is one based on exclusion. In his work on comic books and World War II propaganda, what he refers to as "popaganda," Chris Murray takes issue with Daniels' claim and argues, "Far from representing America as it was, superhero comics represented a view of America that was constructed by and within the ideology of the dominant power structures and institutions," and this representation has to be understood for "not only what was represented, but also what was excluded, and why" (143).[8] Like the genre of the popular immigrant narrative, the superhero comics of the day followed a practice of representation that left out anything that might challenge the popular conception of the construction of the nation. In both genres, the United States remained the "city on a hill," where justice for all is ever present. Even Superman's motto, his fight for "truth, justice, and the American way," equates the nation with righteousness.[9] It is into this legacy of mainstream representations of heroism, justice, and struggle that counterheroes like DAS and Super Doméstica intervene.

It's a Bird . . . It's a Plane . . . It's a Window Washer?

In teaching us a new visual code, photographs alter and enlarge our notions of what is worth looking at and what we have a right to observe. They are a grammar and, even more importantly, an ethics of seeing . . . The most grandiose result of the photographic enterprise is to give us the sense that we can hold the whole world in our heads—an anthology of images.

» Susan Sontag, *On Photography* (3)

One of the most striking visual representations of an alternative narrative of immigration created in the past few years is Dulce Pinzón's photographic series *Superheroes*. The installation is an ongoing project, begun in 2004–2005, that currently includes twenty photographs; it captures Mexican immigrants in superhero costumes performing various forms of labor.[10] *Superheroes* is a visual counternarrative of immigration—a new anthology of images—that incorporates the laboring bodies of immigrant communities into the national construction of heroism. I borrow Sontag's concept of "an anthology of images" to explain how Pinzón is using photography to "enlarge our notions of what is worth looking at" (3). Pinzón created the series as a response to the rise in the use of the rhetoric of "heroes" after the events of September 11, 2001. The label of "hero" was being used to describe the courageous actions of individuals in the face of dangerous events. These emergencies and disasters, and the people designated as heroic because of their resulting actions, were front-page news. Left out of this public discourse of heroism were the sacrifices and labor of individuals quietly working for the common good of others, performing acts of heroism that don't make the daily news. Pinzón was bothered by the ways in which so many people of color were rendered invisible by the dominant constructions of heroism. In her artist statement on her website, she explains:

> The Mexican immigrant worker in New York is a perfect example of the hero who has gone unnoticed. It is common for a Mexican worker in New York to work extraordinary hours in extreme conditions for very low wages which are saved at great cost and sacrifice and sent to families and communities in Mexico who rely on them to survive.
> The Mexican economy has quietly become dependent on the money sent from workers in the U.S. Conversely, the U.S. economy has quietly become dependent on the labor of Mexican immigrants. Along with the depth of their sacrifice, it is the quietness of this dependence which makes Mexican immigrant workers a subject of interest.

Pinzón expands our definitions of what makes an individual heroic and of whose bodies are worth noticing. The invisibility of service workers in a multicultural global space like New York City functions to erase their labor and their contributions to the running of the city. Pinzón does not dismiss the efforts of rescue and aid workers or claim that their actions were not heroic; rather, she points out the problematic practice of only acknowledging the labor of a certain group while ignoring the efforts of those who continue to exist in the margins. In her description of the series, Pinzón critiques a labor system that exploits workers while effectively rendering the exploited individual and his/her labor invisible. For the artist, it is the work that these immigrants perform for the greater good of their communities that makes their actions heroic. They are laboring under difficult conditions, not for their own individual advancement, but for the well-being of those they left behind.[11] Through the visual emphasis on their labor and her focus on the level of personal self-sacrifice practiced by these individuals, Pinzón's representation positions them within the rhetoric of superheroes.

In her statement, Pinzón also makes clear the economic relationship between Mexico and the United States and the ways in which both nations' economies are dependent on the labor of immigrant workers. Pinzón's photo series posits a complex argument that advocates for a more sophisticated understanding of a global system of labor under which workers and capital are mobilized in the interest of a large international economy. Instead of discussing immigration within the parameters of the typical debate that positions it only as an issue that affects the United States, she visibly links the country of origin and the host country in two very specific ways, through the notion of home and by addressing the subject of remittances. By incorporating these two elements into her series, Pinzón encourages her audience to question assumptions they might have about labor, immigration, and acts of heroism. She persuades her viewer to see the series' subjects as modern-day superheroes.

While taking pictures of the workers in the series rejects their invisibility and documents their labor, by visually capturing these workers as superheroes, Pinzón employs a powerful strategy of signification. Through her visual text, she inserts immigrant bodies into the myth of the "American superhero" and, in the process, questions both identities. In her discussion of race and the construction of "America," cultural critic and producer Coco Fusco argues that photography "offers the promise of apprehending who we are, not only as private individuals but also as members of social and cultural groups, as public citizens, as Americans. No other means of representing human likeness has been used more systematically to describe and formulate American identity than photography" (13). Fusco's argument emphasizes the role the visual plays in the creation of a national identity and underscores the specific power the medium of photography has in helping define our own position in the nation. Who gets photographed, how one is photographed, and how those photos are framed tell a story.[12] Pinzón's photographs offer a visual counternarrative of immigration and labor that expands on the "anthology of images" a mainstream audience holds. She is telling a different story, one of community, labor, and transnational connections.

The series photographs available on Pinzón's website display fifteen different workers performing their daily labor while wearing superhero costumes.[13] While the photographs are part of an installation that has toured throughout the United States and Mexico, their availability on the Internet has made them accessible to an even larger audience. The technological advances in the field of digital technology and the power of digital photography to disseminate images have made the genre an incredible tool for the creation of oppositional narratives.[14] Pinzón's photographs also destabilize the colonial logic of popular representations of immigrant bodies as racialized "others," representations that are created and circulated by the same technol-

Name	Superhero	Place of Origin	Remittances	Occupation
Juventino Rosas	Aquaman	State of Mexico	$400/week	Fish market employee
Federico Martinez	Batman	State of Puebla	$250/week	Taxi driver
Minerva Valencia	Catwoman	State of Puebla	$400/week	Nanny
Adalberto Lara	El Chapulín Colorado	State of Mexico	$350/week	Construction worker
Sergio García	Mr. Fantastic	State of Mexico	$350/week	Waiter
Paulino Cardozo	Incredible Hulk	State of Guerrero	$300/week	Greengrocer truck loader
Oscar Gonzalez	Human Torch	State of Oaxaca	$350/week	Cook
Ernesto Mendez	Robin	Mexico City	$200/week	Sex worker
José Rosendo de Jesús	El Santo	State of Guerrero	$175/week	Union organizer
Noe Reyes	Superman	State of Puebla	$500/week	Deliveryman
Maria Luisa Romero	Wonder Woman	State of Puebla	$150/week	Laundromat employee
Róman Romero	Green Lantern	State of Guerrero	$200/week	Construction superintendent
Alvaro Cruz	The Flash	State of Mexico	$75/week	Cook
Luis Hernandez	The Thing	State of Veracruz	$200/week	Demolition worker
Bernabe Mendez	Spiderman	State of Guerrero	$125/week	Window washer

Table 4.1. Original list of characters from Dulce Pinzón's photographic series Superheroes

ogy Pinzón now harnesses. Pinzón's series *Superheroes* is an example of the successful fusion of art, activism, and technology.

The original set of *Superheroes* photographs tells the story of thirteen men and two women. Because my project is centered on the representation of women in narratives of immigration and the representation of domestic workers, it would be easy to concentrate my analysis on the two female immigrant workers represented in the installation. However, because the series works as a whole in creating new meanings, it becomes important to analyze Pinzón's cultural production in its entirety. The installation follows a similar format for each photograph. The subject of the photo is captured in the middle of performing some sort of action—working, protesting, thinking, running—while wearing a superhero costume. Each picture is labeled with the name of the worker, the place of the immigrant's home, and the dollar amount of remittances regularly sent back to the place of origin. The linguistic message communicated by the label combined with the visual message communicated by the photograph functions to create a new narrative that destabilizes the fixed meaning of "superhero" and expands the conventions of the immigrant narrative.[15] The fusion of the linguistic and visual meanings of the photographs offers stories of individuals whose labor and immigration serve the interests of multiple communities.

As a whole, the series invites its audience to imagine different ways of seeing immigrant workers and their labor. The photographs resist the common practice of rendering these workers invisible and place at the forefront their contribution to a global economy. Through her visual use of the superhero rhetoric, Pinzón challenges the construction of superheroes as monolithic—white and masculine—and instead positions the personal sacrifices of these workers as a form of heroism. Gone is the emphasis on "America" as the "shining city upon a hill," the "promised land" of wealth and success. In its stead, the series provides a visual representation of current international networks of labor and the transnational movement of individuals. In 2008, remittances to Mexico from all countries were estimated (in U.S. dollars) to total $25.1 billion, with a drop in 2009 to $21.2 billion as a result of the U.S. recession.[16] Remittances are on the rise again, as World Bank estimates place Mexico at $22.6 billion in total remittances in 2011, third only to India ($55 billion) and China ($51 billion).[17] The captions that identify the superheroes are a powerful example of the transnational movement of capital, in this case between the United States and Mexico. The pictures capture the specific contributions these immigrant workers make to the U.S. economy through their labor and frame New York City as a global city whose need for low-income workers is partially met through immigrant labor. The needs of capital have transformed to meet the needs of what Saskia Sassen refers to as a "global city." With the management of the world economy from these global cities, immigrant workers are needed to meet the service needs of financial managers and other high-income/professional workers. The series uncovers this often-unacknowledged need and rejects both the anonymity and the devaluation of immigrant workers.

While the traditional superhero genre relies heavily on the concealment of the hero's identity, Pinzón provides her audience with the true identity of each photographic subject. The descriptive label works to unmask the superhero and identify her/his alter ego while stripping his/her labor of the level of secrecy under which it normally functions. While some individuals remain masked because of the nature of the hero costume, these individuals are not anonymous. Pinzón's emphasis on the identities of these workers rejects the imperialist practice of capturing images of nameless bodies of color.[18] No longer nameless faces, they are real people, with real names, real lives, and real communities.

Re-Imagining Resistance and Acts of Heroism

With great power, there must also come—great responsibility.

» Spiderman, in *Amazing Fantasy* No. 15 (Lee, Ditko, and Kirby)[19]

The subjects of Pinzón's photograph series are as varied as the super-heroes they represent. Many of the photos marry the iconic costume of the hero with the labor being performed by the subject. Spiderman is a window washer high up on the side of a building, and Superman is a deliveryman with his red cape flying behind him. The Thing, a hero transformed into a rock, is ironically now a demolition work-er. Aquaman slices up fish, while the Human Torch uses fire from a stove to cook. The elastic powers of Mr. Fantastic now function to help serve customers in a restaurant, while the Incredible Hulk's muscles are used to load and unload boxes from a greengrocer truck. The Green Lantern watches over a construction site, working as a super-intendent, a *velador*—a play on the Spanish word, which has mul-tiple meanings, including "superintendent" but also "candleholder" or "one who illuminates." While Batman doesn't have his Batmobile, the importance of his vehicle remains present, as he now drives a cab. All of these superhero representations correspond in interesting ways to the labor being performed by the workers—forms of labor many would consider menial and unimportant, but labor necessary for the functioning of a global city. Four of the other male superheroes, how-ever, are represented performing actions not necessarily connected to their daily labor or their costume, but to other aspects of their lives.

In his photograph, Alvaro Cruz is posed as The Flash, a hero fa-mous for his ability to move with supernatural speed. The use of the Flash costume to allude to his speed helps draw the viewer's gaze to the bright red and yellow body in motion. Cruz is identified as a cook, but his representation is not connected to the labor he performs. Instead, Pinzón shoots Cruz in a line of runners, in mid-stride. What makes the representation distinct is that unlike the other photos, the action of the body is a reference to activity outside of Cruz' labor. The caption informs us that Cruz runs with Los Compadres running team, made up of Mexican immigrants and ex-patriots, part of a New York Running Clubs organization ("New York Area Clubs"). As one looks more closely at the photo, it becomes clear that while Cruz is the only one wearing a costume, he is part of a larger group. The runners in line with him share a similar pose, looking down at their watches, getting ready to time themselves. It would be safe to assume that those runners who are lined up with him are members of Los Compadres. The photograph pushes the viewer to think about the existence of workers outside of their occupations. Cruz, like the other individuals of the series, is more than just his labor.

Cruz is represented as a hero for the remittances he sends home, but his heroism is also in the practice of creating community. The photo bears witness to the existence of community groups who come together for multiple purposes, but share the commonality of their immigrant status. Cruz may be at the center of the photograph, but the staging of the other Compadres runners around him offers a collective shot of various members of the immigrant community, making a marginal community visible and gesturing to the creation of support systems necessary to navigate a space where one's working-class labor is devalued and one's immigrant body is criminalized.

In the series, Pinzón's incorporation of two superheroes famous throughout Latin America, but not necessarily known to a U.S. audience, further expands the convention of the superhero genre. One of the most enduring and endearing characters in Mexican television history is the bumbling superhero El Chapulín Colorado (The Red Grasshopper), created by Roberto Gómez Bolaños. The character was first introduced in the 1970 sketch show *Chespirito* and became so popular that he was given his own weekly show. In the show, the character is used to make fun of the conventions of the superhero genre, as he is neither exceedingly strong nor endowed with supernatural powers, nor even necessarily very smart. He is short and skinny and easily frightened, not the picture one conjures up when first imaging a hero. Stumbling through clues, attempting to solve crimes and mysteries, El Chapulín Colorado is a laughable but lovable character who, while not a traditional superhero, always works toward a greater good.

In *Superheroes*, Adalberto Lara, an immigrant construction worker, is El Chapulín. Lara is photographed pushing a wheelbarrow in the middle of a construction site, and the tomfoolery that normally surrounds the character is completely absent. In his hand, Lara carries El Chapulín's traditional weapon, his squeaky red mallet, but he is also holding onto the wheelbarrow, one tool of Lara's trade. In the television series, the mallet used to foil the bad guys is now rendered obsolete. In the same way in which El Chapulín revises the image of what a hero looks like, Lara as a construction worker revises the meaning of heroic acts through his labor and remittances. In the photo, there is also a high level of irony in the fact that a character known as clumsy and uncoordinated is now a worker who must always be cautious on the worksite. Instead of destroying things in his path, this Chapulín is responsible for the building of structures that help create the city he inhabits—a city that disavows his existence. Lara visually represents a long history of immigrants helping to construct the infrastructure of cities. He is performing the labor portrayed in traditional narratives like *Pocho* and *Christ in Concrete*.

Another photograph in the series that incorporates a hero from outside of the U.S. context is the photo of José Rosendo de Jesús dressed as the masked wrestler El Santo. For those who grew up watching *lucha libre* (Mexican wrestling), Santo is an easily recognized figure whose popularity and fame extended well beyond the wrestling arena. He appeared as a crime fighter in over fifty *lucha libre* films (Levi 103). Living up to his name (which translates to "Saint"), Santo was a crusader for justice, fighting evil on the big screen while defeating lesser wrestlers in the ring. Like other superhero figures, the mystery of Santo's true identity, Rodolfo Guzmán Huerta, was a part of his mythology for many years.[20]

Pinzón's casting of Rosendo de Jesús, whose occupation is union organizing, in the role of Santo makes a powerful statement about the quest for justice.[21] As an advocate for workers' rights, Rosendo de Jesús' labor is part of a collective effort for the greater good of a specific group.[22] His politics are clearly on display and go beyond the issue of labor rights. The sign held up by this Santo reads "Mission Not Accomplished." This is a critical rebuttal of the "Mission Accomplished" banner that flew behind President George W. Bush during his announcement that major combat operations in Iraq had ended in success.[23] The message of the speech and the banner were strongly critiqued for their premature message of victory, especially in light of the violence that escalated after the announcement (Kuhn). Santo's revisionist sign is a strong critique of Bush's failed foreign policies and connects the consequences of unsuccessful policies abroad and the deteriorating working conditions of laborers in the United States. Like the superhero who must step in when the nation cannot protect its citizens, Santo, in his role as union organizer, steps in when the U.S. government fails the working masses. The photograph of Rosendo de Jesús as Santo expands his heroism beyond the remittances he sends home and represents his labor as a union organizer as a form of economic justice, an activism worthy of admiration.

In her decision to incorporate two Mexican mythic figures into the exhibit, Pinzón expands not only our notions of what makes one a superhero, but also the construction of the superhero as "American." Even though the two immigrant workers in these particular costumes are displayed alongside other racialized working bodies, they stand out from those in the more traditional superhero costumes. While many audience members who are unfamiliar with El Chapulín or Santo might be puzzled by their incorporation in the series, for those audience members who know these Mexican superheroes, the photos act as a potent form of cultural intervention. The photographs incorporate a different history and construction of heroism that is most often known only to those who remain in the margins of popular representation.[24] The images of El Chapulín and Santo incorporate non-U.S. bodies into the mythology of the American superhero and, as a result, create a more transnational construction of heroic figures. Including these two Mexican figures in the series is one more way in which Pinzón disrupts her audience's assumptions and encourages a national re-imagining of the meaning behind certain forms of labor, especially labor most often rendered invisible.

While audiences will be familiar with the image of an immigrant as a domestic worker, a construction worker, or a waitperson, the one occupation most will have never thought about is that of the sex worker. The construction of sex work as illicit has ensured the continuation of silence around this occupation. One of the most interesting and potentially controversial photographs in Pinzón's installation is the representation of Ernesto Mendez, a sex worker in Times Square, as Robin, Batman's traditional sidekick.[25] The ironic use of the Robin costume is not lost on those who are aware of the sexual ambiguity that has plagued the Boy Wonder. Since the 1954 publication of Fredric Wertham's *Seduction of the Innocent*, Robin has been the subject of speculation and homophobic mocking.[26] In this representation of Robin, his sexuality is placed front and center, and while we do not know the gender of his clientele, we do know that his occupation is based on his ability to market his body. The clever staging of the photo offers multiple ways to read his labor. Mendez is shot leaning on a streetlight, looking up at a sign for a business whose name begins with "Peep" and which sells books and videos. While the viewer cannot clearly make out what Mendez is facing, the object behind him, a police cruiser, is clearly visible. The juxtaposition of Mendez' body between the police car and what we can safely assume is an adult-entertainment store is fascinating, as it makes a strong statement about the position of Mendez' labor as a sex worker and its presence in spite of its prohibited nature. The inclusion of the police cruiser functions as a reminder of the criminalization of Mendez' work but can also be read as the inability of city officials to fully control the activities of one of the city's most popular tourist destinations. The shiny construction of Times Square—with its glowing billboards and flashing lights—as a tourist destination and center of urban life is based on the erasure of activities that do not fit into the postcard image of the site. Like the Statue of Liberty, Times Square sells a specific image of the city—one of light and glamour. The fact that Mendez' labor takes place in this constructed space encourages the audience to see beyond the happy, shiny image of Times Square, just like his immigrant narrative pushes the audience to look beneath the ideology perpetuated by the Statue of Liberty. Instead, Pinzón's representation of Robin and Times Square strips the audience of previously conceived images of both labor and space.

Robin as sex worker offers an important intervention for the ways in which sex work is framed within popular discourse. One could argue that by representing a form of labor illegal in the state of New York, Pinzón's series runs the danger of reinforcing the stereotype of immigrant workers as criminals. However, by shooting Mendez as Robin, a "good guy," Pinzón refuses to perpetuate the ideology that positions sex workers as immoral and their labor as illicit. The incorporation of the photo in the superhero series rejects the negative moralization of Mendez' occupation and instead positions his work within a larger immigrant labor force. In Pinzón's work, Mendez as Robin is moralized as a hero because his labor results in the remittances he sends home. Mendez' working body also challenges the gendered discourse of sex work that assumes sex workers are always female, reminding us that sex work, like the issue of immigration, is much more complicated than is represented by the media. Which brings us to the two female figures in the series.

A Differently Gendered Superhero

> We needed a female nemesis to give the strip sex appeal, so we came up with a kind of female batman . . . it was kind of the antithesis of a bat. Cats are hard to understand. They are as erratic as women are.
>
> » Bob Kane, quoted in *Catwoman* (Colón 16)

Few comic book figures are as conflicted or contradictory in nature as Batman's nemesis/love interest Catwoman. Known for her seductive gait and witty comebacks, Catwoman straddles the line between good and evil, never easily inhabiting either. Sex worker, thief, and kick-ass vigilante, Catwoman is a mysterious figure that embodies the ambiguous gray space between right and wrong. The famous character, whose alter ego is Selina Kyle, first appeared in 1940. Created by Bill Finger and Bob Kane, Catwoman, introduced as "the Cat" in the first Batman comic (1940), was initially a burglar and jewel thief (Colón 15). As with other comic book figures, Catwoman's character is written by several writers, has multiple origin stories, and is subject to various interpretations.[27] In Frank Miller's 1987 comic book, *Batman: Year One*, Catwoman is a more independent figure, a sex worker who comes from a dysfunctional family and trains in martial arts to defend herself from an abusive pimp. Regardless of which origin story one prefers, Catwoman is a complex female character who is capable of taking care of herself and those in her care. She is a combination of strength and vulnerability—characteristics that captivate Batman and are supposed to be alluring to a mainstream audience.[28]

In Pinzón's series, Minerva Valencia as Catwoman is no longer the dark, sexually alluring figure from the comics or big screen. While she wears an all-black costume, the danger associated with the traditional leather costume and whip is absent. In its stead, we have a maternal nanny figure, a woman paid for her care work. The female character whose life on the street comes as a result of a dysfunctional family life is now represented as being responsible for the well-being of someone else's children. While the choice to cast a vigilante sex worker encased in leather as a nanny might seem contradictory, Pinzón's choice of using the figure of Catwoman to illustrate care work functions with the superhero's need to protect those less fortunate.[29] The photograph takes us into the domestic space in which Valencia labors and we witness a brief moment of her interactions with her young wards. The juxtaposition of the two small white children against the darkness of Valencia's clothing works to highlight the racial difference between the children and their nanny.[30] As she holds one child in her arms, the young girl at her side reaches up, seeking Valencia's attention. While the photo is staged, the audience still gets a glimpse of the multiple demands placed on this Catwoman. The importance of Catwoman as nanny captured inside of the domestic space is clear when one considers the invisibility of the work performed in the home by immigrant laborers. The care work she performs is devalued because of its gendered nature, while the racial hierarchy that dictates the value of nannies creates a wage hierarchy that most deeply affects immigrant workers. It is also an ironic representation of Catwoman, the fierce and free-spirited woman who rejects convention and refuses to be "housetrained."

Valencia is one of countless domestic workers whose labor remains marginalized and hidden behind the discourse of the privacy of the home. The constructed division between the private and public spheres has benefited a labor structure mired in gender stereotypes and hierarchies. The few times the public intrudes on the private practice of having a nanny occurs when high-profile individuals are caught in scandals. Several prominent politicians have seen their aspirations for public office waylaid by the public revelation of their employment practices. Secretary of Labor candidate Linda Chavez, California Senate candidate Michael Huffington, and California gubernatorial candidate Meg Whitman have all been faced with the challenge of defending to voters and fellow politicians their employment of undocumented immigrant domestic workers (Grier 2010).

141

While the practice of hiring undocumented laborers is a widespread and common one, it is only when public figures are discovered employing these workers that the issue comes under media scrutiny. Unfortunately, most of the time the workers remain marginal to the story as the focus remains on the politician.[31]

The antithesis to bad girl Catwoman is, of course, the good girl Wonder Woman, the most famous female action hero in the world of U.S. comics. Created in 1941 by psychologist William Mouton Marston, Wonder Woman was supposed to embody the strength of Superman, but with the "allure of a good and beautiful woman" in order to appeal to readers (Marston, quoted in Daniels 58). Wonder Woman's origin story begins on Paradise Island, a mythical place inhabited by Amazons. After Captain Steve Trevor crashes on the island, the queen decides to send Diana, her daughter and best warrior, to America to help protect democracy. Using the alias "Diana Prince," Wonder Woman battles foes with her supernatural strength and her golden lasso (Daniels 60–63). With her star-spangled briefs and her red-and-white costume, she is the female representation of the American patriotic superhero. Known as much for her sex appeal as she is for her powers, Wonder Woman continues to enjoy a high level of popularity and remains the best-known female superhero in the world of comics.

In Pinzón's work, Wonder Woman has been transformed into Maria Luisa Romero, a commercial laundry employee. Gone are Wonder Woman's invisible jet and her golden lasso of truth, replaced by industrial-strength laundry machines. Like the photograph of Catwoman, Romero's picture makes visible a gendered form of labor that most often takes place within the private space of the home. The audience witnesses her placing clothing into a washing machine while wearing Wonder Woman's iconic costume. Unlike Valencia, whose attention is firmly fixed on the young child in her arms, Romero's attention is not focused on her actions. Instead, we get a picture of a pensive Wonder Woman, staring off into the distance while automatically performing her task. The industrial machines behind her illustrate the movement of a form of labor previously performed in the home to one now being completed in the public space. The Laundromat is a classed space where working-class individuals who lack the space or funds for washing machines must wash their laundry. The Laundromat has also become the place where those who are too busy or who have the privilege of extra funds pay someone else, like Romero, to wash their laundry. As a space, the Laundromat mirrors the multiple meanings around class, gender, and labor that Romero's work embodies.

Even though Marston's Wonder Woman is an immigrant from Paradise Island, her belonging in the nation is never called into question. No one asks for her papers or makes mention of her immigrant status. As a racialized body, however, Pinzón's Wonder Woman is much more suspect. Interestingly enough, the most famous live-action representation of Wonder Woman is Lynda Carter's in the television series *The New Adventures of Wonder Woman* (1975–1979). Carter, whose real name is Linda Jean Cordóva Carter, was born in Phoenix, Arizona, to an Irish American father and a Mexican American mother ("Lynda Carter"). Though she is half Latina, Carter is not visibly marked as Latina. Even though she has never made a secret of her Latina background, her light skin and green eyes allow an audience to construct her as white.[32]

The irony of Wonder Woman performing domestic labor is also not lost on those familiar with the superhero's history. Her superhero activities outside of the private space of the home caused anxiety for many readers at the time of her creation. In her reading of Diana Prince, Roz Kaveney argues that "Wonder Woman was so very obviously a feminist icon that she was condemned by Wertham as a possible lesbian role model from a post–Second World War perspective in which any woman who stepped outside the home and pursued a career was seen as suspect" (18).[33] For individuals like Wertham— the same critic who found Robin's sexuality so dangerous—Wonder Woman's visible presence outside of the domestic sphere gestures toward a challenge to established gender roles. The rejection of the traditional role of housewife gets equated with a rejection of heterosexuality, because, according to Wertham, only a lesbian would ever want to leave the haven of the domestic space. In a similar way in which Pinzón's Catwoman has been enclosed in the domestic space, her Wonder Woman is confined to perform gendered labor in the Laundromat. Unlike middle-class white women, these modern-day immigrant superheroes do not have the privilege of staying in their own homes, but must perform their traditionally gendered labor for others.[34] The photographs illustrate the ways in which the occupational choices of these immigrant workers are limited by their gender, race, and immigrant status.

Another important difference between Pinzón's subjects and the popular superheroes lies in their images. Unlike the superheroes they portray, Romero and Valencia are not reduced to sexualized bodies. As Kaveney points out, "Iconographically, almost all superheroes are good-looking and muscular, and wear costumes that emphasize the fact" (10). For female superheroes, the emphasis on their bodies is magnified by their overall lack of clothing. Pinzón's images reject the practice of placing female bodies in skimpy costumes to appeal to a male audience and, at the same time, refuse to perpetuate the racist stereotype of the hot Latina domestic worker. These women are not glamorous or mysterious or invisible. Their bodies do not represent the Hollywood ideal of beauty or the comic book–drawn temptress. Pinzón's female superheroes are also not defined by their relationships with men—there is no Batman or Captain Trevor. Instead, we get real women with real bodies who put a human face on labor that is most often relegated to the margins. In both of these photographs, the women are captured performing gendered labor, work that becomes visible through the snapshots. The photographs of these female superheroes remind one of the ways in which female immigrants are most often confined to working in labor sectors deemed "feminine." The separation between public/private and male/female continues to operate in more nuanced ways in a larger global context.

At first glance, it might seem like Pinzón's *Superheroes* is skewed in its representation of superheroes as male—especially considering the incorporation of only two female figures. In her article "The Rise and Fall of the 'Migrant Superhero' and the New 'Deportee Trash,'" Ninna Nyberg Sorensen critiques Pinzón's lack of females in the series and argues that the representations reinforce the "popular and official images of the migrant superhero in form of a masculine character" (107). For Nyberg Sorensen, the image of Valencia as Catwoman is not a positive one, but instead represents "an anti-heroine rather than a contributor to development . . . a woman taking care of other women's children, leaving her own behind" (15). The critique doesn't take into consideration the complexity of Catwoman's character and overlooks several important factors, including the lack of female heroes in the public imaginary and the concentration of immigrant female workers in specific occupations and in specific spaces. While superheroes like Batman, Superman, and the Incredible Hulk have enjoyed multiple Hollywood film treatments, the Wonder Woman film project remains in limbo and films centering on female superheroes (e.g., Catwoman, Elektra) have bombed at the box office.[35] The lack of successful female heroes on the big screen is indicative of the gendered nature of the genre. One could blame Pinzón for her lack of female superheroes in the series, but the lack of popular female superheroes in the public consciousness makes an analysis of her representation of Catwoman and Wonder Woman a more useful project. One must also be cognizant of the fact that much of the labor performed by immigrants continues to exist in heavily gendered and segregated spaces. Male immigrants are hired to work in diverse public spaces, while female immigrants predominate in labor that takes place in the more private—and hidden—domestic spaces, which limits the number of possible occupations that can be represented. There is also no specific mention of a family Valencia has left behind, and it is problematic to assume that just because she is a female immigrant, she is a mother who has left her children.

The series also provides an interesting glimpse into the question of documented/undocumented labor and the public debate that surrounds this contentious issue. Pinzón does not specify in the photo series or in her artist statement the immigration status of the workers she photographs.[36] In this absence, audience members have created their own narrative. The photographs have been written about extensively in blogs and online articles. The comments made by readers of various sites reveal tremendous xenophobia around the issue of immigration. Included in the comments are a number of statements regarding the "illegal" status of the workers in the photo series.[37] Many of those who view the series jump to the false conclusion regarding the documented status of the subjects, assuming that because they are immigrant workers they must be undocumented. Perhaps this assumption is based on the fact that these immigrants remain so closely linked to their country of origin. Many people have accepted the traditional immigrant narrative's message that once an immigrant migrates to the United States, she cuts off all connections to her past. Or perhaps in our current moment, individuals are being conditioned to view all immigrants from south of the border as potentially undocumented and therefore criminal.

The disturbing assumptions made about the subjects of Pinzón's series are indicative of a growing anti-immigrant movement in the United States today. The passage of legislation like Arizona's SB 1070 and the vitriol that surrounds the debates around immigration reform have led to the resurgence in the media of the image of the dangerous "illegal immigrant." For many, "undocumented" means "criminals" taking away "American" jobs, and draining "our" resources. The current backlash against Latin@ workers is nothing new and has occurred at multiple times in our history; what makes it different today is the ease with which negative images of immigrants are circulated through the traditional media and the Internet.[38] The technology that now allows for the dissemination of Pinzón's oppositional images is the same technology that circulates xenophobic messages. With the existence of these racist images and the fanning of these racial fears, it is hardly surprising that audience members would assume the individuals in Pinzón's series are undocumented. While identifying them as documented would clear up the issue for some, it wouldn't necessarily resolve the xenophobic lens through which immigrant workers are viewed today. At the same time, however, Pinzón's photographs encourage a more multifaceted dialogue and complicate the debate around immigrant labor. By representing the immigrant worker as a crime-fighting superhero, Pinzón critiques the simplistic media construction of immigrants as inherently immoral.

While it is dangerous to position individuals in a realm where they are superior to others, or to romanticize hardship, Pinzón's series doesn't attribute any superhuman characteristics to her heroes. The superheroes in her series have been stripped of the glamour associated with having super powers and secret identities. There is an absence of wealth and power. Instead, she makes their everyday labor—most often represented as menial and degrading—worthy of admiration.[39] Her series employs the power of photography to create new narratives of immigration that reject the simplistic organizing structure of the traditional immigrant story. The story the series provides viewers is one of opposition that seeks to make visible a complex system of labor and immigration that benefits transnational structures of power. The power of supranational systems to render invisible the working bodies that provide the labor and capital necessary for their everyday survival is uncovered by the photographs of these modern-day superheroes.

"Las Super Domésticas"—No Phone Booth Necessary

> Experience first generated through the body returns to the body in the flesh of the staged performance . . . Theater requires the body to make testimony and requires other bodies to bear witness to it.
>
> » Cherríe Moraga, "An Irrevocable Promise" (45)

In her documentary *Maid in America*, filmmaker Anayansi Prado portrays the use of the superhero figure by domestic workers in resisting exploitation. As discussed in chapter 2, the documentary offers a powerful counternarrative to stereotypical representations of domestic labor and immigration. More than just offering an alternative image of domestic labor, the film also records the efforts of community organizers to educate and empower workers. Prado's filming of Eva's daily life leads to the documentation of the creation of a new superhero: "Super Doméstica." The creation of a community organizer, Super Doméstica is a character that fights for the rights of domestic workers and becomes a teaching tool and figure of resistance. I focus specifically on the use of Super Doméstica to illustrate the possibilities of using superhero rhetoric to empower marginalized workers. The use of the superhero figure by organizations like CHIRLA demonstrates the possibilities for resistance that such rhetoric can inspire.

Prado uses screen captions to linguistically disrupt discourses of invisibility. The first screen caption informs viewers that over one hundred thousand domestic workers labor in the city of Los Angeles. For many, these workers go unnoticed, discernible only as they get on and off the buses that traverse the classed spaces of the sprawling city. The documentary, however, dismisses the common misconception that these workers are simply "happy domestics" or "submissive servants." The audience is witness to the celebration of Domestic Workers Appreciation Day/Feliz Dia de la Trabajadora Domestica, a day designated by the California Assembly for the acknowledgment of the contributions of domestic workers to the state. The designation came about as a declaration, titled Las Super Domésticas, signed by Assemblyman Gilbert Cedillo in 2002.[40]

The real importance of the holiday has nothing to do with the politicians, but instead highlights domestic workers using the day to come together to celebrate their labor and strengthen networks of support. The documentary follows Eva on her first time attending the festivities surrounding the day. For her, it becomes a space in which to make connections with other women like her. Eva vocalizes the isolation of her labor and the ways in which the domestic space encloses one's labor experiences. She explains to the camera that the celebration gives them an opportunity to come together to "talk about what we want to do, that we want to make changes. Just one big voice." The notion of having a unified voice is an important one as it allows for the creation of activism that transcends the isolating structure of domestic labor. The sharing of individual stories of economic and labor hardship promotes the creation of a community narrative of opposition. Through the sharing of their experiences and the creation of a movement for workers' rights, the appreciation day becomes more than a simple day of food and dancing. These women are taking over a public space to make visible the working conditions occurring in the enclosed private space of the home. A few minutes later, the documentary bears witness to the organization that comes about from such gatherings.

The gathering of workers for the purpose of sharing stories of resistance and opposition is a powerful strategy in the organization of labor movements. One of the most powerful scenes of the film occurs as a group of domestic workers practice a play. The piece, written by Eulalia, a retired domestic worker, is based on her experience with an abusive employer. While she might seem like an unlikely storyteller in the mainstream image of cultural producers, Eulalia relies on her own individual oppositional narrative to create a story of resistance for an entire community.[41] The action of the play follows a domestic worker whose employer throws hot coffee in her face and then reports her to the police and to immigration services. Even though she is the one who has been assaulted, we watch as her character begs the abusive employer to forgive her. As she is about to be arrested, Super Doméstica, played by Eva, jumps into the scene and protects her from the immigration official. With her red cape and skirt, she proudly proclaims: "I'm here to defend her. I'm the Super Doméstica!" As she fights off the immigration official, Super Doméstica rejects the claim that as an undocumented immigrant, the domestic worker has no rights. She challenges the authority of the state agent to define justice. Instead, Super Doméstica informs the official and the audience that Eulalia's character "has rights in this country as a worker. And all over the world as a human being." Eva, having taken the persona of superhero, becomes a crusader for justice—she steps in when the nation fails to protect the human rights of individuals. She does not need a fancy costume, just a simple cape and skirt over plain black pants and shirt. Like Pinzón's female superheroes, there is no sexualization of the female body or fetishization of her strength. She lacks the superhuman strength or supernatural abilities of traditional superheroes, but she is not powerless. Her powers come from the strength of her message: all workers have rights, regardless of their immigration status, and all workers deserve to be treated as human beings.

Instead of just playing hero, Super Doméstica democratizes the superhero status by passing on the strength of her knowledge and imparting the domestic worker with the power to advocate for other immigrant workers. Before leaving, Super Doméstica bestows upon Eulalia's character a red cape and declares: "I now pronounce you a Super Doméstica. And you will be an example for those who are facing similar situations." The play connects the exploitation of workers to an immigration structure that privileges employers and makes abuses like the one witnessed in the production a systemic problem. The romantic and problematic notion of immigration leading to a better life for the immigrant is summarily rejected. Instead, it makes visible the abuse that domestic workers face and the fact that the threat of deportation and fear of immigration officials keep many workers from reporting abuse. The production makes the audience, both the one watching the play and the one viewing the documentary, aware of the working conditions that take place behind closed doors.

While the play might seem simple, the message behind it is far more complex. The play functions as a teaching tool that helps immigrant laborers learn about their rights as workers. It is a modern *acto*, keeping alive the tradition of joining performance and a call for change to create activist theater.[42] Eulalia's play is part of a legacy of using performance to inspire change. Her *acto* is a current version of the type of activist theater created by groups such as Teatro Campesino, whose works were instrumental in organizing migrant laborers for the United Farm Workers. In his work on Chicano theater, theater scholar Jorge Huerta argues,

> Even from the beginning of what we can call contemporary Chicano theatre, this was a theatre movement based on the need to make a difference in the community, not through Art but through Action. Social action, political action—any kind of action and activism that could educate and motivate first the community members themselves, and then, if possible, members of the broader society. (4)

While the *actos* performed by Teatro Campesino were, for the most part, witnessed only by those in attendance at their live performances, the audience of Eulalia's *acto* is greatly multiplied because it appears in the documentary. The larger dissemination of the production illustrates the role that technology plays in spreading narratives of opposition. As an audience, we are witness to an act of resistance without having to physically inhabit the space of production. Eulalia's message of solidarity, immigration, economic justice, and human rights transcends the limitations of live theater and gestures to the disruptive possibilities of alternative narratives of heroism.

Like Pinzón's series, the character of Super Doméstica positions ordinary workers as extraordinary human beings because of the labor they perform. Pinzón's photography encourages her audience to rethink their notions of superheroes and immigrant laborers, while the play Prado's documentary captures encourages its audience to become like Super Doméstica and advocate for the rights of immigrant domestic workers. Both provide alternative representations of immigration and labor that reject the stereotypical mainstream portrayals of Latina domestic workers and offer models for using technology to spread messages of resistance and opposition. When the state fails to protect the most vulnerable, new and re-imagined superheroes are needed to step in.

Hiding in Plain Sight: Double Agent Sirvienta

> The advantage of the disadvantaged opponent lies in [DAS's] mobility, flexibility, and speed against the interest of the socially authorized, and through a parasitical kind of squatting on the institutionalized social space that is denied her.
>
> » Laura E. Pérez, *Chicana Art* (187)

In her multimedia series *Double Agent Sirvienta*, Chicana artist Laura Alvarez provides her audience with a powerful image of an immigrant woman who uses the invisibility of domestic labor to infiltrate multiple spaces. Employing the figure of the "costumed superhero" is a visually striking strategy that gets an audience to question its assumptions about the definition of a "hero." In her Double Agent Sirvienta (DAS) series, however, Alvarez positions the traditional maid's uniform, rather than a bright and form-fitting costume, as an important tool in her hero's missions. In her discussion of Batman's nonsupernatural powers, cultural commentator Roz Kaveney argues that "a substantial minority of people without powers . . . share a commitment to the superhero mission, so they are generally regarded as superheroes in spite of their absence of such powers" (4). Like Batman, DAS utilizes technology and gadgets to fight for justice—overcoming the physical limitations of a nonsupernatural body. By using the cover of a domestic worker, a *sirvienta*, which means "servant" or "maid" in Spanish, Alvarez' character is able to infiltrate the private sphere of the home and perform actions that subvert structures of power. The multimedia series is a combination of paintings, prints, films, installations, and songs, creating a rich narrative through Alvarez' ability to employ technology and multiple artistic media.[43] In expanding her story beyond the traditional canvas, Alvarez creates a hybrid, multilayered narrative that uses the conventions of comics and espionage tales to provide her audience with an alternative version of the mysterious double agent.

DAS is, to invoke Gloria Anzaldúa's term, a "border crosser," one who is able to successfully navigate the differences that arise from constructed national boundaries.[44] She is an immigrant who works on both sides of the border and takes advantage of the invisibility of domestic workers in the United States and Mexico to carry out her missions. Her ability to negotiate international spaces makes her particularly suited for the type of intelligence work that seeks to uncover capitalist networks that remain unfettered by national borders.[45] While popular spy figures, like James Bond, use male privilege and visibility to navigate spaces in the interests of official governments, DAS uses the invisibility of her racialized working body to challenge the authority of the two nation-states she inhabits.

Alvarez' decision to locate the DAS series in Mexico and the United States focuses attention on the connections between the corporate interests of the two governments. DAS's undercover work in the private sphere also makes public the labor structure that exists within the domestic space of the home. As Chicana scholar Laura E. Pérez has argued, the DAS series "brings attention to the ways in which the social space of the home is inhabited, gendered, and racialized, from the perspective of the domestic servant" (181). The character DAS is a telenovela actor who has been relegated to playing the role of "servant" on the show. Instead of relying on her popularity to continue her work in telenovelas, DAS learns to use the character she plays to infiltrate various spaces.

Much of DAS's story is told through a rock opera, whose multiple songs Alvarez has made available for her audience on her website. In "Cuidad Soñada" we learn that the young woman has won the guest role on a telenovela through a contest and she leaves her "small colonial town" for Mexico City. The metropolis proves to be a large disappointment as she is typecast, playing only the role of *sirvienta*, and falls in love with a director who not only is ashamed of her low class background, but also hides his marital status. Disillusioned and heartbroken, DAS attempts to find a way of making her life meaningful. In "Bongos Novela," we learn that she is taken to a café, "where she meets socialists, revolutionary taxi drivers, and yoga teachers. She learns of a secret society infiltrating into the forbidden zones of corporations and oppressive zip codes, stealing secrets and blackmailing authorities for the demands of the less fortunate. Inspired and in a moment of clarity, she decides to change the course of her life." DAS becomes a part of this resistance group, which meets at Café Segue, where espresso is served with "sabor a movimiento" (the flavor of a movement), plans are made, and "timers and electricity, alarms, intercepting intra-office email, mobilizing the masses" are discussed ("Café Segue").

While the audience cannot see her specific actions, through her rock opera songs Alvarez provides details of DAS's missions and adventures. The common practice of individuals' ignoring service workers functions in her favor as she is able to use her invisibility to move freely within the private spaces of her targets. She employs the tools of the trade to disguise her actions: "I've opened top secret briefcases with a plunger, y he copiado data con my squeegee scanner, I've hidden what my duster's doing from all those heat activated ojos" ("Mi Corazón"). DAS relies on the fact that most employers would never look twice at cleaning objects like plungers and dusters to avert suspicion and carry out her missions. Her computer-hacking skills are disguised by her acting skills and the assumptions that get made because of her servant's uniform.[46] Through her use of uniform, tools, and transportation, Alvarez is able to create a character capable of navigating exclusive spaces in missions aimed at disrupting a structure that keeps corporations and certain individuals in power.[47]

Like the images presented by Pinzón, Alvarez' DAS art pieces offer alternative representations of Latina immigrants and domestic labor. Even though the narrative of DAS is more fully understood through knowledge of the pieces in the multiple formats that Alvarez employs, the visual pieces provide powerful images of resistance and activism and can stand alone. In her piece *Blow Up the Hard Drive*, an 18 × 26 in. limited-edition silkscreen created in 1999, Alvarez provides an image of DAS performing her computer hacking while under the cover of being a domestic worker. The silkscreen is framed on top with the format of a file folder, with the label "File://Translations.underdone," while computer code surrounds DAS and her apron. The name of the file is significant in how it alters the electronic extension of the file, "underdone," and in the process points to the incomplete translation. The flames in the background allude to the "blowing up," the explosion of data DAS is performing on the computer hard drive. The apron, normally associated with cooking and the space of the kitchen, has at its center what appears to be a microchip. In discussing DAS's body and dress, Pérez argues that "within the double metaphor of the social body as text, dress and body ornamentations are writing on the body, and about it" (51). Unlike the popular representation of Latina immigrants as uneducated and premodern, DAS is well versed in the sophisticated computer code necessary to perform her hacking activities. Indeed, it is her technological savvy, combined with her talent for hiding in plain sight, that give DAS the ability to destroy the information the Café Segue group deems dangerous. The image of DAS, in her maid's uniform, performing a task requiring highly developed skills, offers a rejection of the image of Latina immigrants as "happy domestics" or "hot Latinas." The heat that surrounds DAS has nothing to do with her body or appearance, but with the act of resistance she is performing.

The power of DAS to use technology and deconstruction/destruction to her advantage is evident in multiple pieces. Alvarez provides another image of DAS blowing things up in her painting *I'm with My Nanny*. The piece, a mixture of acrylic, watercolor, paper, ink, and plexiglass on panel, also created in 1999, portrays DAS with a child in her arms, running away from what appear to be small blue bombs. The title of the piece is a reference to the phrase written on the outfit worn by the child and alludes to DAS's multiple roles as domestic worker and the fact that while she might be seen as the "sirvienta," she also plays the role of nanny.[48] As with *Blow Up the Hard Drive*, DAS is framed in the background by flames, again alluding to the destruction of an object or space. This image, however, points to a much more physical blowing up of a space. The viewer does not know if the space she is destroying is public or private, but her domestic worker's uniform renders her invisible to allow for her navigation and transformation of either. She blurs the boundaries between public and private with her presence and her actions. In addition to destabilizing

Laura Alvarez, *Blow Up the Hard Drive*, copyright © 1999. Silkscreen, 26 × 18 in.
(Courtesy of Laura Alvarez.)

the private/public binary, the picture also offers an image of a hybrid combination of technology and spirituality.

The subtle changes Alvarez makes to the uniform DAS wears intervene in the ideological construction of the domestic worker without sacrificing the mobility the uniform offers.[49] She can still navigate multiple spaces in her working-class uniform but, for those who look more closely, her apron resists the typical homogenization of a uniform. While DAS's apron in the previous image has a computer chip in the center, in this representation, the apron has an image of the Virgen de Guadalupe imprinted on it and small crosses hanging from the edges of the garment.[50] The incorporation of the powerful icon into the art piece connects DAS to a longer historical struggle for social and economic justice and draws on a history of combining Chican@ art and activism.[51] DAS's apron is symbolic of an alternative interpretation of the domestic worker's uniform that relies on and

Laura Alvarez, *I'm with My Nanny*, copyright © 1999. Acrylic, watercolor, paper, ink, and plexiglass on panel, 12 × 12 in. (Courtesy of Laura Alvarez.)

contributes to a legacy of femininity and strength. The art piece combines technology, spirituality, and activism to produce a counternarrative to the traditional image of the uniformed maid.[52]

Alvarez' Guadalupe, however, does not follow the traditional image of femininity and motherhood most often read on the body of the Virgen de Guadalupe. While the posture of this Virgen is similar to that of the traditional Guadalupe, her dress is modern and young. Gone is the long, body-covering gown and in its stead we are given a Guadalupe with a mini dress and tall boots, radiating rays of blue and yellow. Like several Chicana artists, including Ester Hernandez, Yolanda Lopez, Santa Barraza, and Alma López, Alvarez' modernizing of the Virgen de Guadalupe is a revisionist strategy that allows the image of Guadalupe to go beyond the traditional submissive mother figure.[53] The image on DAS's apron connects her indigenous Mexican background and faith with her technological savvy and provides the audience with a transnational modern subject.

It seems no coincidence that DAS would be wearing an image of the Virgen de Guadalupe as she holds the young boy in her arms. The edges of DAS's apron are reminiscent of the rays that surround the Virgen and could be seen as an extension of her power, as she watches over DAS. The modern version of Guadalupe remains a powerful reference to faith and motherhood, and the incorporation of the Virgen into the art piece can also be read as the conflict faced by DAS in having to care for the child while believing in the importance of her mission. The tension between her work as a double agent and her cover as a domestic worker/nanny is visible in the ways in which she holds the child. The young boy is facing the bombs, reaching toward them as he is carried away by DAS. It is almost as if DAS is in danger of being separated from the child by her work. In the musical track "The Journey Continues," DAS vocalizes the conflict she feels: "She adores this little angel sidekick blond baby . . . Is it bad that she is involving an innocent child in missions for the underground? . . . Is it wrong or is it right?" There is no easy answer for DAS, and viewers are left to reach their own conclusions.

One of Alvarez' more recent art pieces incorporates the issue of immigration much more overtly. In *Where Do They Come From? Who Are They? Where Are They Going?*, Alvarez provides three images of DAS with her small charge along with the addition of a male gardener. Created in 2005, vivid blues, greens, and browns dominate the 5 × 8 ft. acrylic-on-canvas painting. While the imagery of fire is missing, the familiar shape of flames is reflected in curving tree branches and roots, which mimic tendrils reaching up. In her maid's uniform, holding the baby, DAS is represented performing multiple covert activities, including passing information on to a fellow agent, fittingly undercover as a gardener. Just as DAS is able to use the cover of domestic labor to "hide in plain sight," her fellow agent employs the stereotype of the Mexican gardener to avoid suspicion. There is a clear division between the naturalist foreground and the looming metropolis in the background. Resting in front of the cityscape is Alvarez' representation of the Virgen de Guadalupe. In a revision of the Virgen figure similar to that seen in *I'm with My Nanny*, this religious figure has the traditional rays emanating from her body and is posed with praying hands. Again, Alvarez' use of the figure of Guadalupe is important as it connects the covert activities of the spies with their indigenous Mexican background. Unlike the traditional image of the Virgen, though, Alvarez' Guadalupe is not looking down, but is instead facing DAS, watching over her. By portraying Guadalupe as watching over DAS, in effect giving her approval, Alvarez destabilizes the right of the state to define truth or justice.

The image might separate the more natural landscape from the looming urban space of the city, but the positioning of the immigrant laboring bodies does not render them as premodern. The title of the image, *Where Do They Come From? Who Are They? Where Are They Going?*, is in direct reference to Paul Gauguin's 1897 oil on canvas, *Where Do We Come From? What Are We? Where Are We Going?*, which many believe to be his masterpiece. The description of the painting at the Boston Museum of Fine Arts, where it is permanently housed, tells of Gauguin's leaving France "for Tahiti, seeking in the South Seas a society that was simpler and more elemental than that of his homeland." The image is comprised of multiple Tahitian figures engaged in various activities, including eating, talking, and reclining. The majority of the figures are Tahitian women, individuals portrayed in Gauguin's primitivist art as parts of a naturalist landscape to be gazed upon. While Alvarez includes elements similar to those in Gauguin's piece, hers rejects the Eurocentric, colonialist gaze through which Gauguin views his subjects. We know the subject of her piece and we see her engaged in covert activities as she performs her duties as nanny. Gone are the static blue religious icon, the frolicking animals, and the exotic nude bodies of the Tahitian women. The mountain behind the icon has been replaced by the looming shadow of the city. Gauguin's version of a pre-Western paradise is summarily rejected for a landscape that gestures to the existence of modern bodies of color within the modern world. Placed in conversation with Alvarez' piece, Gauguin's personal lament for the loss of the "primitive" with the encroachment of "civilization" is revealed as one more example of a white savior fantasy. Alvarez uses her canvas to disrupt the accepted

Laura Alvarez, *Where Do They Come From? Who Are They? Where Are They Going?*, copyright © 2005. Acrylic on canvas, 5 × 8 ft. (From the Collection of Lisa Ellis and Mike LeBuffe.)

practice of portraying bodies of color as primitive and consumable. In its stead, her version offers a narrative of labor, immigration, and resistance that stands in stark opposition to the traditional image of racialized bodies on canvas.

Unlike the representation of immigrant workers as childlike and naïve, at one with nature and unable to fully function in the modern world, the undercover gardener and DAS in her multiple representations are using technology for their own purposes. The use of electronic modes of communication and information sharing witnessed on the canvas highlight their technological skills while alluding to the ways in which the agents use the cover of nature to help fulfill their missions. The images of DAS are not like Gregory Nava's innocent and childlike character Rosa, who, in *El Norte*, cannot operate a washing machine and prefers to wash her employer's clothing by hand in the garden. Instead, DAS's body inhabits the space of the "natural" while employing modern technology, bridging the constructed divide between what is considered modern and premodern.

Alvarez' art is part of this longer history of immigrant-rights activism. The title of the image also speaks to the marginality of immigrant workers and the ways in which these workers are not seen as individuals, but as a mass. The change of the "we" to "they" highlights the dehumanizing "othering" that occurs in linguistic discourse. The

157

visual discourse of Gauguin's art piece might not be as widely disseminated as it was during his time, but the linguistic discourse that "others" racialized bodies continues to grow in popularity in ours. Alvarez' painting also makes reference to some of the anxieties surrounding Latin@ immigrants today and the contradiction between visibility and invisibility. Immigrant workers are fine as long as they labor in silence and remain in the margins. As soon as these racialized bodies become visible, however, mainstream America becomes uncomfortable. The concept of the threatening brown mob, unwilling to or incapable of assimilating, is an ideology that is currently enjoying resurgence.[54]

While it is easy for many to view DAS as a criminal, Alvarez' series encourages her audience to see DAS as a revolutionary, acting on behalf of those who have little agency or access to power. Her actions are aimed at disrupting a transnational web of power that exploits workers for the benefit of the few who run these structures. She embodies the fantasy not of the glamorous spy life or of a hero with super powers, but the hope of the marginalized being able to fight back against injustice.[55] Like Pinzón's subjects, DAS does not embody the traditional superhero, but her quest for justice is itself heroic. It is her actions that define her activism and heroism. She takes on missions that place her in danger for the greater good, not for a government, like the traditional hero, but for an organization comprised of everyday individuals devoted to bettering the lives of the working class. Alvarez' use of technology in the series and in the creation of her art illustrates the oppositional possibilities of employing technology for communicating alternative information. In her description of the series, which appears in the collection *Urban Latino Cultures: La vida latina en L.A.*, Alvarez explains, "The intent is not only to elevate the position of the ethnic domestic worker with irony and humor but also to discuss technology as a symbol or tool of wealth, knowledge, and power" (108). In having DAS use technology in her missions, Alvarez is not only changing the image of the Latina immigrant as premodern, but also disrupting the structure that positions technology as the tool of the powerful.

‡

All four cultural producers discussed in this chapter use technology and the politics of the visual to offer alternative representations of Latina immigrants and domestic labor. Using video to document the educational strategies of CHIRLA, Prado joins Vasquez, Pinzón, and Alvarez in creating alternative narratives of immigration and labor.

These artists offer a version of the immigrant narrative that does not easily fit into the traditional paradigm and, in the process, challenge the story of what immigration is today. In their work, the simplistic image of "America" as the "land of opportunity" is replaced by the realities of labor practices that keep immigrant workers at the bottom rung of the nation's economic ladder. By employing the tools most often used against marginalized communities, they are using technology to communicate a much more global story of mobility, one where connections with countries of origin remain intact and where a simple resolution is nonexistent. Instead of positioning their immigrant status as a negative, these superheroes use their ability to inhabit multiple spaces to help their communities. When discussing the characteristics of comic book superheroes, Kaveney argues, "Superheroes are uncanny and exist at the threshold between states—it is the threshold that is important rather than the states it lies between" (5). In the same way that superheroes learn to navigate the threshold, these immigrants become adept at carving out a place for themselves in the liminal space between national identities. As such, the subjects of Pinzón's, Prado's, and Alvarez' work propose new narratives of immigration that embrace a multiplicity of stories and emphasize the processes of transnational movement in the creation of oppositional stories of labor, gender, and immigration.

Resistance

A Growing Movement

Tenemos más de un año, cerca de dos años [working with UNITE HERE]. Ellos nos estan ayudando. Nos apoyan para hablar con nuestras compañeras para que ellas acepten, y haber como podemos ganar mas respeto para nosotros. Y que nos vemos como lo que somos—personas. Y se que tenemos que trabajar, pero no por eso pueden abusar de nosotras, porque no es justo. Nosotros trabajamos, y ellos nos pagan, pero que no abusen de nosotros. Que nos vean como lo que somos—gente que les ayudan crecer sus negocios.

[We have been working with UNITE HERE for close to two years. They are helping us. They assist us in speaking to female coworkers, to get them to join us, so that we can all gain more respect for ourselves. [They help us organize] so that we can see ourselves for who we are: people. And I know that we have to work, but they [the Hyatt] should not just abuse us because of this [being workers]. Because it is not fair. We work and they pay us, but they shouldn't abuse us. They should see us for what we are—people who help their businesses grow. (My translation)]

» Elvia Claudio[1]

The power of stories to shape our understanding of the world cannot be underestimated. From storybooks, to films, to music, to art, the circulation of narratives helps define who we are as a community—at both the local and the national level. In the United States, the perpetuation of the traditional immigrant narrative has played a vital role in the construction of the nation—a construction that assists in the continual dissemination of unfair stereotypes of and ideologies of worthiness for immigrants. The emphasis on the myth of the American Dream and a meritocratic system of success necessarily excludes those stories that expose the myth for what it is—an illusion. The incorporation of such alternative narratives expands our understanding of the construction of the nation and makes visible the integral roles that labor, gender, and immigration play. While mainstream media might favor the perpetuation of the traditional immigrant story, the circulation of alternative narratives is growing. Immigrant stories of opposition are creating a new Latina genealogy of opposition and resistance. These stories are not confined to the pages in books or to the scenes in Hollywood films. Instead, we see these stories in art, in music, in our own communities. They surround us and play a role in our everyday lives—we just have to learn to recognize them and acknowledge their power.

The counternarratives discussed in this project lead us to think critically of what it means to be a racialized and gendered body and an immigrant subject. Through their attention to the multiple forms of exploitation experienced by Latina immigrants, these stories challenge traditional notions of hard work and perseverance as clear pathways to citizenship and belonging. Through their representation of Chicana/Latina subjects, playwrights like Milcha Sánchez-Scott and Lisa Loomer highlight commonalities between differing groups of Latinas but avoid the practice of flattening the important differences between them. Writers like Esmeralda Santiago and Lucha Corpi remind us that we continue to exist within a racist construction of citizenship and that being Chicana or Puerto Rican means not having the privilege of full citizenship. Cultural producers like Dulce Pinzón, Laura Alvarez, Debora Kuetzpal Vasquez, and Anayansi Prado complicate our visual imagery of immigration and labor while encouraging us to see the possibilities for resistance and acts of everyday heroism in our communities. The narratives of opposition analyzed in the previous chapters continue to expand our theorizing of constructed national borders and help add texture to our understanding of what it means to be a part of a transnational system of labor dependent on the working bodies of poor women everywhere.

I conclude my project with the story of Elvia Claudio, a Hyatt Hotels housekeeper in San Antonio. Claudio's immigrant story is one of hard work and struggle, the kind of narrative that gets excluded from popular representations of immigration. Her story is also an inspiring narrative of resistance and hope, one that challenges our understanding of labor and immigration while expanding the parameters of the genre. Claudio's story is the type of narrative that remains invisible in the mainstream media. She is not like Marisa in *Maid in Manhattan*, waiting patiently for her prince to come save her. A woman of strength, Claudio is proud of the work she performs and strongly believes that workers deserve to labor under fair working conditions. She is actively working to make the Hyatt a better working space for herself, her current coworkers, and the women who will follow once she retires. Claudio is advocating for a system of labor that recognizes the humanity of workers and acknowledges the role that individuals like herself play in running the hotel industry. Her narrative intervenes in the ideological construction of the traditional immigrant story that continues to enjoy so much mainstream popularity.

I met Claudio on the streets of San Antonio during a demonstration against Hyatt in July 2011. Along with union organizers, community activists, and her fellow workers, Claudio was utilizing the national action as a platform to share her story and to publicly reveal what she described as the precarious working conditions that employees of the Hyatt must navigate. While those who actively engage in the right to assemble and voice dissent might be accustomed to seeing diverse groups of people come together at protests, many had not seen what met the crowd gathered in front of the San Antonio Hyatt where the protest was being held. In the middle of the protest were two hotel beds. Conspicuously out of place, the beds blurred the boundaries between the public space of the street on which the crowd gathered, the laboring space in which housekeepers work, and the private space hotel guests see as temporarily their own. Those involved with organizing the action knew the purpose of the beds, but the rest wondered at their significance. Were they a simple representation of the hotel room? Were the beds a prop to more closely connect us to the laboring space of the Hyatt housekeepers? Did the beds signify the contradiction of domestic labor in the transnational space of the hotel industry?

After the participants marched and chanted slogans calling out what they labeled the unfair labor practices of the Hyatt, the meaning of the beds as props became clear. As the demonstrators gathered around the beds, community organizers, union workers, and Hyatt housekeepers made multiple speeches, emphasizing the importance of economic justice. At that point, Claudio and a fellow worker began to make the beds.[2] As the crowd watched the women labor, Claudio conveyed her narrative of pain and injury. Claudio discussed the onset of carpal tunnel syndrome caused by lifting the heavy mattresses to make the hotel beds. She disclosed being diagnosed by a doctor with the syndrome and being placed on medical leave. The doctor's orders for leave, however, were rejected by the hotel administration, she said. She had no choice but to work with her injury. The crowd was told of the administration's policies of increasing the workload of the housekeeping staffers and decreasing the amount of time in which they were expected to complete cleaning a room. Similar to a speed-up on a manufacturing assembly line, Hyatt housekeepers, according to the labor union UNITE HERE, were being expected to clean more rooms in less time to increase the amount of production—in this case, clean rooms. Formulated as a form of street theater, Claudio's words and actions weaved a story that publicly broke the silence and reversed the invisibility surrounding domestic labor in the hotel industry.

The use of street theater in the action against Hyatt made several important interventions. Claudio's story bore witness to the labor practices of hotels that place their workers at risk for injuries. It made visible the dehumanizing tradition of casting workers as machines, whose labor output can be simply sped up to increase productivity. Her words and actions made public the private labor performed by immigrant women in the hotel room—a labor we don't see performed. Most hotel guests return to their rooms to be greeted by clean towels and neatly made beds—the results of a labor executed by the nameless women pushing carts along the hallway. The making of the beds on the street shattered the divide between the public and the private—a divide necessary for the hospitality industry's construction of the hotel room as a sort of "home away from home." People who stay in hotels are supposed to enjoy the comforts of home, without the responsibilities of caring for it. They are encouraged to rely on the labor of workers who create this space for them, while remaining invisible. Claudio's words and actions reject the erasure and hold the Hyatt responsible for her exploitation. Her story offers an opposition to industry practices meant to render her voice silent. The public action provided Claudio and her fellow workers the platform from which to share their stories.

Elvia Claudio's story is not the type of immigrant narrative we see represented in the mainstream. A Mexican immigrant, Claudio has worked for the Hyatt for a decade. In that time, she has witnessed the changes the hotel administration has made. In a personal interview, Claudio recalled the shift in the administration's priorities—a shift that encouraged workers to take shortcuts to meet the new room quotas. When customers began to complain, however, the tasks they were initially told were no longer their responsibility were once again added to their workload. Claudio told me how housekeepers now average thirty rooms per shift and are supposed to spend only eight minutes on each room. "En ocho minutos ... tenemos que lavar el baño, limpiar el piso para que no haya pelo en el piso, tenemos que sacudir y tenemos que fijarnos en los detalles para que el cuarto quede aceptable" (In eight minutes ... we have to wash the bathroom, clean the floor and make sure there is no hair on the floor, we have to dust and take care of all the details to make sure the room is acceptable [my translation]). Unfortunately, the increased number of rooms needing to be cleaned, combined with the decreased time allotted, has resulted in added pressure on the housekeeping staff. The labor practices of the hotel, however, are visible only to those who perform the labor and those who are working to change it. The hotel guests have no idea that the women who clean up after them are rushing from room to room to make sure their stay is a pleasant one.

The corporal toll on the women who work as housekeepers in the hotel industry cannot be underestimated. The physicality of the labor, the amount of work required, and the time constraints are a recipe for injuries. Claudio not only suffers from carpal tunnel syndrome, but also has fallen in her rush to clean bathrooms. She tells me,

> *Muchas tenemos que trabajar más a prisa. Tenemos que andar corriendo todo el dia. Y a causa de eso, tenemos accidentes, y siempre estamos cansadisimas, tenemos que estar tomando cualquier pastilla para ayudarnos descansar nuestro cuerpo, porque si no, no podemos levantarnos el proximo dia. Es muy pesado ya para nosotras.*
>
> [A lot of us women have to work very fast. We run around all day. Because of this, we have accidents, we are always tired, we have to take pills to help us relieve our body. If we don't [take pills] we can't get up the next day. It is very difficult for us now. (My translation)]

Claudio and her coworkers must rush around all day, working faster than they should. The pressure to clean as many rooms as possible has led to accidents, she said, and the workers suffer from a level of physical exhaustion and aches that can only be alleviated by taking medication—a strategy of self-medication that helps them get up the next day to perform the same work. These women are caught in a system of labor that uses work to benefit the tourist, the conference participant, the transnational hotel guest.[3] In the hotel industry's quest for profits, the bodies of women like Claudio become collateral damage.

An analysis of a genealogy of oppositional narratives makes visible not only the exploitation of workers, but also the resistance that is possible. Claudio refuses to labor in silence. She works with UNITE HERE to organize her fellow workers to improve their working conditions. For Claudio, it is only through organizing and coming together as a collective that she and her coworkers can effect change: "Y sé que vamos a ganar, y vamos a negociar con el contrato para tener mejores condiciones de trabajo. Porque ya no podemos seguir asi. Queremos que nos bajen la cantidad de cuartos" (I know we are going to win and we are going to negotiate a contract for better working conditions. Because we can't keep going this way. We want them to lower our number of rooms [my translation]). She has no doubt that, as workers unite, they will win. They will gain a contract that will lower the number of rooms that must be cleaned and improve their overall working conditions. Claudio's words illustrate the power that an individual's narrative holds in imagining change. There is strength in her convictions. She is no meek and mild stereotypical domestic worker, standing on the sidelines, no sexually alluring erotic body, waiting to be gazed upon.[4] Claudio is a strong woman, a community leader, a labor organizer who is fighting to create a better world for workers.

In her own words, "Y ahora yo soy líder de la unión, y estoy muy contenta": Claudio describes herself as a union leader, and happy in her role. Her story, however, is one we will never see Hollywood clamoring to capture, nor will we see it featured on a television show. While Claudio refuses to be relegated to the margin, her story, like those of other immigrant domestic workers, remains in the shadows of the hegemonic immigrant narrative that continues to dominate our national discourse.

By incorporating the stories of individuals like Elvia Claudio into our narrative of the nation, we expand our understanding of the immigrant experience and reject the ideological enclosure of the traditional and antiquated narrative of upward assimilation. Claudio's story gives us hope. It reminds us that collective struggle can bring about change, even if it happens slowly. Claudio's ability to see change not as a possibility but as a given forces us to look beyond our own limited visions of change. In conjunction with other stories of opposition, her narrative provides a tangible example of the importance that individual action plays in the resistance to our modern structures of economic exploitation and oppression. Her story is indicative of the growing movement of opposition facing transnational corporations that dehumanize workers in their quest for profit.

The study of the exploitation of women of color in a transnational system of exploitation is not simply a theoretical project. It is a project aimed at increasing awareness of our own participation in an economic system that benefits those of us who have the privilege of enjoying the labor of service workers. Armed with oppositional narratives, we can begin the process of deconstructing ideologies that continue to harm immigrant communities of color. We can reclaim the immigrant narrative as a complex story representing multiple intersecting nodes of oppression, encompassing realities of marginality, exploitation, and violence, and also as a tool of resistance. The new immigrant narrative becomes an oppositional story of survival, one that expands our understanding of what it means to be a gendered and racialized immigrant body in our current moment of globalization. Like Dorothy pulling back the curtain to reveal the true identity of the mighty Wizard of Oz, narratives of opposition help unveil the complicated reality of immigration obscured by the conventional immigrant story. Narratives that reflect the reality of labor, gender, and immigration today—like those of Elvia Claudio—pull back the curtain and remind us of what is at stake in the real world.

Notes

Introduction

1. Winning the lottery would provide Abuela Claudia with the income necessary to make her dreams come true. While the promise of financial security is present, what is important is that those dreams are of work in a place of belonging, a place constructed as "home." It is easy to imagine a woman of Abuela Claudia's advanced age using the winnings to finally rest and live in a level of comfort previously unachievable. After all, isn't the dream of retiring in peace and comfort what Americans are encouraged to work hard to achieve?

2. The Support Our Law Enforcement and Safe Neighborhoods Act, SB 1070 in the Arizona State Senate, was sponsored by Senator Russell Pearce and signed into law by Governor Jan Brewer on Apr. 23, 2010.

3. This discourse also assumes that the border is a rigid and easily identifiable boundary. In questioning the naturalization of the constructed border, I rely heavily on Gloria Anzaldúa's conception of the U.S.–Mexico border as "*una herida abierta* where the Third World grates against the first and bleeds. And before a scab forms it hemorrhages again, the lifeblood of two worlds merging to form a third country—a border culture" (25). Anzaldúa's deconstruction of the border and her argument that the "borderland is a vague and undetermined place created by the emotional residue of an unnatural boundary," one that is "in a constant state of transition," has been instrumental in the theorization of the border as a fluid and complex space of conflict and negotiation (25).

4. In *Hispanic Immigrant Literature: El Sueño del Retorno* (The dream of return), Nicolás Kanellos traces the existence of a large body of literature, which he names "Hispanic immigration literature," during the early part of the twentieth century. His project provides an important opposition to the invisibility of Spanish-language accounts of the immigrant experiences of various Latin@ groups in the past century. Kanellos' definition of immigrant literature, however, differs greatly from mine, as he focuses on literary and cultural texts written by first-generation immigrants in Spanish and does not extend his analysis to representations of immigration by writers who might be the products of immigrant families or who choose to write in English.

5. This is not to say, however, that all immigrant narratives written during this time period fall into the hegemonic narrative of assimilation. For an example of an alternative narrative, see Carlos Bulosan's *America Is in the Heart* (1946).

6. In her analysis of the role nostalgia plays in the immigrant narrative, Natalie Friedman identifies Mary Antin's memoir as a perfect example of "a traditional immigrant narrative: it begins in the homeland, documents the journey to America, and then explores the assimilation of its characters to American culture without once looking back" (80).

7. While this is a "structure," or "schema," of literature, it is also a narrative that is deeply entrenched in the belief systems of many Americans. The narrative is very much about the way individuals imagine themselves and their privilege as a result of the immigrant sacrifice or success of their ancestors, or even themselves. It's a story or narrative that justifies their success as an outcome of their own individual efforts.

8. For McNamee and Miller, "social gravity" forces are among the nonmeritocratic barriers to mobility that create the gap that exists between the ideological construction of meritocracy and the real distribution of wealth and income.

9. For a biting critique of Boelhower's Eurocentric structuralist reading of immigrant narratives, see Lawrence J. Oliver's "Deconstruction or Affirmative Action: The Literary-Political Debate over the 'Ethnic Question,'" 796–797.

10. While some argue that Boelhower's work provides us with a schema that is so

general it continues to apply to today's narratives, I disagree. This argument tends to equate "general" with "universal" and glosses over the fact that Boelhower's schema is predicated specifically on an ethnic white model of immigration that ignores the very real differences that exist among narratives of immigration both today and in the past.

11. In "Immigrant Literatures: A Modern Structure of Feeling," Lisa Lowe argues that immigrant literature allows for an understanding of modernity as a contradiction, a geohistorical process that has always been created/re-created inside and outside of the Western world (3).

12. For an example of the type of transnational community created between immigrants in the host country and people in the country of origin, see Luz María Gordillo's *Mexican Women and the Other Side of Immigration* (2010). Gordillo's historiography examines the transnational community that has been created and remains situated in both the Mexican point-of-origin community of San Ignacio Cerro Gordo, Jalisco, and the receiving community of Detroit, Michigan.

13. For Wallerstein, such an analysis sees "all parts of the world-system as parts of a 'world,' the parts being impossible to understand or analyze separately. The characteristics of any given state at T(2) were said to be not the result of some 'primordial' characteristic at T(1), but rather the outcome of processes of the system, the world-system."

14. The industrialization of the border region in Mexico by the United States as well as Asian and European countries is an example of the moving of manufacturing plants from core to peripheral areas to take advantage of a cheap labor supply.

15. With regard to non-Western immigrants, the narrative schema also serves to reinforce the dominant myth of the American Dream.

16. For a thorough discussion of enclosures, see Peter Linebaugh and Marcus Rediker, *The Many Headed Hydra: Sailors, Slaves, Commoners, and the Hidden History of the Revolutionary Atlantic.*

17. The dislocation of workers has overarching effects, including the disruption of organizing opposition to multiple forms of injustice. For the Midnight Notes Collective, the term "new enclosures" names the "large-scale reorganization of the accumulation process" whose main objective "has been to uproot workers from the terrain on which their organizational power has been built, so that . . . they are forced to work and fight in a strange environment where the forms of resistance possible at home are no longer available" (321).

18. For a detailed analysis of U.S. military aggression in Latin America, see William Blum's *Killing Hope: U.S. Military and CIA Interventions since World War II.*

19. While the work of scholars like Lisa Lowe has changed the ways in which we read narratives of immigration, others continue to situate these narratives within the hegemonic structure. For example, in *New Strangers in Paradise: The Immigrant Experience in Contemporary American Fiction*, Gilbert H. Muller situates immigration in a global perspective, but continues to position the United States as the "Promised Land." In his concluding chapter he writes that new immigrants "embrace democratic vistas and transcend national meanings: opportunity, social mobility, self-reliance, the dreams inherent in their new Promised Land" (238). In the anthology *The Immigrant Experience in North American Literature: Carving Out a Niche*, editors Katherine B. Payant and Toby Rose persist in employing the rhetoric of old/new world in the preface and introduction.

20. Even though the film presents the military violence unleashed on the indigenous community of Guatemala and connects that violence to the economic interests of the growers, it doesn't make visible the role the United States has played in the relationship between capitalist interests and the military in Guatemala.

21. These are the immigrant bodies that Anzaldúa argues inhabit the borderland, *los atravesados*, "the prohibited and forbidden . . . those who cross over, pass over, or go through the confines of the 'normal'" (25).

22. Unlike the representation of immigrants as naïve or idealistic, the women who immigrate today are aware of the difficulties they will encounter on their journey to the border and during their crossing. In fact, female immigrants from Central America will often begin a regimen of birth control months in advance of their departure because they are aware of the probability of being raped (J. Watson).

23. While the importance of ethnic enclaves is present in the traditional immigrant narrative structure, these enclaves are positioned more as transitory spaces that will be left behind once the immigrant successfully assimilates into U.S. mainstream culture.

24. This is not to say that these communities are ideal or that immigrants are necessarily safe within them. They do, however, provide an alternative to the mainstream community, which might reject the immigrant for multiple reasons.

25. Sassen reports that in 1998 remittances sent home surpassed $70 billion and that in countries like the Philippines, "remittances were the third largest source of foreign currency" (*Globalization* 270).

26. In *Children of Global Migration: Transnational Families and Gender Woes*, Rhacel Salazar Parreñas analyses the impact that distance has on Filipino children whose mothers work outside of the Philippines. For a visual documentation of the difficulties experienced by transnational domestic workers, see Nilita Vachani's *When Mother Comes Home for Christmas* (1995). The film documents the struggles that Josephine Perera—a Sri Lankan domestic worker in Italy—faces as she attempts to care for her family from a long distance.

27. One example can be found in Robert J. Thomas' labor study of lettuce harvesters and the role that immigration status and gender play in organizing labor in the agricultural fields of California. Thomas' research illustrates how the intersection of citizenship status, race, and gender functions in the division of labor in the agricultural fields and relates to the level of exploitation encountered by workers.

Chapter One

1. The California DREAM Act, AB 130 and AB 131, passed in 2011, grants undocumented residents of California access to college financial aid, while the federal DREAM Act, which would provide undocumented young people (those who entered the country before the age of fifteen) a path to citizenship through earning a college degree or serving in the military, has failed to pass into law.

2. Hobsbawm identifies three overlapping types of invented traditions: "a) those establishing or symbolizing social cohesion or the membership of groups, real or artificial communities, b) those establishing or legitimizing institutions, status or relations of authority, and c) those whose main purpose was socialization, the inculcation of beliefs, value systems and conventions of behaviour" (9). When thinking about the hegemonic immigrant narrative as a type of "invented tradition," both type a and type c describe the project of socialization the literary genre performs.

3. In 2008 Governor Sarah Palin referenced Reagan's statement in her assertion that "America is a nation of exceptionalism," framing American exceptionalism as a positive characteristic to be emulated by other nations (Bacevich). Reagan's association with Winthrop's phrase is so well known that his son, Michael Reagan, titled his 1997 book *The City on a Hill: Fulfilling Ronald Reagan's Vision for America*.

4. While Rosaura Sánchez is specifically discussing Arturo Islas' *Rain God* in this quote, her argument for the connection of twentieth-century texts to nineteenth-century precursors is especially relevant and applicable to a study of immigrant literature as a genre.

5. Boelhower notes that, "in light of genre expectations, the reader is led primarily to familiarize himself with new ethnic values and traditions and to naturalize these differences as an integral part of the American experience" (12).

6. A popular rhetorical device used when discussing the United States as a welcoming nation that envelops its immigrants through assimilation is the invoking of the "melting pot" myth. The phrase "melting pot" originates with Zangwill's play titled *The Melting Pot*. For more on the play, see Edna Nahshon's commentary included in *From the Ghetto to the Melting Pot: Israel Zangwill's Jewish Plays*.

7. Because the term "Chican@" was not used before the 1960s Chicano Civil Rights Movement, I follow Richard A. Garcia's use of the label "Mexican American," popular during the first half of the twentieth century, when discussing this earlier population.

8. Garcia's text follows the rise of a middle-class consciousness in San Antonio and pays special attention to the role that the League of United Latin American Citizens played in shifting the consciousness of Mexican Americans from "one of only *lo mexicano* . . . to the incorporation of *lo americano*" (4–5). The ideology of *lo mexicano* placed a strong emphasis on remaining connected to Mexico's culture, while that of *lo americano* advocated for an assimilation of the Mexican American into American culture (5).

9. While Sánchez is writing specifically about texts created within the Chican@ community, her argument works well in placing *Pocho* within a larger framework of literature and cultural production.

10. Published twelve years later, Ernesto Galarza's pivotal autobiography *Barrio Boy* (1971) is an example of a more complex, nonfiction immigrant narrative. While Galarza's family also emigrated during the Mexican Revolution, his narrative does not place the same emphasis on individualism as Villarreal's text. *Barrio Boy* is closely informed by Galarza's own background in labor organizing and activism, a history that includes accusations of communism. For more on *Barrio Boy*, see Ramón Saldívar's "Ideologies of the Self: Chicano Autobiography," Raymund A. Paredes' "Mexican American Authors and the American Dream," and Antonio Márquez' "The American Dream in the Chicano Novel."

11. It is in the representation of historical moments in the novel that literary critic Ramón Saldívar finds *Pocho*'s importance. Saldívar also argues that the importance of the novel lies in the fact that unlike earlier Chican@ novels, which emphasized the presence of Mexican Americans in the Southwest before the construction of the nation, *Pocho* positions this Mexican American narrative as beginning outside of the United States and points to the growing presence of Mexicans in the Southwest during the early twentieth century (*Chicano Narrative* 60).

12. Saldívar argues that Juan Rubio "realizes that with the death of Pancho Villa, the grand dream of social and individual dignity will be subverted" ("Dialect of Difference" 74). However, while understanding the historical importance of the revolution, Saldívar situates it in the novel as being mainly of importance to Juan and his beliefs.

13. Ironically enough, the description of Juan Rubio as having "once fair skin" and "blue-grey eyes," along with his last name ("Rubio" means blond), aligns him with whiteness—a marker of Spanish ancestry.

14. In reality, those notions of a liberal democracy were highly dependent on ideologies of Anglo-Saxon superiority and the inferiority of native peoples, slaves, and Mexicans.

15. See chapter 1 in *Manifest Destiny: The Origins of American Racial Anglo-Saxonism* for Horsman's discussion of white Americans' embracing a constructed Anglo-Saxon past.

16. Senator Robert J. Walker and Senator James Buchanan, quoted in Horsman (216–217).

17. The construction of the Mexican government reflecting the inadequacies of its people stands in sharp contrast to the ideological separation created between a corrupt and despotic British government and its enlightened Anglo-Saxon population. For the revolutionary generation, "it was possible to admire the English while hating the British government," and for Americans, the belief that they "were the most distinguished descendants of the Anglo-Saxons grew . . . in the decades after the Revolution" (Horsman 81).

18. It is no coincidence that it was also during this decade that we witness one of the first waves of anti-immigrant sentiment against non-English immigrants (Horsman 225).

19. On the West Coast, immigrants from Asia passing through Angel Island shared the experience of exclusion with southern immigrants. The island has not been constructed as the welcoming gateway to the "city upon a hill," a construction that Ellis Island enjoys.

20. The militarization of the U.S.–Mexico border and the xenophobic rhetoric surrounding the policing of bodies there is evidence of how this binary continues to function.

21. In his article "Mexican American Authors and the American Dream," Raymund A. Paredes comments, "The evidence indicates that Mexican immigrants . . . entered the United States with the modest expectation of finding steady work at a fair wage. For many, the appeal of the American Dream was so low that they hardly considered staying" (73).

22. This representation is very different from that found in the hundreds of *corridos* that depict the hardships encountered by Mexican immigrants (Paredes 74–75).

23. Through its semantic construction, the novel positions these immigrants as responsible for their own undesirability, a representation divorced from a history of racial formation that constructs Mexicans, and as a result Mexican immigrants, as inferior.

24. The connection between American exceptionalism and labor is a long historical construction in our national imaginary. In his 1782 *Letters from an American Farmer*, J. Hector St. John de Crèvecoeur praised what he saw as the unique ability of Americans to succeed based on their hard work and useful labor (55-56).

25. Like the immigrant narratives of Anzia Yezierska, Carlos Bulosan, and Pietro di Donato, *Pocho* places a great emphasis on the difficult labor performed by its immigrant protagonists.

26. At the same time, however, the novel also positions Richard as different from those workers, as evidenced by his decision to support a grower and his daughter during a work stoppage. Unlike the adult workers, who follow the union's directives, Richard is represented as more insightful and capable of differentiating between "good" and "bad" growers. Even at a young age, Richard is cast as an individual, able to think for himself and avoid becoming part of a collective that ends up being represented as misguided.

27. Paredes observes that "the cornerstone of the American Dream is acquisition and retention of property, and Mexican Americans, despite their traditionally less grandiose expectations, have cherished property as much as have Anglos" (71).

28. The Rubios' status as homeowners cannot protect them from the economic precariousness of their immigrant status, or from the dissolution of Juan and Consuelo's marriage and the separation of the family—a dissolution Richard believes is caused by an inability of the women of the family to assimilate "correctly."

29. In his discussion of the quest for the American Dream, Márquez argues that "the second generation takes advantage of the educational opportunities not available to its parents, rises above the socioeconomic conditions it was born into, and achieves a degree of financial success" (14). This, of course, is not always the case.

30. In a moment of revisionist history in the narrative, Richard writes that being arrested by the police in high school "was the first time in his life he felt discriminated against" (163).

31. In his essay "On Bootstraps," Alexander Ewing traces the origins of the bootstrap idiom and examines how it is currently being employed by public figures.

32. For example, literary critic and immigrant Alfred Kazin's reading of Theodore Roosevelt's autobiography deeply influenced his formation of a concept of what a makes a "real" American man. In an interesting connection, Richard Rodriguez has discussed his benefiting from Kazin's work as a young boy. On reading of Kazin's death, Rodriguez mused, "I remembered Alfred Kazin, a boy in Brooklyn, myself a boy as reader, the two of us intent on assuming an American voice, on joining our voices to the chorus that

has sounded through generations before us" ("Cultural Legacy"). Rodriguez recalled the power that Kazin's immigrant story had in helping create his own ideas of national belonging and assimilation. Like they were for *Pocho*'s protagonist, books proved to be instructive in the young Rodriguez' formation.

33. Ironically enough, the books are given to him by a woman who tells him "he should work hard to be a gardener and someday he could work on a rich person's estate" (107). Richard rejects her advice and instead focuses on Alger's message of individual success through hard work and perseverance.

34. The fact that Alger was writing in the nineteenth century and his books are no longer as well read has not diminished the power of the ideologies behind them. The popularity that the bootstraps model of success continues to enjoy today illustrates the longevity of such ideologies. In fact, even today, several organizations exist that persevere in actively promoting the ideologies of Alger's work. For example, the Horatio Alger Association of Distinguished Americans asserts that Alger's works "told everyone, no matter how poor, or orphaned or powerless, that if they persevere, if they do their best, if they always try to do the right thing, they can succeed" (www.horatioalger.org). Alger's novels came to exemplify what it means to achieve the American Dream. Even more importantly, the Alger Association maintains that "through his body of work, Horatio Alger, Jr., captured the spirit of a nation and helped clarify that spirit." The association's argument that Alger's work helped define the spirit of the nation is vital because the American Dream ideology has been heavily promoted as an objective that one achieves by working hard to become a productive member of the nation. *Pocho*'s close following of the immigrant narrative of assimilation includes mention of Richard's reading Alger's texts. While Richard rejects the idea of honor and always doing the "right thing" promoted by Alger's texts, he readily subscribes to the "pulling oneself up by the bootstraps" mentality.

35. For Sánchez, Richard's rejection of his family and community help set him up for the pursuit of more middle-class aspirations. She argues that "in accepting the myth of individualism, the Chicano of the early forties in effect accepted the ideological representations, discourse, and power configurations of entrepreneurial capitalism" (115).

36. Consuelo believes Richard will "ruin his eyes" with so much reading, and she begins to see his questioning of the family's religious beliefs as blasphemous, not understanding that Richard is curious about the world in which he lives.

37. It is ironic that Richard sees his mother as ignorant and uneducated, but the text has Consuelo use advanced vocabulary that does not fit with the image Richard holds of her. Unfortunately, the protagonist's point of view is what gets emphasized in the novel.

38. Richard's misogynist tendencies are further revealed in his actions toward his sisters, the other female inhabitants of the home, whom he views as incredibly ignorant and having questionable morals.

39. Juan leaves the home after a family fight in which he strikes Consuelo and his daughter Luz. In attempting to assert his patriarchal power, he tries to police Luz' sexuality. When that fails, he leaves and reasserts his masculinity by moving in with a recent Mexican immigrant, Pilar. A young woman close to Richard's age, she is a "good" Mexican woman who does not challenge Juan's patriarchal power. While Juan initially tries to set her up with Richard, he ends up impregnating her—further proof of his own virility.

40. In their overview of Latin@s' patriotic history in the United States, Refugio I. Rochin and Lionel Fernandez report that approximately 500,000 "Spanish-surnamed" persons served in the armed forces during World War II (15).

41. For Thomas Vallejo, Richard's decision to enlist "can be interpreted as an indecisive step into a death-like void" (7), but I would argue that it is his life with his family that Richard perceives as existing in a void.

42. Rochin and Fernandez make the connection between military service and national loyalty when they write that "the Latino community has consistently demon-

strated that when the U.S. is engaged in a military conflict, they have been the 'first ones in and the last ones out.' The Latino community has a long history of immigration to this country. Latino sons and daughters have not hesitated to defend their family's honor and have shown their allegiance to this nation through military service" (3).

43. Released in the fall of 2004 and distributed by Columbia Pictures, *Spanglish* had an opening weekend gross of $8.8 million. By the end of January 2005, the film had grossed over $42 million domestically (*"Spanglish* Domestic Gross").

44. While depictions of fatherhood function to further demonize Latino men, motherhood functions as a way of making a moral statement about a female protagonist. In both *Spanglish* and *Maid in Manhattan* (discussed in chapter 3), the character of the child is employed to act as a moral compass for the mother, ensuring the mother's characterization as moral and dignified. This allows for the mother to be associated with the "good" girl in the virgin/whore dichotomy, which remains so prevalent in commercial productions. Of course, the representation of the moral mother comes at the expense of the absent father: the irresponsible and possibly deviant Latino male.

45. Hollywood films are also the products of numerous individuals who change and edit stories in ways that make them more commercial.

46. For an in-depth discussion of the current militarization of the border and the violence faced by immigrants from the south, see chapter 2.

47. As Perea points out, proficiency in the English language has long been a precursor to becoming a naturalized subject (568). The film frames communication between Flor and the Claskys as a negotiation based on linguistic and cultural differences that can be overcome with the willingness of both parties, a literal and metaphorical speaking of "Spanglish" (a combination of Spanish and English). This negotiation, however, can only occur once Flor learns English, while the Claskys are never expected to learn Spanish.

48. See chapter 2 for a more in-depth discussion of the rhetoric of family and domestic labor.

49. In her pivotal text on domestic work, Judith Rollins observes that "the female employer, with her motherliness and protectiveness and generosity, is expressing in a distinctly feminine way her lack of respect for the domestic as an autonomous, adult employee" (186).

50. In the film, Flor is played by Paz Vega, an award-winning actress in her native Spain, well known for her beauty and sex appeal. By casting a Spanish actress to play a Mexican character, the film collapses the differences that exist between Latinas. The widespread practice of using Spanish actors to play Mexican characters perpetuates the idea that all Latin@s are the same, and the only difference that exists is the racial one that separates them from white America.

51. This is not to say that a film can't have a beautiful protagonist and tell a powerful story at the same time. For example, *La Misma Luna* (2007) has at its center an immigrant domestic worker and her child. Like *Spanglish*, the film has a gorgeous protagonist and a love interest, but this is where the similarities end. Mexican director Patricia Riggen presents a much more uncomfortable story of immigration, one of family separation and heartache. While the film provides a happy reunion between Rosario and her son, Carlitos, it does not attempt to offer an uncomplicated conclusion to the narrative. The individuals encountered on Carlitos' trip are not forgotten and the sacrifice of his reluctant travel companion Enrique renders a simple happy ending impossible.

52. Flor is upset because Deborah has arranged for a sleepover for Cristina at her home without her permission, and John has just found out that Deborah has been unfaithful. Both are feeling manipulated by Deborah and are joined through their sense of anger and betrayal.

53. While the possibility of achieving a college education does exist for the children of domestic workers (for example, see Mary Romero's introduction to *Maid in the U.S.A.*),

it is much harder than the film portrays it to be. In her research on domestic labor, Rollins reports that "all of the mothers of the domestics I interviewed, except one, had been domestics themselves," illustrating that the daughters of domestic workers are not always able to achieve a higher level of social/economic status than their mothers (112).

54. While the U.S. House of Representatives passed the DREAM Act, the Senate voted 55–41 in favor of the bill, five votes short of the sixty needed to pass it (Wong and Toeplitz).

55. This dehumanization is one reason for the refusal by many to employ the term "illegal alien" when discussing undocumented, or unauthorized, individuals.

56. Among some critics of the act are those who object to the ways in which the DREAM Act, while important, creates a binary between "worthy" and "unworthy" undocumented young people. It ignores the reality of the number of students who fall through the cracks of an educational system that fails them. Those who lack the resources or opportunities to attend college are left with the military option, which is also closed to anyone who does not finish high school or obtain a GED. Criticism of the act has been especially vocal from community members who oppose its military-service aspect. Unlike the two-year college degree, which would satisfy the requirements of the act, the military does not have two-year contracts, a fact many might not be aware of. As the Chicano scholars and activists Jorge Mariscal and Mónica Jaúregui point out, "The current crisis in higher education will lead not only to higher fees and tuition, but also to capped enrollments and reduced academic support services, thereby making it more difficult for working-class students to persist and graduate . . . Military staffing needs will remain high . . . and even though rising unemployment is making the recruiter's job easier, DREAMers still make up a highly desirable pool of not just warm bodies but bilingual, well educated, and highly motivated bodies."

Chapter Two

1. In *From the Other Side: Women, Gender and Immigrant Life in the U.S., 1820–1990*, Donna Gabaccia offers a study of migration during the nineteenth century that centers on the lives of female immigrants and examines the importance that gender plays in the construction of immigrant subjectivities.

2. The 1965 Immigration Act altered official immigration by abolishing the national-origins system and prioritizing "family reunification." The law eliminated the national-origin quotas created under the Immigration Act of 1924, which favored Western European immigrants and barred immigration from the Asia-Pacific Triangle. With its emphasis on the reunification of families, the 1965 act allowed for the immigration of family members of past immigrants, including spouses, children, and siblings. The image of immigrants as predominantly male, however, has remained popular.

3. For example, in *Mexican Workers and American Dreams*, Camille Guerin-Gonzales documents the recruitment practices of U.S. labor agents in their quest to provide the railroad companies with cheap labor from Mexico (33–34).

4. Guerin-Gonzales points out that Mexican immigrants were constructed as "birds of passage," temporary labor to work the agricultural fields in California. This made them desirable because growers believed that "Mexicans who returned to their home country each year . . . would not change the racial, cultural, or social character of California" (24). Guerin-Gonzales' work dispels this myth and helps delineate a much more complicated history of Mexican immigration in California.

5. The 1942–1964 guest-worker program known as the Bracero Program imported Mexican laborers to the United States for the purpose of supplying the agricultural industry with cheap labor. The number of Mexican workers who entered the country as braceros is estimated to be about two million (Mize and Swords 3). The program came to an end

in 1964, but its legacy continues as it formalized a model of exploitative labor practices and perpetuated the construction of immigrant workers as transitory and disposable.

6. Senators Ted Kennedy and John McCain used Bush's proposal to promote legislation that would create a path to permanent legal status for undocumented workers (Gibson).

7. The current xenophobic discourse about "anchor babies" is a present-day manifestation of the perceived threat that the reproduction of racialized immigrant bodies poses to a monolithic construction of the nation begun at its founding.

8. The case of Chinese women immigrants, however, is different. The Chinese Exclusionary Act of 1882 reflected the popular rhetoric of the time that assumed that all Chinese women were prostitutes and posed a danger to "decent" white families. For an in-depth analysis of the different ways in which Chinese and Japanese women were constructed in the late nineteenth and early twentieth centuries, see Catherine Lee's *Prostitutes and Picture Brides*.

9. In *Seven Days a Week*, historian David M. Katzman points out that in the period between 1870 and 1910, immigrant women, who often were unable to find other work, replaced the large numbers of native-born women leaving domestic service "to marry, have children, or enter other occupations" (46). Among immigrant women in that period, service work was particularly popular with Irish, Scandinavian, and German immigrants (49).

10. In her film *When Mother Comes Home for Christmas* (1996), Nilita Vachani documents one such training program. The government-run program aims to teach Sri Lankan women the skills necessary to clean a home, including introducing them to household technology like vacuum cleaners and microwave ovens.

11. For example, Nicolás Kanellos points out that, in the case of Latin@ narratives of immigration, the number of recovered narratives by women is significantly smaller than that written by men. The majority of representations of immigrant Latinas come to us not through the women themselves, but through Latino writers (101–102).

12. For example, in his immigrant-literatures recovery project, Kanellos discusses Puerto Rican writer Luisa Capetillo's work as part of a legacy of literature that helped insert gender into the body of Hispanic-immigrant texts. Her written work, including multiple theater texts, was heavily focused on educating workers about their rights. Sánchez-Scott's play is also part of a history of activist Chican@ *teatro* as laid out by the work of Teatro Campesino and Luis Valdez.

13. *Cactus Blood* is the second of four novels in Corpi's mystery series, which follows the exploits of Chicana feminist detective Gloria Damasco.

14. The film also received a John D. and Catherine T. MacArthur Foundation grant ("*Maid in America*: Synopsis"). Along with the prestige of the award, the fact that the documentary aired on the widely available PBS allowed Prado's documentary a much wider viewership than that enjoyed by the theatrical productions or Corpi's novel.

15. "*Maid in America*," *Impacto Films*, 2004, Web.

16. Commissioned by the Mark Taper Forum, the play premiered in January 2003 (Loomer 5).

17. Since it is a play, however, access to *Living Out* is limited, as only a few individuals actually see the text performed. Even when published, plays do not have access to the same number of audience members that commercial projects, such as films, enjoy.

18. By framing the violence on the border as part of a larger militarized conflict, we can connect the current violence perpetrated on the bodies of women of color to a much longer, colonial practice of gendered violence and oppression.

19. The fact that the doctor gave Chuchita's uncle money is confirmed later in the novel when María Baldomar, the mother of Carlota's friend Josie, tells Gloria that Carlota "was sold to the doctor by her best friend's—Chuchita's—uncle" (88).

20. In 2010, the number of Mexican emigrants living abroad was an estimated 11.9 million, or 10.7 percent of the nation's population (World Bank 3, 178). In 2011, "nearly 11.7 million Mexican immigrants resided in the United States" (Stoney and Batalova).

21. In her article on the ways in which rape is used as a weapon of war on the border, Sylvanna Falcón offers a glimpse into the practice of border patrol agents' and immigration officials' raping immigrant women. For Falcón, the rape of immigrant women is a product of the militarized border system ("Rape as a Weapon").

22. One of many examples of violence against immigrants includes the death of eighteen-year-old Guillermo Martinez-Rodriguez, a Tijuana resident who was shot in the back by a border patrol agent on Dec. 30, 2005. The actions of the agent were justified by the INS as being part of the administration's "zero tolerance" policy (Van Uken). In 2011, the humanitarian aid organization No More Deaths released an online report, *A Culture of Cruelty*, documenting over 30,000 incidents of human-rights abuses by U.S. Border Patrol agents against undocumented immigrants between 2008 and 2011. In addition to physical and verbal abuse, incidents included denial of access to water, food, and medical care. For No More Deaths, the "mistreatment and abuse in Border Patrol custody are not aberrational. Rather, they reflect common practice for an agency that is part of the largest federal law enforcement body in the country" (5).

23. In January 2011, the fence project was ended by the Obama administration after yielding only fifty-three miles of protection and costing nearly $1 billion (Gamboa).

24. Daniel Good reports that "some $2.4 billion has been spent since 2005" and that "$6.5 billion will be needed to maintain the new fencing over the next 20 years" ("Billions for a U.S.–Mexico Border Fence").

25. In *No One Is Illegal*, historians Mike Davis and Justin Akers Chacón draw important parallels between the Minutemen Project and a long U.S. history of white vigilante violence.

26. Bejarano's observations are part of her reply to Rob Guerette's 2007 article "Immigration Policy, Border Security, and Migrant Deaths."

27. Julie Watson reports on the practice of female migrants' taking birth control several months before their migration to avoid becoming pregnant as a result of rape. In his article on the denial of abortion access to detained immigrant women, Kevin Sieff reports that in 2008, 10,653 women were detained by Immigration and Customs Enforcement and that 965 of these women were pregnant, "many of them . . . raped on their way to the United States—a journey known to be dangerous for any willing to take it, but especially so for women." Sieff's report narrates the story of Maria, a Honduran immigrant who attempted to enter the United States to find work as a housekeeper and who was raped on the journey. After being detained by the border patrol, Maria discovered she was pregnant but had no access to abortion services.

28. Sassen points out that "legal immigration to the United States increased to 500,000 entries a year in the 1980s, up from 265,000 in 1960. The 1970 U.S. Census recorded 9.6 million immigrants, representing 4.7 percent of the population. The 1980 Census recorded 13.9 million immigrants representing 6.2 percent of the population" (*Mobility* 43).

29. For example, Saucedo documents the case of Guadalupe Sanchez, who was raped by her employer (the head of a janitorial company in San Francisco) and who was threatened with being reported to the INS if she left her job or complained (136).

30. A particularly chilling example of the ways in which racialized bodies remain suspect and particularly susceptible to violence is the case of nine-year-old Brisenia Flores and her family. On May 30, 2009, in Arivaca, Arizona, anti-immigrant vigilante Shawna Forde and her accomplices stormed the home of Brisenia and murdered the young girl and her father and injured her mother. Forde assumed because of their proximity to the border and their background that Brisenia's parents were drug dealers and attacked their home in an effort to rob them of drugs and money to fund her anti-immigrant vigilante group, the Minutemen American Defense Fund (Riccardi). No proof of drugs was discovered in the home.

31. For her insightful discussion of Alice Childress' titular short story and the ways

in which the rhetoric of family has worked in the construction of race and notions of nationhood, see Patricia Hill Collins' "Like One of the Family: Race, Ethnicity, and the Paradox of US National Identity."

32. According to her official biography on ABC.com, Jo Frost is "our modern day Mary Poppins." Her television show *Supernanny* premiered in the United Kingdom in 2004 and made its U.S. television premiere in 2005.

33. Telma tells the camera that she has been offered jobs that pay more, but she chooses to remain with the Marburys because they respect her and treat her well, a choice that is consistent with Hondagneu-Sotelo's findings that Latina domestic workers "prefer an employer who takes personal interest in them to an employer who pays more and treats them disrespectfully and coldly. They want to keep their dignity on the job" (195).

34. Katzman traces the shift in the racial composition of domestic workers during the late nineteenth and early twentieth centuries from working-class native-born women, to European immigrants (especially Irish), to African American women (70–73).

35. See chapter 7 in *Seven Days a Week* for Katzman's discussion on domestic service and the industrialization of the nation.

36. In her article "America's Dirty Work: Migrant Maids and Modern-Day Slavery," Joy M. Zarembka documents the widespread sexual harassment and sexual assault of domestic workers (142–153).

37. In *Pocho*, Villarreal represents the women in Richard's life as such stereotypes.

38. In a critique of Hollywood casting practices, Sánchez-Scott makes specific reference to the fact that the only roles Sarita can get cast to play are Latina victims of violence: "barrio girl who gets raped by a gang in *Police Story*, a barrio young mother who gets shot by a gang in *Starsky and Hutch*, a barrio wife who got beat up by her husband who was in a gang in the *Rookies*. I was even a barrio lesbian who got knifed by an all girl gang" (89). The three staples of Latin@ stereotypes—violence, the barrio, and gangs—are present in all of her roles.

39. Carlota's narrative makes visible the violence that is perpetrated on the body of the immigrant domestic worker, but at the same time, it represents active resistance to that violation. Corpi's text refuses to portray Carlota as a passive victim. She isn't physically able to stop the rape, but Carlota doesn't allow Dr. Stephens' position as her employer, or his physical strength, to silence her objections.

40. The prosecution of sexual offenders is often based on the notion of the state as the prosecutor's "client." In his discussion of the complicated relationship between rape victims and prosecutors, Jeffrey J. Pokorak argues, "The core role of the prosecutor is to represent the interests of the government and only indirectly to represent the interests of individual citizens. In her most blunt incarnation, the victim of a crime is relevant to a prosecutor only as a witness and as a symbol of the threat the defendant poses to society" (695). Because Carlota is undocumented, she is the one who is considered a threat to the nation, while Dr. Stephens is protected by his privilege of citizenship.

41. Jose Antonio Vargas' very public "coming out" as an undocumented immigrant drew national attention to the presence of undocumented immigrants in the public realm. The narrative of this Pulitzer Prize–winning journalist challenged the myth of the American Dream and dispelled the negative stereotype of undocumented immigrants as uneducated and a drain on resources.

42. Prado, quoted in *"Maid in America*: Updates," http://www.pbs.org/independentlens/maidinamerica/updates.html.

43. Unfortunately, it seems Judith was unable to keep this promise. In the follow-up on the women of the series, Prado reports, "After moving back to Guatemala, Judith returned to the U.S. in March 2005." Her daughters remained in Guatemala.

44. During the time *Latina* takes place, the INS was responsible for the detection and detainment of undocumented migrants. The year after the creation of the Department

of Homeland Security in 2002, the enforcement duties of the INS were transferred to the jurisdiction of the newly created Immigration and Customs Enforcement. For more information on the consequences of this restructuring, see chapter 2 in Tanya Maria Golash-Boza's *Immigration Nation*.

45. In her work on human rights and immigration policies, Golash-Boza describes interior enforcement as consisting of "policing strategies designed to find undocumented migrants within the borders of the United States" (45).

46. In the essay "Constructing Rhetorical Borders," Lisa A. Flores traces the role that the media and discourse played in creating rhetorical borders between the United States and Mexico during the repatriation campaign.

47. Loomer's play, however, also gives the audience representations of several employers whose attitudes toward, and treatment of, their domestic employees are resoundingly similar to those found in *Latina*, highlighting the pervasive view of domestic workers as inferior and replaceable.

48. For example, Nancy meets fellow mothers Wallace and Linda, who give her advice on having a nanny, including using a Nanny Cam (16–17) and leaving money on the counter to test the nanny's honesty (16–17). Wallace makes derogatory statements about immigrant Latina nannies being unable to read.

Chapter Three

1. While the original story is heteronormative, the fantasy holds universal appeal.

2. The *New York Times* headline "I.M.F. Chief, Apprehended at Airport, Is Accused of Sexual Attack" announced the arrest to the world (Baker and Erlanger).

3. The name of the housekeeper was initially withheld, but once her name became public, the personal attacks on her character ensued. Diallo's African immigrant status made her the target of racist and xenophobic comments, including the rumor that she lived in a "residence for people with H.I.V. or A.I.D.S.," a claim denied by her attorney (Zernike).

4. In his first television interview after the charges were dismissed, Strauss-Kahn referred to the event as "an inappropriate relationship . . . an error . . . a moral failing" and claimed it was consensual ("Dominique Strauss-Kahn Rues").

5. Strauss-Kahn's legal problems are far from over. After the prosecutor's office dropped the charges against him, Diallo filed a civil suit against him and is currently in litigation. He is also under investigation for possible involvement in a "hotel prostitution ring" in Lille, France. While admitting his attendance at the sex parties in question, he denies knowing that "the women involved in the orgies were hired prostitutes" ("Dominique Strauss-Kahn Claims").

6. The analysis of housekeeping labor in the hotel industry is important because of the rising number of workers employed by hotels. The lodging industry is the third largest retail industry in the country and employs about 1.3 million workers, one-fourth of whom are housekeepers ("Latina Housekeepers Hurt").

7. Loach worked closely with the Justice for Janitors community when making the film. The decision to premiere the film on June 15 (Justice for Janitors Day) in Century City, California, is illustrative of the strong connection between the storytelling of the film and the stories the film attempts to capture. It was specifically screened for the individuals who inspired it: "dressed in bright red 'Justice for Janitors' t-shirts, the workers arrived in busloads, carrying mops and brooms and shouting their slogan, 'Si se puede!'" ("Janitors Relive").

8. In the case of the U.S. hospitality industry, "hotels and other accommodations provided 1.9 million wage and salary jobs in 2008," and most of that employment "is concentrated in cities and resort areas" (Bureau of Labor Statistics).

9. In its analysis of the Census Bureau's 2009 American Community Survey, the Pew Hispanic Center examined the occupational distribution among foreign-born workers. In the "Cleaning and Maintenance" category, the percentage of foreign-born workers was 8.5, more than twice the percentage of native-born workers (3.5). The popularity of this industry for Latin@ immigrants is evidenced by the higher concentration of immigrants from Mexico (14.1 percent), Central America (16.5 percent), and South America (10.6 percent), in comparison to South and East Asia (2.5 percent), the Middle East (1.3 percent), and the Caribbean (7.5 percent) ("Statistical Portrait").

10. While the hospitality industry continues to grow, its growth results in fewer new jobs than that in many other industries. The Bureau of Labor Statistics predicts that "wage and salary employment in hotels and other accommodations is expected to increase by 5 percent between 2008 and 2018, compared with 11 percent growth projected for all industries combined" (http://www.bls.gov/oco/cg/cgs036.htm).

11. One limitation of spoken-word texts is that they are often available only to those who attend performances, but with the recording of NORTE/word, the number of people with access to the text is much larger. In "Migrant Melancholia," Alicia Schmidt Camacho notes that "Norte chose to circulate her work in a format that would make it available to a broader audience and would also retain the texture of her voice" (851).

12. For an important analysis of the significance of Norte's original chosen genre and the creation of art in the public space, see "Heterotopias and Shared Methods of Resistance: Navigating Social Space and Spaces of Identity," by Jennifer A. González and Michelle Habell-Pallán.

13. In her essay on NORTE/word, Michelle Habell-Pallán argues that the text is "eloquently bilingual, is about women and girls on the 'outside'—women and girls outside of the home, outside of loving relationships, outside of adequate education and health care systems, and outside of the mass media" (163).

14. For an interesting history of domestic labor in El Paso, see Vicki L. Ruiz' "By the Day or Week: Mexicana Domestic Workers in El Paso."

15. El Paso is also the site where, in 1933, five hundred domestic workers organized to form the Domestic Workers' Association. While short lived, their organization made visible the low wages and poor working conditions of domestic workers in the area (Ruiz 65).

16. As a result of industrialization projects, the population of Juárez grew dramatically during the latter part of the twentieth century. Janice A. Corbett, in "Ciudad Juárez 4th Largest City," reports that the city's population in 1970 was estimated at 407,370, while current estimates place it at 1.3 million and growing by 170,000 to 190,000 people annually because of the migration of workers. Unfortunately, the escalating violence against women (identified as feminicide by multiple scholars including Rosa Linda Fregoso, Cynthia Bejarano, and Alicia Schmidt Camacho) and the out-of-control drug war have made Juárez one of the most dangerous cities in the nation, which has affected the number of people living in the city and migrating to the area.

17. Mary Romero reports that "researchers estimate that anywhere from 18,000 to 26,000 domestics are [currently] employed in private residences in El Paso" (121).

18. As Amel Adib and Yvonne Guerrier point out, under this system, "women may predominate in certain hotel jobs, not so much because they are regarded as particularly appropriate for women, but because these jobs are regarded as appropriate only for those disadvantaged in the labour force. Certainly, the largest proportions of female workers are found in the lowest skill, lowest status and 'dirtiest' hotel jobs" (419).

19. In her essay on her documentary Brincando el charco, Frances Negrón-Muntaner explains that the phrase "brincando el charco" (jumping the puddle), used by Puerto Ricans to describe their migration to the U.S. mainland, "aims to minimize the impact of crossing . . . although it is widely acknowledged that one is never the same afterwards"

(512). It is a linguistic strategy that alludes to the anxiety around the ambiguous positioning of Puerto Ricans in the United States.

20. I use the term "im/migration" to allude to the complex position of Puerto Ricans as both migrants (who hold official U.S. citizenship status) and immigrants (as subjects of a colony). By using the term I am also acknowledging the contradictions of being a Puerto Rican subject who has legally limited rights of citizenship.

21. The question of statehood and Puerto Rico's bilingualism made headlines when 2008 Republican presidential candidate Rick Santorum suggested that Puerto Rico must adopt English as its official language, even though no such requirement exists in the U.S. Constitution. According to Santorum, "To be a state in the United States, English has to be the main language" (quoted in Summers). As reporter Juana Summers points out, though, such a requirement "would go beyond what's required of U.S. residents."

22. The film earned $93.8 million at the U.S. box office (*"Maid in Manhattan* Domestic Gross"*).

23. For a discussion of the importance that Chris Marshall's political affiliation with the Republican Party plays in the overall meritocratic message of the film, see Stephen Knadler's insightful critique in "'Blanca from the Block': Whiteness and the Transnational Latina Body."

24. Marisa's ambition to move into hotel management at such an exclusive hotel seems misguided at best, considering the fact that managers at top hotels are often recruited from hotel-management programs such as the School of Hotel Administration at Cornell University and Les Roches School of Hotel Management, but the plotline works well within a discourse on meritocracy.

25. Lopez' racialized body has garnered especially high levels of attention. For an example of how her body has been constructed, see "Brain, Brow, and Booty: Latina Iconicity in U.S. Popular Culture," by Isabel Molina-Guzmán and Angharad N. Valdivia, and Knadler's "'Blanca from the Block.'"

26. For example, in the film *Selena* (1997), Lopez played the title character, a Mexican American singer, while in *The Wedding Planner* (2001), Lopez was cast in the role of an Italian American woman. Her production company is named Nuyorican Productions, highlighting her identification as Nuyorican.

27. Lopez has at times tried to market herself as just a girl from the barrio who has been able to achieve success. For example, her song "Jenny from the Block" discusses her background. While she grew up in a middle-class home, Lopez rewrites her personal story to more dramatically fit it within the discourse of the American Dream.

28. Ironically, in what can only be described as a way of "whitening" Lopez, emphasis has been placed on the fact that while both of her parents were born in Puerto Rico and met in New York City, one of them is in fact of "European ancestry" ("Jennifer Lopez"). While some websites report that it is just one of her parents, others claim that both of the parents' families included European immigrants.

29. Judith Rollins discusses the practice of rendering domestic workers invisible and the ways in which it makes the domestic worker a "non-person." She points to the fact that it is a practice with a long history and argues that "the servant as a non-person is a perfect fit: the position is subordinate by definition, the person in it disrespected by centuries of tradition" (210).

30. In her brilliant short narrative "Myth of the Latin Woman: I Just Met a Girl Named Maria," Judith Ortiz Cofer discusses the construction of the "Maria" stereotype and the consequences that the continued perpetuation of the myth holds for Latina women.

31. This representation is quite different from the one offered by Hotel Workers Rising's statistics on occupational injuries suffered disproportionately by housekeepers in the hotel industry ("Housekeepers Are Organizing").

32. In one scene, Marisa literally tries to hide behind a toilet while cleaning Chris' room. Her housekeeping uniform helps render her invisible and allows her love interest to remain "blind" to her working body. It is only out of her uniform that her body becomes hypervisible to Chris.

33. For Alicia Schmidt Camacho, the tourist couple are playing out a "heterosexual adventure against the neocolonial backdrop of the luxury hotel" ("Migrant Melancholia" 856).

34. "On the basis of the stereotype that all Mexican women are named Maria, white employers in the Southwest frequently refer to all Latina domestics as 'Maria'" (Romero 146).

35. In her text on the effects of tourism on the Caribbean population, Polly Pattullo reports that in 2002 Puerto Rico was the American tourist's favorite destination in the Caribbean, with 28 percent of all stayovers (169).

36. América and Ester represent the gendered workforce (75 percent of employees are female) who labor in the interest of tourism in the Caribbean, as discussed in detail in Enloe's research (34).

37. While América's ability to move to the mainland might be rare, the care work she performs for the Leverrets during their vacation is not. Alicia Swords and Ronald Mize report that "child care is increasingly being displaced onto hospitality workers so that parents can enjoy their vacation, relax, and abandon all their responsibilities, including parenting" (54).

38. For another example of the physical toll of domestic labor on the body, see Barbara Ehrenreich's chapter "Scrubbing in Maine" in *Nickel and Dimed: On (Not) Getting By in America*.

39. Celia Alvarez, a housekeeper who worked for the Hyatt Regency for nineteen years, describes the long-term effects of hotel labor on a worker's body: "Cleaning between 25 and 30 rooms a day demands working fast and this is how I hurt my body. I am permanently injured in my lower back and shoulder and I can no longer work as a housekeeper. I have pain every day" (quoted in "Latina Housekeepers Hurt").

40. Pattullo reports that "throughout the Caribbean, an estimated one in seven jobs is to be found in the tourist industry; a higher percentage than in any other region of the world" (66). In her work on tourism and gender, Janet Henshall Momsen finds that "the main form of employment for women in the tourist industry is as maids in hotels" (112).

41. Mimi Sheller theorizes that the representation of the Caribbean region as Edenic and bountiful, "where others labour and living is easy," has encouraged tourists "to believe that they can engage guiltlessly in sensuous abandon and bodily pleasure," a practice she identifies as "hedonism" (177–178).

42. América's refusal to see herself as "American" is not only due to the fact that she lives in Puerto Rico. Once she migrates to New York, she continues to identify herself as Puerto Rican.

43. For a brief history of U.S. imperial policies in Puerto Rico and the effects on the Puerto Rican economy, including the inception of Operation Bootstrap and the development of the petrochemical industry, see chapter 1 in Francisco L. Rivera-Batiz and Carlos E. Santiago's *Island Paradox: Puerto Rico in the 1990s*.

44. In their essay on tourism and consumption of land in Puerto Rico and Mexico, Swords and Mize report that in 2004, Puerto Rico "totaled 3.5 million visitors, and the receipts generated from this tourism amounted to US $3.024 billion" (56). For a visual documentation of the connection between tourism and structural-adjustment policies, see Stephanie Black's powerful film on Jamaica, *Life and Debt*. See also Jacqui Alexander's chapter on Bahamian tourism, "Erotic Autonomy as a Politics of Decolonization," in *Pedagogies of Crossing*.

45. See chapter 2 for a discussion of the history of immigrants and women of color in domestic work in the United States and the visual connection to this history made in *Maid in America*.

46. Such a history also complicates the "fantastic" nation that Negrón-Muntaner argues Puerto Ricans have constructed under American colonialism (520).

47. For an account of the role that foreign interests, including the International Monetary Fund, have played in making Caribbean nations dependent on tourism, an industry that often only benefits transnational corporations, see George Gmelch's chapter "Island Tourism" in *Behind the Smile: The Working Lives of Caribbean Tourism*.

48. The fantasies, of course, are based on a nostalgic construction of colonialism that erases a history of genocide and slavery (Swords and Mize 58).

49. Maintaining an atmosphere of a past colonial time for tourists is a dangerous practice because, as Sheller argues, "depictions of Caribbean edenism underwrite performances of touristic hedonism by naturalizing the region's landscape and its inhabitants as avatars of primitivism, luxuriant corruption, sensual stimulation, ease and availability" (170).

50. When Paul Laverty was writing the screenplay for the film, he specifically sought out the advice of Rocio Saenz, a union leader of the Justice for Janitors campaign. Saenz also met with Loach and was cast in the film as a union organizer. In his article on the film, Duncan Campbell notes, "In the scene in which Rocio delivers her rallying speech, many of the extras were workers she had been responsible for organizing in real life." Saenz later became president of Service Employees International Union, Local 615.

51. For more information on the Lawrence strike, see Bruce Watson's *Bread and Roses: Mills, Migrants and the Struggle for the American Dream*.

52. What makes the current movement different from the original Bread and Roses labor movement is the role that undocumented immigration plays in creating a new level of fear. The threat of losing one's job does not pose the same danger as the threat of being deported.

53. Loach's film offers the audience the opportunity to, in Edward Said's words, "see things that are usually lost on minds that have never traveled beyond the conventional and comfortable" (63).

54. See chapter 2 for a longer discussion on border violence beyond the physical space of the border and the use of rape in controlling immigrant women's bodies.

55. In a scene that demands complete suspension of disbelief, Marisa ends up trying on a Dolce & Gabbana outfit that guest Caroline Lane asked to have returned to the hotel shop. As the proper heroine of the story, however, she makes it clear that the idea is not hers, but Stephanie's. Stephanie urges her to try on the clothing because, after all, "When will you or I ever get to try on a five-thousand-dollar anything?" Marisa's reluctance to try on the designer outfit assuages the viewer's discomfort at the idea of a domestic worker's going through a hotel guest's possessions. It also helps to set her apart from the other maids because her lying is not seen as necessarily immoral because she is inadvertently caught up in the situation. The scene is so reminiscent of the Cinderella fairy tale that Wang even has Marisa try on Caroline's shoes, which conveniently don't fit because Caroline's feet are too big.

56. See Isabel Molina-Guzmán's chapter 4 in *Dangerous Curves* for a discussion on the class politics of the film and what she refers to as "deracialized class mobility" (165).

57. One positive result of the visibility of the Strauss-Kahn case has been the attention it has brought to the issue of housekeepers' safety in the industry. Greenhouse's *New York Times* article was directly connected to coverage of the case and is an example of how media outlets used the high visibility of the story to discuss the widespread harassment of housekeepers.

58. For an interesting reading of *Bottle Rocket* as part of Anderson's authorial logic, see Devin Orgeron's "La Camera-Crayola: Authorship Comes of Age in the Cinema of Wes Anderson."

59. Lumi Cavazos is probably best known to a U.S. audience for her role as Tita in *Like Water for Chocolate* (1992).

60. Compared to that of Catalina, a similar character in the television show *My Name Is Earl*, Inez' sexualization is much more subtle. The first time the audience is introduced to Catalina, a hotel maid played by Nadine Velazquez, the camera focuses on her body, clad in a sexy maid's uniform, and Randy Hickey calls "dibs," laying a claim to her. While the practice of calling "dibs" on women in the show is made in humor, the vocal hailing, combined with her physical image, reduces Catalina to the typical hot Latina stereotype.

61. In his discussion of the function of the motel in film, Randall Teal argues that it "is often seen as a place separate from the context it is associated with, suspended somewhere between civilization and wilderness. This is not so different from how we tend to experience the motel. This portrayal helps to make these images believable, as they are both recognizable and seductive" (72). Anthony's introduction to Inez at the motel falls comfortably within Teal's discussion of the motel as an in-between space, especially since Inez' body is reduced to such a recognizable stereotype.

62. This visual strategy is also present in the sexualization of Flor during the beach scene in *Spanglish*.

63. For example, in an earlier scene, Anthony discusses his stay in a mental hospital with sorority girl Stacy Sinclair, who responds to Anthony's story with a smile and the trite "You're really complicated, aren't you?" From her college education to her pearls and preppy clothing, Stacy is represented as the modern type of woman that inhabits Anthony's privileged, but boring, world.

64. In his discussion of the creation of community in Wes Anderson's films, Brannon M. Hancock argues that "Anderson and Wilson's central characters have in common the preference for an idealized fantasy in contrast to the stark realities of their lives . . . These characters all have the startling ability to view their lives according to their own desires, seeing things the way they *want* to see them, which is not always consistent with reality as observed from the outside."

65. Hancock reads the male characters in *Bottle Rocket* as part of Anderson's practice of creating characters that have the ability to construct and reconstruct their own reality and to share in the recognition of the self that occurs through the participation in a specific community.

66. Bob is constantly being beaten up by his older brother, Future Man, and it is his helplessness in this relationship that motivates him to join Dignan and Anthony. Dignan's obsession with Mr. Henry (his former boss and local crime lord) and his need for acceptance render him a weak character who is unable to act on his own needs and desires. For an interesting reading of Dignan's worship of Mr. Henry, see Orgeron's "La Camera-Crayola" (46).

67. Loach's decision not to reduce Maya to a sexual object, however, does not mean she isn't still read as such. For example, in his review of the film, Peter Matthews refers to Maya as "feisty" and as a "Latin spitfire" ("Beyond Our Ken"). Matthews simply reduces Maya to the stereotype that continues to exist in the minds of viewers.

68. Darío offers an alternative representation to the violent masculinity represented by Correa. Instead of giving just the stereotypical representation of deviant Latino masculinity, the novel offers multiple representations of Latino males who challenge this stereotype without being idealized or romanticized.

69. Even more tragic than Maya's story is Rosa's immigrant narrative, as we discover that her family's dependence on her remittances forced her into sex work for years. During a fight over Rosa's betrayal of the union, Rosa informs Maya of the actions she has been reduced to perform for the survival of the family, including sleeping with the supervisor of Angel Services to secure Maya a job. Rosa's confrontation with her sister acts as a powerful disruption in the conventional narrative's emphasis on the myth of meritocracy.

70. After meeting with the New York Hotel and Motel Trades Council, the Pierre and

183

the Sofitel have agreed to arm their housekeepers with panic buttons, a practice the union hopes will be mandated at all New York hotels. The Pierre also held self-defense courses for its housekeeping staff. Even though these measures will help, they still position house-keepers as responsible for their own safety (Hollander, El-Ghobashy, and Shallwani).

Chapter Four

1. This slogan was shown being uttered by Citlali on a protester's sign at the UNITE HERE action in San Antonio discussed in this chapter. The sentence, which translates to "Don't mess with my people," appears on various T-shirts and images featuring Citlali.

2. The action was part of a national UNITE HERE campaign against Hyatt that took place in multiple cities, including Los Angeles, San Antonio, Chicago, and Boston. I took part in the San Antonio action.

3. Citlali is the daughter of two female goddesses, and as such she makes visible a queerness, a radical sexual politics that often remains in the margins of Chican@/Latin@ cultural productions.

4. The hundreds of community activists, workers, and supporters were under the constant surveillance not only of the Hyatt's security forces, but also of the San Antonio Police Department. The police force present seemed incommensurate with the peaceful actions of the demonstrators. The only arrests made were of eleven activists who linked arms and sat across an intersection, practicing a form of peaceful civil disobedience.

5. As Roz Kaveney points out, whether or not the superhero possesses special powers, the superhero mission remains the same: "the fight for truth, justice, and the protection of the innocent" (4).

6. This is not to say that superheroes cannot be subversive or that superheroes re-main static figures. I am specifically referencing the popular rendering of superheroes in mainstream media like television and film.

7. For more information on specific origin comics of DC characters, see Les Daniels' *DC Comics: Sixty Years of the World's Favorite Comic Book Heroes*.

8. Murray argues that among those excluded from the construction of "America" in these comics were women, minorities, and non-heteronormative individuals.

9. The motto was first introduced during Superman's debut on television in the early 1950s. In a dramatic story line—featured in the 2011 Action Comics No. 900—the char-acter of Superman goes before the United Nations to renounce his U.S. citizenship in order to embrace an international notion of justice (Gustines).

10. Sixteen of the photographs are available for viewing on the artist's website: www.dulcepinzon.com/en_projects_superhero.htm.

11. This type of superhero falls in with Kaveney's definition of the superhero without extraordinary powers who nonetheless shares the commitment to a superhero mission (4).

12. We need only look at the historical relationship between photography and pseudoscientific constructions of race to understand the very complicated role the visual has played in creating and perpetuating ideologies about people of color. Fusco goes further to argue that "the representations of race in photography have never been restricted to denigra-tion of racialized subjects; racial difference has also been seen as a spectacle and a commodity over the course of a century . . . Photography renders and delivers interracial encounters that might be dangerous, forbidden, or unattainable as safe and consumable" (20).

13. Batman is featured in two photographs, bringing the total number of photos to sixteen.

14. Walter Benjamin's famous essay "The Work of Art in the Age of Mechanical Reproduction" gestured toward the possibilities of the democratization of art that pho-tography held, but he could not have foreseen the role technology would play in the circulation of images.

15. In his discussion of press photographs, Roland Barthes argues that it is "only

when the study of each structure [of communication] has been exhausted that it will be possible to understand the manner in which they complement each other" (*Image—Music—Text* 16). While Barthes is specifically discussing the written caption that accompanies a press photograph, Pinzón's labels function in a similar manner.

16. "Top Remittance-Receiving Countries" (World Bank, *Migration and Remittances* 13).

17. "Mexico" (World Bank, *Migration and Remittances* 178).

18. In her discussion of Fred Wilson's installation photography, Jennifer A. González argues that Wilson's deployment of labels highlighted "the racist implications of photographs taken by Europeans of non-Europeans, [and] reiterated the relations of categorization and control imagined in the photographs, while also drawing attention to the act of labeling itself as a method for circumscribing meaning" (72).

19. For Pinzón's superheroes, the responsibilities to those communities left behind are made a focus of their heroism through the description of their remittances in each photograph caption.

20. El Santo removed his mask on Feb. 3, 1984, revealing his face in public for the first time in over forty years, and died of a heart attack two days later (Levi 103–104).

21. Pinzón herself worked as a union organizer in New York City ("A Conversation with Dulce Pinzón").

22. While many argue that unions are corrupt or serve only the interests of a few, the importance of organizing labor remains as vital today as it was in the beginning of the twentieth century. To understand the dire conditions of unions today, all we have to do is look at Wisconsin governor Scott Walker's aggressive anti-union proposal introduced to the state senate that "would strip government workers, including school teachers, of nearly all collective bargaining rights" (Bauer). The law, Act 10, passed in 2011, killed collective-bargaining rights for union workers whose unions opposed Walker's 2010 gubernatorial campaign. It faces yet another legal challenge, as the Wisconsin Supreme Court has agreed to hear another appeal against it (Gruenberg).

23. Bush's announcement came during his May 1, 2003, speech aboard the USS *Abraham Lincoln* ("President Bush").

24. The photographs also function as a way of centering a marginalized cultural heritage. As cultural critic Luz Calvo argues in her essay on Alma López' *Our Lady*, the "subaltern's specialized knowledge produces a particular kind of viewing pleasure for those who 'get it'" (110).

25. In the identifying label, Pinzón refers to Mendez as a "gigolo," the more commonly used word for sex worker. I choose to use "sex worker" to describe Mendez to avoid negative-value-laden terms. "Sex worker" is a more positive term that emphasizes respect for human dignity and value.

26. Wertham argued that "only someone ignorant of the fundamentals of psychiatry and of the psychopathology of sex can fail to realize a subtle atmosphere of homoerotism which pervades the adventure of the mature 'Batman and his young friend "Robin"'" (190). In his analysis of the relationship between Batman and Robin and the aesthetics of camp, Andy Medhurst argues, "If one wants to take Batman as a Real Man, the biggest stumbling block has always been Robin" (159). The truth of Medhurst's claim has been strongly asserted by recent film projects. In the latest filmic interpretation of Batman, director Christopher Nolan agreed to exclude Robin to ensure that Christian Bale would agree to play the title role in three films ("*The Dark Knight Rises*").

27. For example, Julie Newmar, who played Catwoman in six television episodes, described her interpretation of the character as "all things feminine. Was she a feminist? Hell, no! She was feminine. That's way above feminist" (quoted in Colón 22).

28. Batman's "re-heterosexualization," to use Medhurst's descriptive term, has involved the banishment of Robin and the introduction of female love interests like Vicki Veil and Catwoman (159).

29. For example, Selina Kyle (Catwoman's alter ego) develops a protective relationship with her thirteen-year-old roommate, Holly, a sex worker, who is later taken to live with Selina's sister, Maggie, a nun.

30. In discussing Catwoman, the issue of race is especially relevant, considering the television casting of Eartha Kitt in the role. While the casting of an African American actor for the role was seen as progressive by some, Kitt herself dismissed the question of race: "Was it a radical victory, a black woman portraying a traditionally white character? I don't think of myself in terms of a race. I'm an artist" (quoted in Colón 22).

31. In a direct departure from other undocumented workers, Nicky Diaz, Whitman's employee, refused to simply fade into the background.

32. Carter recalls her experiences with her Mexican grandmother: "Some of the best memories of my childhood were of being with my grandmother when she was making tortillas, having to cut the tripe when she made menudo, or sorting the sticks and stones out of the beans on her table" ("Lynda Carter").

33. In fact, Wertham found Wonder Woman quite dangerous: "The homosexual connotation of the Wonder Woman type of story is psychologically unmistakable . . . For boys, Wonder Woman is a frightening image. For girls she is a morbid ideal. Where Batman is anti-feminine, the attractive Wonder Woman and her counterparts are definitely anti-masculine" (192–193).

34. While the entrance of middle-class women into the workforce during World War II was extremely important for the feminist movement, working-class women (including white women, immigrants, and women of color) have always had to work and have not constructed labor outside of the house as necessarily a form of liberation.

35. With a budget of $100 million, Halle Berry's *Catwoman* grossed only a little over $40 million domestically ("*Catwoman* Domestic Gross"), and Jennifer Garner's *Elektra* grossed less than $25 million domestically ("*Elektra* Domestic Gross"). The 2011 Wonder Woman television incarnation was canceled after only a couple of episodes aired.

36. "Pinzón's photographs depict documented economic migrants, a group that is sometimes talked about and confused (willingly or innocently) with undocumented migrants. She is reluctant to discuss the politics of labor migration, partly because she does not live in the United States any longer but also, one suspects, because her photographs are her message" (Brook).

37. Just a few examples of the comments on the photo series are: on *PetaPixel*, user "Jpashain" argues, "The ILLEGAL immigrants are not, nor should they be portrayed, as heros!" (Zhang); *Blog the Beat* user "rich" says, "Interesting . . . we praise (illegal) mexican immigrants for working in conditions that were deemed unfair several decades ago" ("Dulce Pinzón's Superheroes"); and on *Blastr*, users like "Mary" and "illegalmeansillegal" are taken to task by other commenters for assuming the photographs are of undocumented workers (Edelman).

38. For example, the massive mobilization efforts of multiple community organizers and media personalities led to immigration rallies throughout the country in 2006. While these rallies helped to raise awareness around HR 4437, the Border Protection, Anti-terrorism and Illegal Immigration Control Act (2005), and helped create connections between different immigrants' rights groups, the images of millions of mobilizing brown bodies were used by pundits like Glenn Beck to instill fear in his audience.

39. This is not to say that the series has not faced valid criticism. In her discussion of the changing status of deported immigrants, Nyberg Sorensen argues, "From being a migrant superhero, provider of family and community development . . . [forced-return migrants] become deportee trash over night" (110). Nyberg Sorensen's critique of the Central American governments' use of superhero rhetoric to secure continuous remittances from immigrant workers abroad is a valid one, but it is dangerous to equate state strategies of manipulation with individual strategies of resistance. While I agree

that the strategy that positions immigrant workers as heroes by national governments is a self-serving and problematic practice, it is not necessarily fair to compare Pinzón's work to government propaganda. The impetus behind her use of the superhero is different and must be taken into account. Pinzón's series is intended for an American audience, to intervene in the erasure of immigrant workers' labor. It is not intended to absolve the Mexican government for its inability to provide for its citizens or to encourage Mexican citizens to immigrate for the good of their country. Collapsing the differences is a dismissive gesture that fails to account for the use of the superhero image for resistance. I also find Nyberg Sorensen's use of the terms "garbage" and "trash" to describe immigrant workers problematic. While I understand the ways in which she is being critical of the ease with which immigrants are deported and rejected, the use of such rhetoric works only to further dehumanize them. For example, see Alicia Schmidt Camacho's critique of the fatalistic discourse used in the description of the feminicide victims in Juárez, Mexico, and the ways in which such a discourse further victimizes individuals ("Body Counts").

40. Because declaring the day a holiday does not include any tangible changes to working conditions, wages, or health-care coverage, it would be easy to dismiss the holiday as just one more empty gesture made by politicians looking for votes. The use of the term "Super Domésticas" can be seen as a patronizing move, a pat on the head to domestic workers, a strategy of giving them a nice title while denying them any real reform or acknowledgment of worker rights. However, it is a small step in recognizing the hard work that domestic workers perform on a daily basis and the impact that their labor has on the running of the city.

41. The film captures the creative process of embodying experience for testimony that Cherríe Moraga sees as a possibility in the space of the theater (45).

42. The *acto*, or act, was a popular form of theatrical production employed by Luis Valdez and Teatro Campesino in the 1960s and 1970s in their effort to educate and mobilize migrant workers. The performances often took place on the side of the road and utilized the workers in the productions to make the plays a true community effort. For more information on Teatro Campesino, Valdez, and *actos*, see Jorge Huerta's *Chicano Theatre: Themes and Forms* and Yolanda Broyles-González' *El Teatro Campesino: Theater in the Chicano Movement*.

43. Alvarez' website is http://paradisoarts.com/htdocs/lauraalvarez.html.

44. In *Borderlands: The New Mestiza = La Frontera*, Anzaldúa argues for a new *mestiza* consciousness, one that is based on the negotiation of multiple subjectivities. The border crosser is one who employs this consciousness to inhabit what seem like contradictory locations; she learns now to survive in the in-between spaces borders try to demarcate.

45. For example, DAS infiltrates the houses (one in Mexico City and one in Los Angeles) of the telenovela director; his having a home in the United States alludes to the fact that his investments and financial interests are not limited to just the Mexican side of the border ("Prime Time Sirvienta" and "The Journey Continues," both songs in the DAS series).

46. In each of the visual pieces, DAS wears a different version of her uniform. A Mexican immigrant in a ball gown might be too conspicuous for a public more used to the image of immigrant Latinas as maids. Instead, her costume gives her access to spaces that would most commonly be concealed from public view (bedrooms, home offices, etc.), but would need to be cleaned on a regular basis. In effect, DAS is employing the strategy of hiding in plain sight.

47. She uses the bus to traverse the classed spaces that exist between the traditional service worker and her employer. In an interesting blurring of boundaries between art and reality, Alvarez informs her web visitors that "DAS has been featured as life-size paintings at the San Francisco Muni bus stops."

48. See chapter 2 for a more in-depth discussion on unpaid care work.

49. For an insightful artistic critique of the use of the domestic-worker uniform in constructions of race and gender, see Yolanda López' installation *The Nanny*, from her 1994 series *Women's Work Is Never Done*—discussed in Pérez' chapter 2.

50. The image of Guadalupe on the apron functions similarly to Pinzón's incorporation of the Mexican superheroes. Those images provide a viewing pleasure for individuals who recognize and identify with them.

51. The image of the Virgen de Guadalupe proved extremely important in the creation of solidarity for the union efforts of the United Farm Workers in the 1960s. Cesar Chavez used the Virgen as a symbol for the community to rally behind.

52. As Pérez points out, "The use or representation of dress and body ornamentation in visual, installation, or performative art practice is . . . both symbolic and productive" (50).

53. Luz Calvo argues that the Virgen de Guadalupe, "precisely because she is always already a polyvalent sign—is especially available for retooling and radical configuration by Chicana artists" (115). In her response to the uproar surrounding her digital print *Our Lady*, Alma López writes that when she sees her print and other Chicana artists' visual works portraying the Virgen, she sees "Chicanas creating a deep and meaningful connection to this revolutionary cultural female image that appeared to an inspired indigenous person at a time of genocide, and as an inspiration during liberation struggles such as the Mexican Revolution and the Chicano civil rights movement. I see Chicanas who understand faith" (253). The faith López alludes to is not a patriarchal one that inhabits the space of the church, but a much more syncretic one that allows for female agency and subjectivity.

54. In his controversial and much-quoted essay "The Hispanic Challenge," Samuel P. Huntington argues that the unwillingness or inability to assimilate by Hispanic immigrants poses a threat to the very construction of the nation and could tear the nation apart. See Sánchez and Pita's essay "Theses on the Latino Bloc" for a critique of the rhetoric espoused by Huntington. The authors also take on the difficult task of identifying the vital commonalities and differences that exist within the heterogeneous Latin@ community.

55. Pérez argues that the DAS series is "at once a fantasy about social empowerment and an allegory of the artist as provocateur within hegemonic culture's own 'home'" (181). In fact, for Pérez, Alvarez herself is a sort of "spy in the art world," learning how to use the conventions of a field to subvert it (186).

Conclusion

1. Elvia Claudio, personal interview, Oct. 11, 2011.

2. While most of us are familiar with the tedious task of making a bed, we do not have to make over thirty beds a day.

3. Claudio is also very cognizant of the role that tourism plays in the city's economy and in the hotel industry: "Y aparte de que no es nada mas ocuparnos de nuestro trabajo, es tambien preocuparnos por la gente porque necesitamos que la gente siga visitando a San Antonio. Necesitamos que se queden en los hoteles porque necesitamos trabajo. Si la gente no viene, nosotros no tenemos trabajo" (Besides worrying about our jobs, we also worry about the customers because we need people to continue to visit San Antonio. We need them to stay in the hotels because we need the work. If people don't come, we don't have work [my translation]).

4. Claudio also does not see UNITE HERE as coming in and "saving" her and her fellow workers. She sees the union as helping them achieve change.

Bibliography

"A Conversation with Dulce Pinzón." *The NYMPHOTO Blog.* 7 Jan. 2010. Web. 10 Apr. 2011.

Adib, Amel, and Yvonne Guerrier. "The Interlocking of Gender with Nationality, Race, Ethnicity and Class: The Narratives of Women in Hotel Work." *Gender, Work and Organization* 10.4 (2003): 413–432. Print.

Alba, Richard, and Victor Nee. "Rethinking Assimilation Theory for a New Era of Immigration." *International Migration Review* 31.4 (1997): 826–874. Print.

Alexander, Jacqui. *Pedagogies of Crossing: Meditations on Feminism, Sexual Politics, Memory, and the Sacred.* Durham, NC: Duke UP, 2006. Print.

Alvarez, Laura. *Double Agent Sirvienta* (multimedia series). 1996-2005. *Paradiso Arts.* Web. 14 Oct. 2013.

———. "Double Agent Sirvienta." *Urban Latino Cultures: La vida latina en L.A.* Ed. Gustavo Leclerc, Raul Villa, and Michael J. Dear. Thousand Oaks: SAGE Publications, 1999. 108-111. Print.

"America Is a Shining City upon a Hill." *SourceWatch.* 25 June 2007. Web. 1 May 2012.

Anderson, Bridget. *Doing the Dirty Work?: The Global Politics of Domestic Labour.* London: Zed, 2000. Print.

Anderson, Wes, dir. *Bottle Rocket.* Columbia Pictures, 1996. Film.

Anzaldúa, Gloria. *Borderlands: The New Mestiza = La Frontera.* 2nd ed. San Francisco: Aunt Lute, 1999. Print.

Archibold, Randal C. "Arizona Enacts Stringent Law on Immigration." *New York Times* 23 Apr. 2010. Print.

Bacevich, Andrew. "Sarah Palin and John Winthrop." *Huffington Post.* 3 Oct. 2008. Web. 1 May 2012.

Baker, Al, and Steven Erlanger. "I.M.F. Chief, Apprehended at Airport, Is Accused of Sexual Attack." *New York Times* 14 May 2011. Web. 2 May 2012.

Barthes, Roland. *Image—Music—Text.* Trans. Stephen Heath. New York: Hill and Wang, 1978. Print.

———. *Mythologies.* 1st ed. Trans. Annette Levers. New York: Farrar, Straus and Giroux, 1972. Print.

Bauer, Scott. "Wisconsin Senate to Vote on Anti-union Bill." *Yahoo!* 17 Feb. 2011. Web. 17 Feb. 2011.

Bejarano, Cynthia. "Senseless Deaths and Holding the Line." *Criminology and Public Policy* 6.2 (2007): 267–274. Print.

Benjamin, Walter. "The Work of Art in the Age of Mechanical Reproduction." *Illuminations: Essays and Reflections.* Ed. Hannah Arendt. Trans. Harry Zohn. New York: Schocken, 1969. 217–252. Print.

Black, Stephanie, dir. *Life and Debt.* Tuff Gong Pictures Prod., 2001. Film.

Blum, William. *Killing Hope: U.S. Military and CIA Interventions since World War II.* Monroe, ME: Common Courage, 1995. Print.

Boelhower, William Q. "The Immigrant Novel as Genre." *MELUS* 8.1 (1981): 3-13. Print.

Brook, Pete. "Photog Gives Migrant Workers the Superhero Treatment." *Wired.* 14 Sept. 2010. Web. 3 May 2012.

Brooks, James L., dir. *Spanglish.* Columbia Pictures, 2004. Film.

Broyles-González, Yolanda. *El Teatro Campesino: Theater in the Chicano Movement.* Austin: U of Texas P, 1994. Print.

Budoff Brown, Carrie. "Gov. Candidates in 20 States Endorse Anti-immigration Laws." *Politico.* 2 Sept. 2010. Web. 30 Apr. 2012.

Bulosan, Carlos. *America Is in the Heart.* Seattle: U of Washington P, 1973. Print.

Bureau of Labor Statistics. *Career Guide to Industries, 2010–11.* U.S. Dept. of Labor. Web. 5 July 2011.

Calvo, Luz. "Art Comes for the Archbishop: The Semiotics of Contemporary Chicana Feminism and the Work of Alma López." *Our Lady of Controversy: Alma López's "Irreverent Apparition."* Ed. Alicia Gaspar de Alba and Alma López. Austin: U of Texas P, 2011. Print.

Campbell, Duncan. "The Story That Inspired Ken Loach to Shoot a Film in LA." *The Guardian.* 19 Apr. 2001. Web. 3 May 2012.

Castañeda, Antonia. "History and the Politics of Violence against Women." *Living Chicana Theory.* Ed. Carla Trujillo. Berkeley, CA: Third Women, 1998. 310–319. Print.

Castles, Stephen, and Mark J. Miller. *The Age of Migration: International Population Movements in the Modern World.* London: Macmillan, 1998. Print.

"Catwoman Domestic Gross." *Box Office Mojo.* 2004. Web. 3 May 2012.

Chang, Grace. *Disposable Domestics: Immigrant Women Workers in the Global Economy.* Cambridge, MA: South End, 2000. Print.

Childress, Alice. *Like One of the Family: Conversations from a Domestic's Life.* Boston: Beacon, 1986. Print.

Claudio, Elvia. Personal interview. 11 Oct. 2011.

Colón, Suzan. *Catwoman: The Life and Times of a Feline Fatale.* San Francisco: Chronicle, 2003. Print.

Corbett, Janice A. "Ciudad Juárez 4th Largest City." *TradePort.* 3 Nov. 2000. Web. 25 July 2001.

Corpi, Lucha. *Cactus Blood: A Mystery Novel.* Houston: Arte Público, 1995. Print.

Cortés, Carlos E. "Who Is Maria? What Is Juan? Dilemmas of Analyzing the Chicano Image in U.S. Feature Films." *Chicanos and Film: Representation and Resistance.* Ed. Chon A. Noriega. Minneapolis: U of Minnesota P, 1992. 74–93. Print.

Coscarelli, Joe. "Brisenia Flores Is Still not Quite National News: Why?—New York News—Runnin' Scared." *Village Voice.* 1 Nov. 2011. Web. 23 Jan. 2012.

Cranford, Cynthia. "Constructing Union Motherhood: Gender and Social Reproduction in the Los Angeles 'Justice for Janitors' Movement." *Qualitative Sociology* 30:4 (2007): 361–381. Print.

———. "Gendered Resistance: Organizing Justice for Janitors in Los Angeles." *Challenging the Market: The Struggle to Regulate Work and Income.* Ed. Jim Stanford and Leah F. Vosko. Montreal: McGill-Queen's UP, 2004. 309–329. Print.

Crèvecoeur, J. Hector St. John. *Letters from an American Farmer.* London: Davies and Davis, 1782. Print.

Daniels, Les. *DC Comics: Sixty Years of the World's Favorite Comic Book Heroes.* 1st ed. New York: Bulfinch, 1995. Print.

"*The Dark Knight Rises* (2012): Did You Know?" *IMDb.* Web. 4 Apr. 2012.

Davis, Mike, and Justin Akers Chacón. *No One Is Illegal.* Chicago: Haymarket, 2006. Print.

di Donato, Pietro. *Christ in Concrete.* New York: New American Library, 1993. Print.

"Dominique Strauss-Kahn Claims Diplomatic Immunity in Maid Case." *BBC News.* 28 Mar. 2012. Web. 2 May 2012.

"Dominique Strauss-Kahn Rues New York Hotel Maid Liaison." *BBC News.* 18 Sept. 2011. Web. 3 May 2012.

"Dulce Pinzón's Superheroes." *The Beat: The News Blog of Comics Culture.* Web. 3 May 2012.

Edelman, Scott. "Why Migrant Workers Are Dressing Up as Superheroes." *Blastr.* 10 Nov. 2009. Web. 3 May 2012.

Ehrenreich, Barbara. *Nickel and Dimed: On (Not) Getting By in America.* New York: Holt, 2001. Print.

Ehrenreich, Barbara, and Arlie Russell Hochschild, eds. *Global Woman: Nannies, Maids, and Sex Workers in the New Economy.* New York: Holt, 2002. Print.

"Elektra Domestic Gross." *Box Office Mojo.* 2005. Web. 3 May 2012.

Enloe, Cynthia. *Bananas, Beaches, and Bases: Making Feminist Sense of International Politics.* Berkeley: U of California P, 1989. Print.

Ewing, Alexander. "On Bootstraps." *More Intelligent Life.* 8 Apr. 2009. Web. 3 Mar. 2012.

Falcón, Sylvanna. "'National Security' and the Violation of Women: Militarized Border Rape at the U.S.–Mexico Border." *Color of Violence: The INCITE! Anthology.* Cambridge, MA: South End, 2000. 119–129. Print.

———. "Rape as a Weapon of War: Advancing Human Rights for Women at the U.S.– Mexico Border." *Social Justice* 28.2 (2001): 31–50. Print.

Fernandez, Ronald. *The Disenchanted Island: Puerto Rico and the United States in the Twentieth Century.* Westport, CT: Praeger, 1996. Print.

Fischer, William, et al., eds. *Identity, Community, and Pluralism in American Life.* New York: Oxford UP, 1997. Print.

Flores, Lisa A. "Constructing Rhetorical Borders." *Critical Studies in Media Communication* 20.4 (2003): 362–387. Print.

Foucault, Michel. "7 January 1976." *"Society Must Be Defended." Lectures at the Collège de France, 1975–1976.* Ed. Mauro Bertani and Alessandro Fontana. Trans. David Macey. New York: Picador, 2003. 1-22. Print.

Fregoso, Rosa Linda. *MeXicana Encounters: The Making of Social Identities on the Borderlands.* Berkeley: U of California P, 2003. Print.

Friedman, Natalie. "Nostalgia, Nationhood, and the New Immigrant Narrative: Gary Shteyngart's *The Russian Debutante's Handbook* and the Post-Soviet Experience." *Iowa Journal of Cultural Studies* 5 (2004): 77–87. Print.

Frontera NorteSur. "Latin America Border Series: The Century of the Woman Migrant." *New Mexico State University Frontera NorteSur: Online News Coverage of the US–Mexico Border.* 7 March 2006. Web. 5 June 2010.

Fusco, Coco. "Racial Times, Racial Marks, Racial Metaphors." *Only Skin Deep: Changing Visions of the American Self.* Ed. Coco Fusco and Brian Wallis. New York: International Center of Photography/Harry N. Abrams, 2003. 13–50. Print.

Gabaccia, Donna. *From the Other Side: Women, Gender and Immigrant Life in the U.S., 1820–1990.* Bloomington: Indiana UP, 1994. Print.

Galarza, Ernesto. *Merchants of Labor: The Mexican Bracero Story: An Account of the Managed Migration of Mexican Farm Workers in California, 1942–1960.* San Jose, PR: Rosicrucian, 1964. Print.

Gamboa, Suzanne. "Obama Administration Scraps Border Fence." *MSNBC.* 14 Jan. 2011. Web. 2 May 2012.

Gans, Herbert J. "Toward a Reconciliation of 'Assimilation' and 'Pluralism': The Interplay of Acculturation and Ethnic Retention." *International Migration Review* 31.4 (1997): 875-892. Web. 11 July 2011.

Garcia, Richard A. *Rise of the Mexican American Middle Class: San Antonio, 1929–1941.* College Station: Texas A&M UP, 2000. Print.

Gauguin, Paul. *Where Do We Come From? What Are We? Where Are We Going?* 1897. Museum of Fine Arts, Boston. *Museum of Fine Arts.* Web. 3 May 2012. <http://www.mfa.org/collections/object/where-do-we-come-from-what-are-we-where-are-we-going-32558>

Gibson, William E. "Bush Renews Proposal for Guest-Worker Program." *Sun Sentinel* [Fort Lauderdale, FL] 19 Oct. 2005. Print.

Gmelch, George. *Behind the Smile: The Working Lives of Caribbean Tourism.* Bloomington: Indiana UP, 2003. Print.

Golash-Boza, Tanya Maria. *Immigration Nation: Raids, Detentions, and Deportations in Post–9/11 America.* Boulder, CO: Paradigm, 2011. Print.

Gómez Bolaños, Roberto. "Chespirito." *Chespirito.* 2004. Web. 2 May 2012.

González, Jennifer A. *Subject to Display: Reframing Race in Contemporary Installation Art.* Cambridge, MA: MIT P, 2008. Print.

González, Jennifer A., and Michelle Habell-Pallán. "Heterotopias and Shared Methods of Resistance: Navigating Social Space and Spaces of Identity." *Inscriptions* 7 (1994): n. pag. Web. 2 May 2012.

Good, Daniel B. "Billions for a U.S.–Mexico Border Fence, but Is It Doing Any Good?" *Christian Science Monitor* 19 Sept. 2006. Web. 3 May 2012.

Gordillo, Luz María. *Mexican Women and the Other Side of Immigration: Engendering Transnational Ties.* Austin: U Texas P, 2010. Print.

Greenhouse, Steven. "For Hotel Housekeepers, Sexual Affronts a Known Hazard." *New York Times* 20 May 2011. Web. 3 May 2012.

Grier, Peter. "Meg Whitman and the Perils of Employing Illegal Help: Six Memorable Cases." *Christian Science Monitor* 29 Sept. 2010. Web. 3 May 2012.

Gruenberg, Mark. "Walker's Anti-Union Law Heads for New Test in Court." *People's World.* 19 June 2013. Web. Oct. 2013.

Guerin-Gonzales, Camille. *Mexican Workers and American Dreams: Immigration, Repatriation, and California Farm Labor, 1900–1939.* New Brunswick, NJ: Rutgers UP, 1994. Print.

Guerrete, Rob T. "Immigration Policy, Border Security, and Migrant Deaths: An Impact Evaluation of Life-Saving Efforts under the Border Safety Initiative." *Criminology and Public Policy* 6:2 (May 2007): 245-266. Print.

Gustines, George Gene. "Superman Renounces His U.S. Citizenship." *Arts Beat: The Culture at Large.* 29 Apr. 2011. Web. 29 Apr. 2011.

Habell-Pallán, Michelle. "Marisela Norte, *NORTE/word.*" *Reading U.S. Latina Writers: Remapping American Literature.* Ed. Alvina E. Quintana. 1st ed. New York: Palgrave Macmillan, 2003. 163–172. Print.

Hancock, Brannon M. "A Community of Characters: The Narrative Self in the Films of Wes Anderson." *Journal of Religion and Film* 9.2 (2005): n. pag. Web. 3 May 2012.

Hanska, Jan. *Reagan's Mythical America: Storytelling as Political Leadership.* New York: Palgrave Macmillan, 2012. Print.

Hill Collins, Patricia. "Like One of the Family: Race, Ethnicity, and the Paradox of US National Identity." *Racial Studies* 24:1 (2001): 3-28. Web. 14 Oct. 2013.

Hobsbawm, Eric, and Terence O. Ranger, eds. *The Invention of Tradition.* Cambridge: Cambridge UP, 1992. Print.

Hollander, Sophia, Tamer El-Ghobashy, and Pervaiz Shallwani. "After Hotel Attacks: Panic Buttons." *Wall Street Journal* 1 June 2011. Web. 3 May 2012.

Hondagneu-Sotelo, Pierrette. *Doméstica: Immigrant Workers Cleaning and Caring in the Shadows of Affluence.* Berkeley: U of California P, 2001. Print.

Horatio Alger Association of Distinguished Americans. "Horatio Alger, Jr." N.d. Web. 13 Jan. 2004.

Horsman, Reginald. *Manifest Destiny: The Origins of American Racial Anglo-Saxonism.* Cambridge: Harvard UP, 1981. Print.

"Housekeepers Are Organizing for Safe and Secure Workplaces." *Hotel Workers Rising!* UNITE HERE. N.d. Web. 13 Oct. 2013.

Hsu, Spence H. "In Border Fence's Path, Congressional Roadblocks." *Washington Post* 6 Oct. 2006. A01. Web. 3 May 2012.

Huerta, Jorge A. *Chicano Theater: Themes and Forms.* Ypsilanti, MI: Bilingual Press, 1982. Print.

Humane Borders. "Migrant Deaths, Rescue Beacons, Water Stations 2000–2011." *Humane Borders/Fronteras Compasivas.* Mar. 2012. Web. 2 May 2012.

Huntington, Samuel P. "The Hispanic Challenge." *Foreign Policy* 1 Mar. 2004. Web. 30 Apr. 2012.

"Janitors Relive Story of Their Struggle." *New York Times* 18 June 2000. Web. 2 May 2012.

"Jennifer Lopez." *IMDb*. Web. 3 May 2012.

Kanellos, Nicolás. *Hispanic Immigrant Literature: El Sueño del Retorno*. Austin: U of Texas P, 2011. Print.

Kanhai, Rosanne. "'Sensing Designs in History's Muddles': Global Feminism and the Postcolonial Novel." *Modern Language Studies* 26.4 (1996): 119–130. Print.

Katz, Basil, and Bernd Debusmann Jr. "Egyptian Pleads Guilty to Abusing NY Hotel Maid." *Reuters* 27 June 2011. Web. 3 May 2012.

Katzman, David M. *Seven Days a Week*. Champaign: U of Illinois P, 1981. Print.

Kaveney, Roz. *Superheroes!: Capes and Crusaders in Comics and Films*. 1st ed. New York: Tauris, 2008. Print.

Knadler, Stephen. "'Blanca from the Block': Whiteness and the Transnational Latina Body." *Genders* 41 (2005): n. pag. Web. 3 May 2012.

Koch, Kathleen. "Bush OKs 700-mile Border Fence." *CNN.com*. 26 Oct. 2006. Web. 19 Apr. 2011.

Kuhn, David Paul. "'Mission Accomplished' Revisited." *CBS News* 5 Dec. 2007. Web. 3 May 2012.

"Latina Housekeepers Hurt." *Hotel Workers Rising!* UNITE HERE. 14 Apr. 2010. Web. 2 May 2012.

Lazarus, Emma. "The New Colossus." *National Park Service*. Web. 2 May 2012.

Lee, Catherine. *Prostitutes and Picture Brides*. San Diego: University of California Center for Comparative Immigration Studies, 2003. Print.

Lee, Stan, writ.; Steve Ditko, illus.; and Jack Kirby, penc. *Amazing Fantasy No. 15*. Marvel Comics, 1962. Print.

Lenz, Brooke. "Postcolonial Fiction and the Outsider Within: Toward a Literary Practice of Feminist Standpoint Theory." *NWSA Journal* 16.2 (2004): 98–120. Print.

Levi, Heather. *World of Lucha Libre: Secrets, Revelations, and Mexican National Identity*. Durham, NC: Duke UP, 2008. Print.

Linebaugh, Peter, and Marcus Rediker. *The Many-Headed Hydra: Sailors, Slaves, Commoners, and the Hidden History of the Revolutionary Atlantic*. Boston: Beacon, 2000. Print.

Loach, Ken, dir. *Bread and Roses*. Lionsgate, 2000. Film.

Loomer, Lisa. *Living Out*. New York: Dramatists Play Service, 2003. Print.

López, Alma. *Our Lady*. 1999. Digital. *www.almalopez.com*. 2001. Web. 14 Oct. 2013.

———. "Silencing Our Lady: La Respuesta de Alma." *Aztlán* 26.2 (2001): 249–268. Print.

López, Yolanda. *The Nanny*. 1994. Mixed media. *Persimmon Tree*. Web. 14 Oct. 2013.

Lowe, Lisa. *Immigrant Acts: On Asian American Cultural Politics*. Durham, NC: Duke UP, 1996. Print.

———. "Immigrant Literatures: A Modern Structure of Feeling." *Literature on the Move: Comparing Diasporic Ethnicities in Europe and the Americas*. Ed. Dominique Marcais. Heidelberg, Germany: Universitätsverlag C. Winter Heidelberg, 2002. 1–14. Print.

Lydersen, Kari. *Out of the Sea and into the Fire: Immigration from Latin America to the U.S. in the Global Age*. Monroe, ME: Common Courage, 2005. Print.

"Lynda Carter." *IMDb*. Web. 3 May 2012.

"*Maid in America*: Synopsis." *Impacto Films*. Web. 8 Apr. 2011.

"*Maid in America*: The Women." *Impacto Films*. Web. 8 Apr. 2011.

"*Maid in Manhattan* Domestic Gross." *Box Office Mojo*. Web. 3 May 2012.

Mariscal, Jorge, and Mónica Jaúregui. "Still Waiting, Still DREAMing." *Committee Opposed to Militarism and the Draft (COMD)*. Mar. 2010. Web. 2 May 2012.

Márquez, Antonio. "The American Dream in the Chicano Novel." *Rocky Mountain Review of Language and Literature* 37.1-2 (1983): 4–19. Print.

Matthews, Peter. "Beyond Our Ken." *BFI Sight & Sound*. May 2001. Web. 3 May 2012.

McNamee, Stephen J., and Robert K. Miller. "The Meritocracy Myth." *Sociation Today* 12.1 (2004): n. pag. Print.

Medhurst, Andy. "Batman, Deviance and Camp." *The Many Lives of Batman: Critical Approaches to a Superhero and His Media*. Ed. Roberta E. Pearson and William Uricchio. New York: Routledge, 1991. 149–163. Print.

Midnight Notes Collective. *Midnight Oil: Work, Energy, War, 1973–1992*. New York: Autonomedia, 1992. Print.

Miller, Frank. *Batman: Year One*. DC Comics Database Wikia. N.d. Web. 13 Oct. 2013.

Miranda, Lin-Manuel. "Hundreds of Stories." *In the Heights*. Perf. Olga Merediz. Ghostlight, 2008. Audio CD.

———. "Paciencia y Fe." *In the Heights*. Perf. Olga Merediz. Ghostlight, 2008. Audio CD.

Mize, Ronald L., and Alicia C. S. Swords. *Consuming Mexican Labor: From the Bracero Program to NAFTA*. Toronto: U of Toronto P, 2010. Print.

Molina-Guzmán, Isabel. *Dangerous Curves: Latina Bodies in the Media*. New York: New York UP, 2010. Print.

Molina-Guzmán, Isabel, and Angharad N. Valdivia. "Brain, Brow, and Booty: Latina Iconicity in U.S. Popular Culture." *The Communication Review* 7.2 (2004): 205–221. Print.

Momsen, Janet Henshall. "Tourism, Gender and Development in the Caribbean." *Tourism: A Gender Analysis*. Ed. Vivian Kinnaird and Derek R. Hall. Chichester, England: Wiley, 1994. 106-119. Print.

Moraga, Cherríe. "An Irrevocable Promise: Staging the Story Xicana." *Radical Acts: Theatre and Feminist Pedagogies of Change*. Ed. Ann Elizabeth Armstrong and Kathleen Juhl. San Francisco: Aunt Lute, 2007. 45–56. Print.

Muller, Gilbert H. *New Strangers in Paradise: The Immigrant Experience in Contemporary American Fiction*. Lexington: UP of Kentucky, 1999. Print.

Murray, Chris. "Popaganda: Superhero Comics and Propaganda." *Comics and Culture: Analytical and Theoretical Approaches to Comics*. Ed. Anne Magnussen and Hans-Christian Christiansen. Copenhagen: Museum Tusculanum, 2000. 141–156. Print.

My Name Is Earl, "Pilot." *My Name Is Earl: Season 1*. Writ. Gregory Thomas Garcia. Dir. Marc Buckland. Twentieth Century Fox Home Entertainment, 2006. DVD.

Nahshon, Edna, ed. *From the Ghetto to the Melting Pot: Israel Zangwill's Jewish Plays: Three Play Scripts*. Detroit, MI: Wayne State UP, 2006. Print.

Nakano Glenn, Evelyn. *Forced to Care: Coercion and Caregiving in America*. Cambridge: Harvard UP, 2010. Print.

Nava, Gregory, dir. *El Norte*. Cinecom Pictures, 1984. Film.

Negrón-Muntaner, Frances. "When I Was a Puerto Rican Lesbian: Meditations on *Brincando el charco*: Portrait of a Puerto Rican." *GLQ: A Journal of Lesbian and Gay Studies* 5.4 (1999): 511–526. Print.

"New York Area Clubs." *New York Road Runners*. Web. 9 Apr. 2012.

No More Deaths. *A Culture of Cruelty*. 2011. Web. 3 May 2012.

Norte, Marisela. "Act of the Faithless." *NORTE/word*. New Alliance Records, 1991. Audio CD.

Nyberg Sorensen, Ninna. "The Rise and Fall of the 'Migrant Superhero' and the New 'Deportee Trash.'" *Border-Lines: Journal of the Latino Research Center* 5 (2011): 90–120. Web. 3 May 2012.

Oliver, Lawrence J. "Deconstruction or Affirmative Action: The Literary-Political Debate over the 'Ethnic Question.'" *American Literary History* 3.4 (1991): 792–808. Print.

Orgeron, Devin. "La Camera-Crayola: Authorship Comes of Age in the Cinema of Wes Anderson." *Cinema Journal* 46.2 (2007): 40–65. Print.

Ortiz Cofer, Judith. "Myth of the Latin Woman: I Just Met a Girl Named Maria." *The Latin Deli: Telling the Lives of Barrio Women*. Athens: U of Georgia P, 1993. 148–154. Print.

Paredes, Raymund A. "Mexican American Authors and the American Dream." *MELUS* 8.4 (1981): 71–80. Print.

Parreñas, Rhacel Salazar. *Children of Global Migration: Transnational Families and Gender Woes*. Stanford, CA: Stanford UP, 2005. Print.

Pattullo, Polly. *Last Resorts: The Cost of Tourism in the Caribbean*. London: Latin American Bureau, 2005. Print.

Payant, Katherine B., and Toby Rose, eds. *The Immigrant Experience in North American Literature: Carving Out a Niche*. Westport, CT: Greenwood, 1999. Print.

Perea, Juan F. "American Languages, Cultural Pluralism, and Official English." *The Latino/a Condition: A Critical Reader*. Ed. Richard Delgado and Jean Stefancic. New York: New York UP, 1998. 566–573. Print.

Pérez, Laura E. *Chicana Art: The Politics of Spiritual and Aesthetic Alterities*. Durham, NC: Duke UP, 2007. Print.

Pérez y González, María E. *Puerto Ricans in the United States*. Westport, CT: Greenwood, 2000. Print.

Pew Hispanic Center. "Statistical Portrait of the Foreign-Born Population in the United States, 2009." *Pew Research Center*. 17 Feb. 2011. Web. 2 May 2012.

Pinzón, Dulce. *Superheroes*. 2005. *dulce pinzón*. Web. 3 May 2012.

Pokorak, Jeffrey J. "Rape Victims and Prosecutors: The Inevitable Ethical Conflict of De Facto Client/Attorney Relationships." *South Texas Law Review* 48 (2007): 695–728. Web. 25 Jan. 2012.

Prado, Anayansi, dir. *Maid in America*. Impacto Films, 2004. Film.

"President Bush Announces Major Combat Operations in Iraq Have Ended." 1 May 2003. *George W. Bush White House Archives*. Web. 3 May 2012.

Riccardi, Nicholas. "Brisenia Flores: Mother Describes Border Vigilante Killings in Arizona." *Los Angeles Times* 1 Nov. 1925. Web. 23 Jan. 2012.

Riggen, Patricia, dir. *La Misma Luna*. Twentieth Century Fox, 2007. Film.

Rochin, Refugio I., and Lionel Fernandez. "U.S. Latino Patriots: From the American Revolution to Afghanistan, An Overview." 2002. *Pew Research Center*. Web. 3 May 2012. <http://www.pewhispanic.org/files/reports/17.3.pdf>.

Rodriguez, Richard. "Cultural Legacy." *PBS Online Newshour*. 30 Aug. 1998. Web. 3 Mar. 2012.

Rollins, Judith. *Between Women: Domestics and Their Employers*. Philadelphia: Temple UP, 1985. Print.

Romero, Mary. *Maid in the U.S.A.* New York: Routledge, 1992. Print.

Ruiz, Vicki. "By the Day or Week: Mexicana Domestic Workers in El Paso." *Women on the U.S.–Mexico Border: Responses to Change*. Ed. Vicki L. Ruiz and Susan Tiano. Boston: Allen and Unwin, 1987. 61-76. Print.

Said, Edward. *Representations of the Intellectual: The 1993 Reith Lectures*. New York: Vintage, 1996. Print.

Saldívar, Ramón. *Chicano Narrative: The Dialects of Difference*. Madison: U of Wisconsin P, 1990. Print.

———. "A Dialect of Difference: Towards a Theory of the Chicano Novel." *MELUS* 6.3 (1979): 73–92. Print.

———. "Ideologies of the Self: Chicano Autobiography." *Diacritics* 15.3 (1985): 23–43. Print.

Sánchez, Rosaura. "Ideological Discourses in Arturo Islas's *The Rain God*." *Criticism in the Borderlands: Studies in Chicano Literature, Culture, and Ideology*. Ed. Héctor Calderón and José David Saldívar. Durham, NC: Duke UP, 1991. 114–126. Print.

Sánchez, Rosaura, and Beatrice Pita. "Theses on the Latino Bloc: A Critical Perspective." *Aztlán* 31.2 (2006): 25–53. Print.

Sánchez-Scott, Milcha. *Latina. Necessary Theater: Six Plays about the Chicano Experience*. Ed. Jorge Huerta. Houston: Arte Público, 1989. 76-141. Print.

Sandoval, Chela. *Methodology of the Oppressed*. Minneapolis: U of Minnesota P, 2000. Print.

Santiago, Esmeralda. *America's Dream.* New York: Harper Collins, 1996. Print.

Sassen, Saskia. *Globalization and Its Discontents.* New York: New York Press, 1998. Print.

——. *The Mobility of Labor and Capital.* Cambridge: Cambridge UP, 1990. Print.

——. "Women's Burden: Counter-geographies of Globalization and the Feminization of Survival." *Journal of International Affairs* 52.2 (2000): 503–524. Print.

Sassen, Saskia, and Arlie Russell Hochschild. "Global Cities and Survival Circuits." *Global Woman: Nannies, Maids, and Sex Workers in the New Economy.* Ed. Barbara Ehrenreich and Arlie Russell Hochschild. New York: Holt, 2002. 254–274. Print.

Saucedo, Renee. "INS Raids and How Immigrant Women Are Fighting Back." *Color of Violence: The INCITE! Anthology.* Ed. INCITE! Women of Color against Violence. Cambridge, MA: South End, 2000. 135–137. Print.

Schmidt Camacho, Alicia. "Body Counts on the Mexico–U.S. Border: Feminicidio, Reification, and the Theft of Mexicana Subjectivity." *Chicana/Latina Studies: The Journal of Mujeres Activas En Letras y Cambio Social* 4.1 (2004): 22–60. Print.

——. "Migrant Melancholia: Emergent Discourse of Mexican Migrant Traffic in Transnational Space." *South Atlantic Quarterly* 105.4 (2006): 831–861. Print.

"Sealing Our Border: Why It Won't Work." *Arizona Daily Star* Sept. 2006. Web. 3 May 2012.

Sheller, Mimi. "Natural Hedonism: The Invention of Caribbean Islands as Tropical Playgrounds." *Beyond the Blood, the Beach and the Banana: New Perspectives in Caribbean Studies.* Ed. Sandra Courtman. Kingston, Jamaica: Ian Randle, 2004. 170–185. Print.

Sieff, Kevin. "Access Denied: Government's Harsh Limits on the Reproductive Rights of Immigrant Women." *AlterNet.* Web. 8 Mar. 2009.

Sontag, Susan. *On Photography.* New York: Picador, 2001. Print.

"*Spanglish* Domestic Gross." *Box Office Mojo.* Web. 3 May 2012.

Stoney, Sierra, and Jeanne Batalova. "US in Focus: Mexican Immigrants in the United States." *Migration Information Source.* Migration Policy Institute. Feb. 2013. Web. 10 Oct. 2013.

Summers, Juana. "Rick Santorum on Official Language: Puerto Ricans Should Speak Spanish Too." *Politico.* 15 Mar. 2012. Web. 3 May 2012.

Supernanny. ABC. 2005. Web. 19 Apr. 2011.

Swords, Alicia, and Ronald L. Mize. "Beyond Tourist Gazes and Performances: U.S. Consumption of Land and Labor in Puerto Rican and Mexican Destinations." *Latin American Perspectives* 35.3 (2008): 53–69. Print.

Teal, Randall. "Between the Strange and the Familiar: A Journey with the Motel." *PhaenEx: Journal of Existential and Phenomenological Theory and Culture* 3.2 (2008): 71–91. Print.

Thomas, Robert J. *Citizenship, Gender, and Work: Social Organization of Industrial Agriculture.* Berkeley: U of California P, 1985. Print.

Thornton Dill, Bonnie. *Across the Boundaries of Race and Class: An Exploration of Work and Family among Black Female Domestic Servants.* New York: Garland, 1994. Print.

Undocumented Students: Unfulfilled Dreams. Los Angeles: UCLA Center for Labor Research and Education, 2007. Print.

United Nations Population Fund. "State of World Population Report 2006: A Passage to Hope: Women and International Migration." *UNFPA.* 2006. Web. 3 May 2012.

Vachani, Nilita, dir. *When Mother Comes Home for Christmas.* Filmsixteen, 1996. Film.

Vallejos, Thomas. "Ritual Process and the Family in the Chicano Novel." *MELUS* 10.4 (1983): 5–16. Print.

Van Uken, Bill. "Killing Fuels Mexican Anger over U.S. Immigration Policy." *World Socialist Web Site.* 7 Jan. 2006. Web. 15 Jan. 2012.

Vargas, Jose Antonio. "My Life as an Undocumented Immigrant." *New York Times* 22 June 2011. Web. 24 Jan. 2012.

Vasquez, Debora Kuetzpal. "Citlali: La Chicana Superhero." *Lucha Vista Magazine*. Oct. 2009. Web. 3 May 2012.

Villarreal, Jose Antonio. *Pocho*. New York: Anchor, 1970. Print.

Waldinger, Roger D., et al. "Helots No More: A Case Study of the Justice for Janitors Campaign in Los Angeles." *UC Los Angeles: The Ralph and Goldy Lewis Center for Regional Policy Studies* 15 (2006): n. pag. Web. 3 May 2012.

Wallerstein, Immanuel. "The Rise and Future Demise of World-Systems Analysis." *Ninety-first Annual Meeting of the American Sociological Association*. New York, 1996. Web. 3 May 2012.

Wang, Wayne, dir. *Maid in Manhattan*. Columbia Pictures, 2002. Film.

Watson, Bruce. *Bread and Roses: Mills, Migrants and the Struggle for the American Dream*. New York: Viking Penguin, 2005. Print.

Watson, Julie. "More Women Are Risking Rape, Death." *Washington Post* 27 Apr. 2006. Web. 10 May 2013.

Wertham, Fredric. *Seduction of the Innocent*. New York: Rinehart, 1954. Print.

Williams, Linda. *Playing the Race Card: Melodramas of Black and White from Uncle Tom to O. J. Simpson*. Princeton, NJ: Princeton UP, 2001. Print.

Wong, Scott, and Shira Toeplitz. "DREAM Act Dies in Senate." *Politico*. 18 Dec. 2010. Web. 3 May 2012.

World Bank. *Migration and Remittances Factbook 2011*. Washington, DC: World Bank, 2011. Web. 20 Jan. 2012.

Yezierska, Anzia. *The Bread Givers: A Novel*. Foreword and Introduction by Alice Kessler-Harris. New York: Persea, 2003. Print.

Zarembka, Joy M. "America's Dirty Work: Migrant Maids and Modern-Day Slavery." *Global Woman: Nannies, Maids, and Sex Workers in the New Economy*. Ed. Barbara Ehrenreich and Arlie Russell Hochschild. New York: Holt, 2002. Print.

Zernike, Kate. "Harsh Light on Two Men, but Glare Falls on Women." *New York Times* 18 May 2011. Web. 2 May 2012.

Zhang, Michael. "Migrant Workers Photographed as Superheroes." *PetaPixel*. 15 Sept. 2010. Web. 3 May 2012.

Zlotnik, Hania. *The Global Dimensions of Female Migration*. Washington, DC: Migration Policy Institute, 2003. Print.

Index